Books by Edith Simon

THE CHOSEN

BITING THE BLUE FINGER

WINGS DECEIVE

THE OTHER PASSION

THE GOLDEN HAND

THE HOUSE OF STRANGERS

THE TWELVE PICTURES

THE SABLE COAT

THE PIEBALD STANDARD

THE GREAT FORGERY

THE MAKING OF FREDERICK THE GREAT

THE MAKING OF

FREDERICK THE GREAT

FREDERICK
as a young man

THE MAKING OF FREDERICK THE GREAT

By Edith Simon

WITH MAPS AND ILLUSTRATIONS

LITTLE, BROWN AND COMPANY

Boston *Toronto*

LIBRARY OF CONGRESS CATALOG CARD NO. 63-8963

FIRST AMERICAN EDITION

PRINTED IN THE UNITED STATES OF AMERICA

For my parents

CONTENTS

ILLUSTRATIONS

ILLUSTRATIONS

Maps

For every State, from the smallest to the greatest, the principle of enlargement is the fundamental law of life.

Frederick II, *History of my Time*, 1743.

THE MAKING OF

FREDERICK THE GREAT

PREFACE

Frederick II of Prussia, called the Great, was once a national hero by adoption in England—partly because the Colonial War was won as much on the battlefields of Frederick's third Silesian or Seven Years War (1756–1763) as in America, partly for the heroic spectacle of little Prussia's lone stand against a coalition of the three mightiest powers in Europe (France, Austria, Russia), and partly because of the appeal of his wry, multi-faceted personality. His fame was world-wide, and traces of his cult appeared in places as remote from context as the Algerian interior.

Today every vestige of that cult and any popular memory of that personality have vanished, save in his own country. The liveliness of Frederick's immortality in Germany contrasts the more with his oblivion elsewhere, in view of his pronounced anti-German attitudes and un-German humour, the previous diffusion of his popularity, and the lurid drama of his formative years, which one might have thought calculated to endure as a classic case history.

It is these formative years, the years of action in reaction, taking Frederick right up to the age of thirty-five and as he wrongly believed the close of his military career, the forces and causes that made the crabbed hero of legend, which are the subject of this book.

Fame or oblivion apart, few historic figures have experienced so many fluctuations in the regard of posterity; none has lent himself to more divergent assessments, independently of geographic-ideological divisions. The touchstone of Frederick's title to greatness, and of his image as either hateful or glorious, is of course the question of a united Germany. Consistent in apparent inconsistency, judgment on Frederick has been relative to current views of all-German political union. For Frederick, by breaking up the thousand-year-old Holy Roman Empire of the German Nation, paved the way for that more organic, modern German Empire under Prussian leadership, which, founded eventually in 1871, had long been sought as a basic condition of progress and prosperity, and which, before its renewed partition in 1945, became prime mover in two world wars. Wherever and whenever such a state was held desirable, Frederick would be admired, and vice versa.

Thus Frederick is associated with the rise of Prussia and what is sometimes described as Prussianism. It takes a mental effort to see both at an embryonic stage, discernible only in retrospect. At Frederick's birth, the Kingdom of Prussia was precisely eleven years old, in the position of a puny stepchild among the family of nations, poor in natural resources, its largest city more like a collection of villages, its monarch treated by his colleagues somewhat as an arriviste figure of fun—except insofar as he was the possessor of an army which had often in the past proved its auxiliary usefulness to other states. In retrospect, nothing could be clearer than the seeds of aspirations coupled at once with fanatical industry and growing militarist orientation, arising from a sense of inferiority.

So, to play for a moment the unlimited parlour game of apportioning historical responsibility, it might be said, not too unjustly, that without the contempt and chicanery which Frederick William I suffered principally at the hands of Emperor Charles VI, the gifts of Frederick William's son very likely would never have taken him far outside the drawing-room. While the development of Frederick William's character owed much to the tortures of gout and bitter anguish about a son and heir incomprehensibly cast in an alien mould, it needed the endless frustration of his political endeavours finally to screw him up to a pitch of uninhibited malignancy which led many to class him as a demented monster. It needed the maniacal rigour of his treatment to screw up Frederick's urge for self-assertion to a pitch where nothing less than the impossible was worth achieving.

What would have happened had Frederick married a Princess of England and enjoyed without a struggle the civilized life he hankered after—to say nothing of a possible union, then, of England and Brandenburg—comes under the still more fertile game of speculation, in which everybody is his own umpire and anything goes.

The feeling that first comes over one when looking at Frederick's career and antecedents is trepidation: since the story brings home again and again the extent to which men's fate has been in the hands of single human-beings whose qualities and moods impinge directly on their work—often, indeed, impelling it—work which happens to be the government of nations. Although this is one of those truths with which we are familiar by nodding acquaintance, its stark proximity comes as a shock. Again and again, the more impersonal motive causes of land hunger, commercial rivalry, proselytism—respectable and sane by comparison—are, if not submerged, overlaid with considerations of amour propre and the hazards of sentiment. Popular nationalism, once a liberalizing force, by taking over those same wayward stimuli and rationalizing them on a mass scale, turns into chauvinism and perpetuates the vicious circle of aggression. One might despair, but for the reflexion that good as well as ill, emancipation, welfare, wisdom as well as wars, also accrue to societies and peoples ultimately through such frail, individual, human channels, and that the adage may be fairly inverted to read, 'plus c'est la même chose, plus ça change.'

By a conflux of circumstances large and small, exterior and interior, the individual, Frederick, became an embodied symbol of the evolution of his country.

No foolproof method of disentangling the influences of heredity and environment has yet been devised, nor can we accurately test the claim that character is irrevocably determined in the first years of infancy. Whether by inborn or acquired instinct, whether by reason of innate affinity or of custom, from archetypal emotion or because Frederick William's craving for love proved at last inescapable—Frederick loved his father, and so came to identify himself with his father. In the end it was a case of conquest by assimilation; in the end what would emerge was a super-Frederick William, a colossal magnification of the all too human original.

The mystery of Frederick's sex life is interesting but of secondary importance. The theory that he was maimed and spurred on to great deeds by a fear of appearing effeminate would admirably fit in with the whole picture of his life as King. It is so pat in its general structure, so convincing and seductive in detail, as to be hard to dismiss. But all the evidence is purely circumstantial, and those other events of Frederick's youth which are incontestably documented are by themselves sufficient to account for his obsessive drive and the directions it took. The physiological explanation is a convenient, pleasing extra—but still just an extra.

Although the absence of women from Frederick's mature life* led to a variety of concurrent rumours, the statement that by clumsy medical treatment in his youth Frederick had been rendered impotent but not castrated was first put forward in 1790 by a Swiss physician named Zimmermann, who had attended Frederick in his last illness (1786). In Prussia it was taken as an insult to the great King's memory, and by official request Frederick's surgeons in ordinary, Engel, Ollenroth, Rosenmeyer, and Liebert, signed affidavits denying the allegation. Under the circumstances neither can appear conclusive.

Inconclusive also are the arguments for and against Frederick's having been a practising homosexual, likewise based on hearsay, inference, and third-party depositions. Again, the possibility cannot be ruled out, but would not substantially affect the course of Frederick's self-rehabilitation as charted in the present study, save by further underlining his need. My aim has been to trace that need in relation to the events with which it marched.

Here the main difficulty lay in considerations of space and viewpoint, which are really one: for unless one central focus is selected and adhered to, there is no limiting a survey of this kind to portable dimensions. So while I have tried to indicate some leading trends of policy in countries other than Prussia

* With the transient and solitary exception of the dancer Barberina, whose vivacious conversation Frederick said constituted her charm for him: Voltaire attributed it to her thighs which, *he* said, reminded Frederick of his dragoons.

at the time, inevitably little is said about other countries and other wars, except as they touch those of Frederick. Equally there are of course many incidents and elements, and above all much political detail, of the reigns of Frederick and his father, which have been left out as diverging from the straight line of exposition. The bibliography should help to fill any gaps in which—as I hope—interest may be roused.

Regarding Frederick's battles, I have dwelt more on the first two with their psychologically important bearing, than on the later ones, especially Hohenfriedberg and Soor, which rank as set-pieces of their kind and have been exhaustively treated many times over in the literature of war.

In rendering recorded speech and correspondence into English, I have on the whole followed—as closely as possible—the spirit rather than the letter: colloquialisms that seem strangely modern; ungrammatical, unorthographic, and muddled expressions that seem to border on illiteracy, are faithful translations in that sense, throughout.

Masculine names are mainly given in their English version, save for minor characters or occasionally to avoid confusion between bearers of the same name.

As for currencies and monetary values, interpretation in present-day terms is a forbiddingly complex task. 'Ducats' and 'Pistoles' merely signify gold coins as such in popular parlance; 'Thaler' were silver coins, first minted in the sixteenth century and then somewhat equivalent to the original English silver penny, later to the five shilling piece; usually 'Reichsthaler', the coinage of the Empire, are meant.* Apart from this, some comparative figures may convey a rough idea of purchasing power.

The cost of feeding 23,038 head of infantry, 8,883 cavalry, and 1,213 artillery, in Prussia, for the year 1739 was 1,635,914 Thaler. The price of rye in 1740 was 1 Thaler 21 Groschen per bushel; wheat stood at 2 Thaler 18 Groschen, barley at 1 Thaler 6 Groschen, oats at 21 Groschen. Frederick's losses in the two Silesian Wars were reckoned to be '20,000 men at

* There were at one time 24, later 30 Groschen—a smaller silver coin—to the Thaler; the Groschen equalled 12 (copper) Pfennige.

100 Thaler each'. The following is an extract from the account of the Crown Prince's expenditure for September, 1719:

	Thaler	*Groschen*
For the collecting bag	—	16
For H.H. the Crown Prince	—	16
For the tailor that made the green dress	2	—
For the girls that made the beds at Wusterhausen	—	16
For having pipe prepared	—	4
For two paint boxes	—	16
For six pounds of [hair] powder	—	12
For boot buttons	—	2
For 12 ells hair riband	1	6
For the poor box	—	1
For the boy in the field whom the dogs bit	—	4
To a Musketeer of the 2nd Battalion who asked H.H. to stand godfather	2	—
For a live woodcock	—	2
To a shepherd boy that carried the dead dog away	—	1
Powder and gratuity for the cannoneer who fired at Schulzendorf	1	8
For a robin	—	2
For nails and wrapping paper to pack the globe in	—	4
Shoe repairs	—	1

I am grateful to my sister, Inge Goodwin, for her work in collecting the illustrations; also, for their kind co-operation in the same cause, to Dr G. Eckardt, custodian of the Palaces and Gardens of Potsdam-Sanssouci; Dr Börsch-Supan of the Administration of Palaces and Gardens, Berlin-Charlottenburg; Dr Fedja Anzelewski of the Kupferstichkabinett, Berlin-Dahlem; Dr Richter, Director, Deutsche Fotothek, Dresden; and Dr Erwin M. Auer, Director, Kunsthistorisches Museum, Vienna. Owing to war damage and post-war changes, it was not always easy to obtain this material, which therefore is not as complete as I should have liked to see it. Certain discrepancies between portraits and the verbal descriptions of their subjects—for example the grim and 'savage-looking' Old Dessauer, who in Pesne's paintings appears suavely handsome;

'Fatty' Frederick William who appears merely portly; and Elizabeth Christine who conforms to her time's fashion plate ideal of the pretty princess—are explained by the perennial difficulties of the court painter. Nevertheless some grain of character lurks in each, and it helps to have some visual reference to their persons.

E.S.

CHAPTER 1

THE YOUNGEST KINGDOM

In 1712, three years before his gloomy death, Louis XIV was still the gadfly of all princely consciousness in Western Europe. He had set a standard of royal being which other rulers strained every nerve and every resource to keep up with—an endeavour foredoomed by their different quality and by the sheer quantity of them also: for the German Empire alone comprised well over three hundred separate states, whereas the Sun King reigned unrivalled over the whole of a united France.

Thus Louis's example, proving as it did inimitable, had strengthened the active power of personal sentiments like envy, pique, ambition, in the conduct of international affairs, until the community of nations reflected all too accurately the petty provincial courts by which it was mostly represented. Apart from Paris and London, the capitals of Europe were typical small towns, appearing none the larger and no more metropolitan for having each its pseudo-Versailles, complete with waterworks and maîtresse en titre.

Among the smallest and rudest of these towns was Berlin, seat of the Margrave-Elector of Brandenburg who had recently achieved the title of King (King *in*, not as yet *of* Prussia) and rejoiced in the birth of a grandson to perpetuate his line. The infant's navel cord was deposited in a silver-gilt capsule with the inscription, 'Friederich, Prince de Prusse et d'Orange et né le 24 Janvier 1712 à 11½ heures du Matin', and preserved among the family records. This primitive act was followed by a christening ceremony traditionally involving such pompous rigours that at least one of the baby's two predeceased elder brothers was believed to have perished from the after-effects of baptism.

The week-old prince seemed delicate, as well he might, having all but had the life crushed out of him soon after birth by the violence of his father's embrace. Upon the yet unfused bones of his small head there sat a crown, and the christening robe was of cloth of silver, studded with diamonds and having a train that required the services of six countesses. Two margraves and one margravine carried him to the chapel royal, where he was placed in the arms of his grandfather the King and baptized by the Calvinist Bishop Ursinus von Bär—in happy if somewhat over-emphatic symbolism, seeing that the bear was the emblem of Berlin and the founding father of the Brandenburg Margravate had been called Albrecht the Bear. *Friedrich*, however, was the name of most frequently distinguished association with the present dynasty. In addition to it the latest scion received only the name of *Karl*,* in compliment to the Habsburg Emperor Charles VI who figured as one of the godfathers.

There were five in all, including Tzar Peter the Great, the Elector of Hanover who was grandfather to the child on the mother's side, the States General of Holland with whom also there was a family link through the Princes of Orange, and the Swiss Republic of Berne, southern outpost of Protestant independence. The godmothers were make-weights: the German Empress Dowager, the Electress and the Dowager Electress of Hanover, the Duchess of Brunswick, the Dowager Duchess of Mecklenburg—underlining the array without adding to it. In spite of the strong religious convictions of the House of Brandenburg, the social and political significance of the choice of sponsors was somewhat dominant. There was no representative of Sweden, though another bastion of the Protestant faith, and none from any German Catholic state except the Emperor whose real dominions strictly speaking lay

* Koser concludes that only one name, Frederick, was given, but his evidence does not seem to me convincing. The Emperor himself subsequently addressed the Prince as Charles Frederick.

outside Germany. As for the Greek Orthodox Tzar, from every religious point of view his participation was an entire irrelevance.

The royal family of Brandenburg consisted of the following: King Frederick I (formerly Elector Frederick III), labouring under the disadvantages of spinal deformity, ill health, and the overpowering memory of a famous father; his third wife, shut away in her apartments with a species of religious mania; his only son the Crown Prince Frederick William, father of the newly christened child, and its mother, Sophie Dorothee of Hanover, with their three-year-old daughter Wilhelmine; and the two Margraves of Brandenburg-Schwedt, half-brothers to the King, who saw no reason at this early date to give up hope of diverting the succession to their own thriving progeny. They had a powerful if clandestine supporter in the reigning Prince Leopold of Anhalt-Dessau—an indirect connexion of the House but pursuing a vested interest in it on behalf of the senior Margravine of Schwedt who was his sister. This apparently bluff and forthright veteran of thirty-six—veteran of Namur, Kaiserswerth, Venlo, Bonn, Hochstädt, Blenheim, Cassano, Turin, Tournay, Malplaquet, and Mörs—this eminently open-air type treading the devious indoor paths of intrigue, was a characteristic ingredient of the atmosphere surrounding the nativity of the future Frederick the Great.

To indicate the rest of the baby's immediate forbears, with skeletons in the cupboard to boot—his paternal grandmother was also his great-aunt, being sister to the maternal grandfather: the late Queen Sophie Charlotte, Princess of Hanover, friend and pupil of Leibniz ('Leibniz today talked to me of the infinitely little—as if I did not know enough of that here!'); the maternal grandmother was Sophie Dorothee 'the elder', divorced since by the Elector of Hanover and future George I of England, for adultery with the ill-fated Königsmarck, and now styled Princess of Ahlden after her place of perpetual banishment in the moorlands of Lüneburg Heath. The paternal great-grandparents on the male side were the Great Elector of Brandenburg, pattern-hero and already something of a patron saint to his descendants, and his first wife Louise

Henrietta of Orange, a spirited and practical lady. The genealogical table shows the remaining pairs of great-grandparents as only two, since Sophie Charlotte of Brandenburg and George I of Hanover-England both were children of Ernest Augustus of Calenberg-Hanover and his wife Sophia. Through the latter, a daughter of that mercurial couple the 'Winter' King and Queen of Bohemia, the pedigree goes back to Mary Queen of Scots and thence beyond further profitable pursuit of direct hereditary influences.

The environmental influences were the ones shortly to appear the most striking and decisive: to the point of hair-raising melodrama.

Meanwhile the general interest was centred on the new baby's powers of survival. By summertime the old King was able to record six teeth in his grandson—all without teething troubles, too: surely a sign of 'Predestination', he wrote thankfully. Other omens multiplied in prophecy that the puny child would flourish: like the sudden hectic growth of an American aloe planted in the residential pleasure gardens forty-four years since, which now for the first time pushed up a central stem to the height of thirty-one feet and produced 7,277 blossoms, amid enormous public excitement.

Then thirteen months after the christening, the old King died. He had been ailing for some time, but his illness took its mortal turn in consequence of that third marriage he had contracted —unnecessarily in the event as well as fruitlessly—to see what he could himself do further for the succession. His mad Queen one morning escaped from her guardians and came dashing herself through the glass door of his chambers, dressed only in her shift and petticoat, that is, *all in white*. The King mistook her for the family ghost, the White Lady, was prostrated by the shock, and never rose again.

His son gave him a magnificent funeral. No cost was spared, no pretentiousness avoided. But as soon as it was all over, the second Prussian King went home and turned his palace upside down, that ornate mountain built upon a molehill, so showing what he really thought of his prodigal Papa.

Off came the Spanish peruque, long a bane of Frederick William's life, off came his coat; in his shirtsleeves, within hours of his father's burial, he lent a hand in stripping the place of dust-catching, decadent superfluities. Hangings, carpets, upholstery were outlawed. A five room suite was retained for the use of himself and his family, the rest turned into offices where the new King could keep an eye on every department of the civil service and pounce on his officials at any moment of the day or night, with a private staircase affording easy vigilance over the cellars which he made his treasury: the wines were sold. Sold, too, were quantities of diamonds with which the old King had loved to embellish his ill-favoured person, most of his menagerie, and all but a few of his fleet of showy coaches.

Overnight the court hierarchy was reduced from 141 to not much above a dozen, mostly domestics. Scores of heralds and musicians were dismissed, though the court painters were kept on under a revised arrangement, by which against a lump annual sum they must deliver a fixed number of pictures per year. As for the higher functionaries, enough posts were abolished to cause epidemic unemployment and real hardship among the aristocracy. The saddest case among those perforce hastening to reduce their households, sell their carriages, and retire to their simple country estates, was that of Frederick I's Master of Ceremonies, so highly trained in the science of etiquette as to be wholly unfitted for any other pursuit. It took him many months of search and heartrending petitions to find another job, at the court of Augustus the Strong of Saxony (where also the diamonds and the wild beasts found a new home).

'Tell the Prince of Anhalt,' Frederick William, rebuffing a precipitate enquiry, wrote in the first known letter of his reign, 'that I am Minister of Finance and Commander-in-Chief to the King of Prussia.'

And his Majesty's Chancellor, Minister of Agriculture, Justice, Education, Transport, Commerce, not to mention Matters Ecclesiastical, he might have added, with a measure of spare-time police activity thrown in. He took to patrolling the streets on his daily constitutional, to give lounging labourers a personal drubbing or burst into a private house where a marital squabble was in progress to force the contenders to kiss and make up.

No detail was unworthy of his notice; before the large must come the small; the sound foundation required for great projects demanded first of all the stopping-up of every channel of waste. Waste of time, waste of money and substance meant waste of opportunity, meant loss: a cosmic deficit, crime against God and Nature. For thrift, solvency, diligence, and success were the great Protestant virtues, the vindication of Adam standing now on his own feet. Where the Catholic Church had multiplied the calendar of religious feasts in order to cut down strife and bloodshed, the Reformed Churches systematically cut down on feasts to eliminate the evils of idleness. What the Thirty Years War had broken down must be made good.

So the quainter of Frederick William's edicts—compelling the market women to knit stockings as they sat offering their wares, setting a strict time-limit on Sunday sermons, imposing a tax on wigs—were evidence not only of a positive genius for infinitesimal organization and myopic combinative powers, but also of an omnifaisant paternalism in emulation of the Deity. To work was to pray, to save was to walk in righteousness, to make Brandenburg-Prussia great was a spiritual duty to strengthen the Protestant bloc and thus spread the Kingdom of Heaven over the earth.

To make Prussia great two inter-connected things were needed: economic prosperity and strength of arms.

Frederick William was in the blest condition of always knowing himself to be right; also, it happened that his personal inclinations did on the whole square with the welfare of his country, his people. He was unfortunate, however—as were his country, his people, and above all his family—in suffering from an inordinate desire to be loved and appreciated, a hunger which the frustration of his talents in the old King's lifetime had steadily sharpened. Like a man long-famished suddenly having bread, Frederick William made to swallow the whole loaf at once. The result was universal indigestion.

Until the last year or so of his father's reign, Frederick William's administrative genius had been bottled up with the stopper of filial piety, his stupendous energy allowed no outlet save in war and procreation. He had been married at nineteen and before that had served with the Brandenburg contingent under Marlborough in the Netherlands, returning again as a volunteer at twenty-one, by which time he had fathered two of his fourteen children (not counting miscarriages), with another on the way. ('I hear the good work [to beget an heir] goes on night and day at Berlin,' wrote Frederick William's grandmother, the Electress of Hanover.) The acquired taste for war became a passion—one in which he was later to be thwarted, not by outside influences as in so many other things, but by his own probity. To the end of his life he celebrated the anniversary of Malplaquet as a pinnacle of nostalgic glory.

Debarred from business of state by his father's touchy vanity, Frederick William had been given an army regiment to occupy him at home, the Potsdam Grenadier Guards, on which he lavished the creative attention due to an obsessive hobby. But here already his abiding gift of killing never less than two birds with one stone had emerged. Compensating Frederick William for his want of authority and his unimpressive physique, his Grenadier Guards were made over into a body of giants, none under six feet tall and not a few approaching seven feet; but in addition the regiment became employed as an experimental unit to test out the various technical innovations of his whilom comrade-in-arms and trusted crony, the redoubtable Prince Leopold.

Now that he had a clear field all round, Frederick William threw himself into his task with the élan of his years, which numbered twenty-five. He was very much a young King, for all that his methods have made him seem forever middle-aged. The 'old' King, too, was no more than fifty-six at his death. Neither was that old King guilty of quite such misrule as his successors attributed to him. While his finances were in no tidier shape than those of other potentates, contemporary travellers were struck by the healthy appearance of his dominions. When all was said, moreover, it was he and no other who had succeeded in acquiring the royal dignity for his House, which his ancestors had long striven for in vain.

Although the Margravate of Brandenburg had been established since the Middle Ages—with incumbents of the Hohenzollern stock for the past three hundred years—it had retained something of its original character as the Empire's outpost against the heathen Slavs, its suzerains somewhat in the rôle of frontiers-men, pioneers labouring to turn a waste of sand, scrub, and boggy marshes into viable land, one hand at the plough, the sword in the other. Their territory had grown, and with it their power, but not as much as the abstract sum of their possessions might suggest: for much of it was scattered incontiguously, without more actual cohesion than a system of garrisons could furnish. From this system stemmed a certain militarist preoccupation, and a larger and more efficient army than was common in countries of similar size—and which in turn contributed to extension of power. But there was a point beyond which material power could not progress without the immaterial stiffening of prestige and recognition: precisely Frederick I's argument when the Emperor had tried to talk him out of wanting to become a king.

The implicit blackening of Frederick I's character, largely an emotional urge with his son, became a literary necessity with the propagators of the Prussian Mythos which arose from that phenomenon, his grandson. But for the extraordinary career of Frederick II, Frederick I might have received less grudging treatment at the hands of posterity—even though at his obsequies no more trenchant (or durable) epithet was found for him than 'The Magnanimous'.

Frederick William, on the other hand, was to become immortalized as 'The Soldier King', just as he would have wished. In his day, however, he had to suffer—and he did suffer greatly—under such appellations as 'The Drill Sergeant', 'The Plus-maker' (from his constantly reiterated aim 'ein Plus zu machen', to make a little over, put a little something by), or, worst of all, 'The Arch-Sandcaster of the Empire'. Much of his country's soil was sand, sand to blot wet writing was an indispensable adjunct to paper work, and he, poor war-loving prince of peace, spilt a great deal more ink than blood for the aggrandizement of his nation.

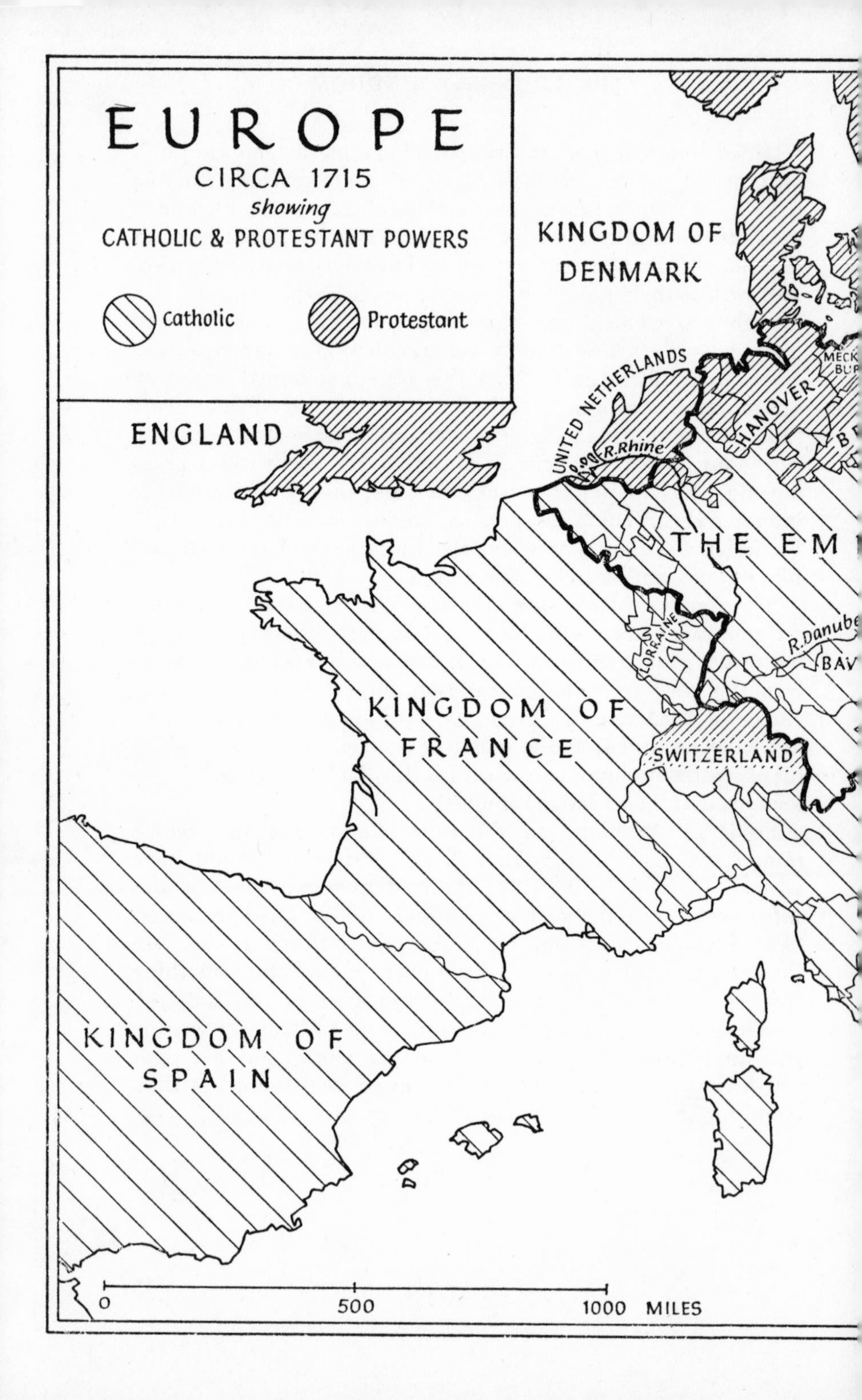
EUROPE
CIRCA 1715
showing
CATHOLIC & PROTESTANT POWERS
Catholic
Protestant
KINGDOM OF
DENMARK
ENGLAND
UNITED NETHERLANDS
R. Rhine
HANOVER
THE EM
R. Danube
LORRAINE
KINGDOM OF
FRANCE
SWITZERLAND
KINGDOM OF
SPAIN
0
500
1000 MILES

RUSSIAN
EMPIRE
K. OF PRUSSIA
DENBURG
KINGDOM OF
POLAND
SILESIA
IRE
OHEMIA
AUSTRIA
KINGDOM OF
HUNGARY
R. Danube
OTTOMAN EMPIRE
KINGDOM
OF THE
TWO SICILIES

CHAPTER 2

THE BACKGROUND

The infant Crown Prince, everyone agreed, was an angel. He had fair curly hair, big blue eyes, he was a boy, and lived. (Two other royal children had been born, in 1713 and 1714, one living only a few months, and both in any case female.) His father saw in him not only the hope of their race but also the brother he himself had never had. His mother, having with his help confounded a prognosis vigorously spread about by the King's relations, that she would never produce an heir, blossomed with refreshed disdain for the clodhoppers surrounding her. His sister, who had furiously rejected her first baby brother* was inseparable from the second. His governesses adored him, and the people glorified him as a promise of better days.

The King's guiding 'Instruction' for the upbringing of his son contained some sapient, almost revolutionary ideas.

The first principle, impossible to repeat too often, was that 'Fritzchen' should be taught to regard his father as his best friend. Filial respect should spring, not from slavish submission, but from a brotherly love and trust. In case of any little childish waywardness, not on any account was one to threaten the Prince with his Papa's displeasure: but use the mother as a threat, by all means.

In his education, Fritzchen should not suffer as his father had once under a curriculum overloaded with bombast and

* Died aged ten months.

impractical learning. Instead of stuffing the little head full of inflated notions concerning the grandeur of his House and with the apocrypha of the Ancients, one should stock it tidily with modern political history, geography, and economics, besides arithmetic and the elements of strategy. The study of Latin, obligatory on the German Electors under their charter of 1356, known as the Golden Bull, was unnecessary in this day and age; likewise the theory of grammar was of not the smallest utility. All a modern sovereign of Brandenburg would need was a fluent command of French and German and ability to write a lucid style. (Certainly Frederick William always saw to it that he made himself clear, without benefit of grammar or of spelling for that matter.)

Most important of all, however, let the child be imbued with love of war and glory, let him grow up in the knowledge that not to be a soldier was contemptible, let him learn to abhor luxury and profligacy of every kind. Let him also be reared in the Law of God, a model Christian of the Evangelical persuasion, with some information concerning the fundamental errors of Catholicism, but untroubled with details as to the lesser sectarian creeds.

To be sure, the Prince must learn to walk before he could run; meanwhile, until he grew out of long clothes and feminine government, one might harden his valour by the expedient of a cannon fired under his window to wake him in the mornings, and harden his constitution by a Spartan diet, notably of beer soup.

'Instructions' of this kind were not in themselves a novelty. The one laid down for Frederick William's own childhood had been composed with the assistance of none less than the great Leibniz. No 'Schwarzscheisser', however, no ink-excreting bookworm to use a favourite word of Frederick William's, had a hand in this revised version.

Frederick William's hatred of all things intellectual was not so arbitrary as it might appear. It was all of a piece with his hatred of waste, sham, and impiety. 'Reason' was a bad word. Luther had coined the phrase of 'the harlot, Reason', and the verb 'raisonnieren', *to reason* in Germanized French, had come to mean *to grumble against Authority*. Authority was the expression on earth of the Divine scheme. Reason was the antithesis of

Faith. The efforts on the part of the new school of professional thinkers, to bring religion into alignment with Reason, were as the red rag of blasphemy to the orthodox on both sides of the schismatic fence.

Moreover, the flowers and fruits of contemporary culture had mostly grown from the rich soil of France. French, the international language of the upper classes and the educated, was the principal vehicle of cultural transmission. The German Empire, a patriarchal concept to which Frederick William clung with heart and soul, was in a state of permanent resistance to the expansionist tendencies of France. He therefore equated book-learning with the arch-enemy and with the supercilious elegance of a whole civilization that looked down on him because he lacked its graces.

Frederick William I was short, dumpy, florid; nasal of voice, humourless, and incapable of turning the neat aphorisms which were the hallmark of sophistication. While he would have scorned to ape what he disapproved, even had he been able, he could not help exhibiting the aggressiveness that comes of sour grapes.

At the same time, an anti-French bias and a spirit of rebellious inferiority were something of a family tradition, as were also a policy of religious toleration, a sense of historic mission, and a passionate industry on the spur of indigence. Most of these had crystallized in recognizable form under the Great Elector, Frederick William's grandfather and namesake: a prince of heroic cast, lively intelligence, and the distinction of having come out of the Thirty Years War without loss. ('Not the War, the Peace was what ruined *me*,' the Great Elector drily complained, not without justice, cheated of his conquests under pressure by France at the Peace of Westphalia.) But the inception of that assertive urge lay much further back.

For one thing, there had always been a disparity of function and rank, inherent in the very office of Margrave. The Margraves of the Empire, guardians of its frontiers and instruments of Imperial law and order, within their jurisdiction had full sovereign rights, yet without ever quite shedding an air of mere policemen in the feudal hierarchy. While the office had now lost most of its original significance, the tie between Brandenburg and the Imperial Crown largely remained one of service and reward; and while the binding power of archaic loyalty yet retained its strength, it was too often strained. For as the services of Brandenburg had grown in value, so necessarily had the rewards: and with that there had likewise grown an Imperial reluctance to pay up. Frequently the promised reward materialized only in part, or depreciated by delay, sometimes transmuted into specious compensation, sometimes even revoked. The Imperial Crown, having its centre of gravity in the Catholic south, could not desire any undue accumulation of weight in the Protestant north. As a result, the House of Brandenburg had become geared to a habitual necessity of struggling for possession of what had been already earned.

Withal Brandenburg's increase in size and influence had been sure if slow, supplemented by deals of barter and inheritance. But to take only the latest and largest of its acquisitions, the former Duchy of East Prussia lay three days' journey away (if one hurried) from the nearest point of Brandenburg's eastern boundary, separated by the country of West Prussia which belonged to Poland. Hence the style of King *in* Prussia—Prussia being a geographical, not a national entity.

There were all manner of complications, the legal and the personal in many ways overlapping. Prussia was outside Germany, in that it did not come within the Imperial jurisdiction. Thus, although without the consent of the Emperor the Margrave-Elector of Brandenburg Fredrick III could not have become King Frederick I 'in' Prussia, in his capacity of King he was theoretically independent; while in his capacity of margrave, elector, and numerous other titular denominations he continued directly answerable to the Emperor.

The Holy Roman Empire of the German Nation, first founded by agreement of Charlemagne and Pope Leo III in A.D. 800, was a conceptual superstructure—*Roman* by faith, *German* by language—rather than an organic commonwealth. There had long ceased to be any effective central control; the Imperial Crown was little more than a source of symbolic authority, fountainhead of honours and privileges to be sure, but from every material aspect a luxury—and an expensive one.

But nations, any more than men, do not live by bread alone.

The office of Emperor was as highly prized as ever it had been, and it was figuratively upheld by all the hundreds of German States which in practice did everything they could to render it executively impotent.

Although the Imperial throne had been occupied by the House of Habsburg for close on three hundred years, technically it was not hereditary but elective. The College of Electors consisted of the sovereign Archbishops of Mainz, Cologne, and Treves, and the secular rulers of the Palatinate, Saxony, Bohemia, Brandenburg, Bavaria, with Hanover furnishing a ninth since 1692, so that the formal truce of the religions was honoured by two Protestant votes (Brandenburg and Hanover) in an institution conceived and maintained under Catholic auspices. However, the Catholic and Protestant States of the Empire were at one in resistance to the foreign Catholic influences of the Papacy and the House of Bourbon. Other than this they had no stable interest in common. The political constellations were in constant flux, accompanied by a huge general output of treaties that became obsolete before the ink was dry.

At Frederick William's accession, Brandenburg-Prussia's position vis-à-vis the principal rival powers was good, every one canvassing assistance of one sort and another. Whilst it was the foremost conscious aim of the second Prussian King to improve his country's standing among the nations, primarily by building it up internally into a kingdom worthy of the name, he had no intention of neglecting his chances in regard to several outstanding territorial claims.

The most important of these were three: first, the Great Elector's conquests in Pomerania, legitimate spoils of war as no one had ever denied; second, the twin duchies of Jülich and Berg on the Rhine, which were due to fall to Brandenburg under a compact still requiring guarantors before it could come into force; and third, the district of Schwiebus in the Habsburg-Austrian province of Silesia.

These were sore points one and all; but the issue of Schwiebus was perhaps pre-eminent in this respect, incidentally illustrating yet another family tradition of Brandenburg—that of conflict between father and son in peculiarly acute form.

The issue was rooted in a covenant of 1537, under which the Electors of Brandenburg and the Dukes of Liegnitz were to succeed to each other's lands in the event of failure of heirs of the blood to either. The Duke of Liegnitz had briefed power to 'give away, sell, pawn, exchange or [otherwise] dispose of, by written or verbal testament', his dominions of Liegnitz, Brieg, and Wohlau, all situated in Silesia, where Brandenburg then already had a foothold, the Duchy of Jägerndorf.

In the event, Jägerndorf was forfeited under escheat not long after, and the Brandenburg-Liegnitz covenant was simply vetoed by Emperor Ferdinand II (1619–1637). However, the signatory Duke of Liegnitz had left a codicil to his will affirming the contract's everlasting validity, and his Brandenburg partner had never in fact surrendered the Deed.

In 1675 the line of Liegnitz expired and the matter came up for discussion again, without concrete upshot. But ten years later the Imperial Crown, in need of military aid against the Turks, proposed a compromise. In return for 80,000 troops the Great Elector of Brandenburg was to receive Schwiebus, a very much smaller portion of Silesian territory than Liegnitz-Brieg-Wohlau (not to mention Jägerndorf), but to be regarded as a bird in the hand for all that. Under divers pressure, the Great Elector accepted—little knowing that his son and heir, the future King Frederick I, was making nonsense of the bargain.

The age-old antagonism of the generations, the mutual jealousy and suspicion between the tribal patriarch and his coming supplanter, had for some time appeared in the Hohenzollern dynasty with an almost mechanical starkness. Again and again the reaction of son against father produced men of apparently wholly different stamp. Even as the Great Elector in his day had rebelled against his father, his son repeated the situation; each in turn had sought refuge in exile for a time. In exile, and heavily in debt, the Great Elector's son secretly pledged himself to return Schwiebus to Austria at his father's death, against immediate financial help.

No sooner was the Great Elector dead than his successor repudiated an agreement which, he said, he had not previously had power to conclude: no promise of his made before his

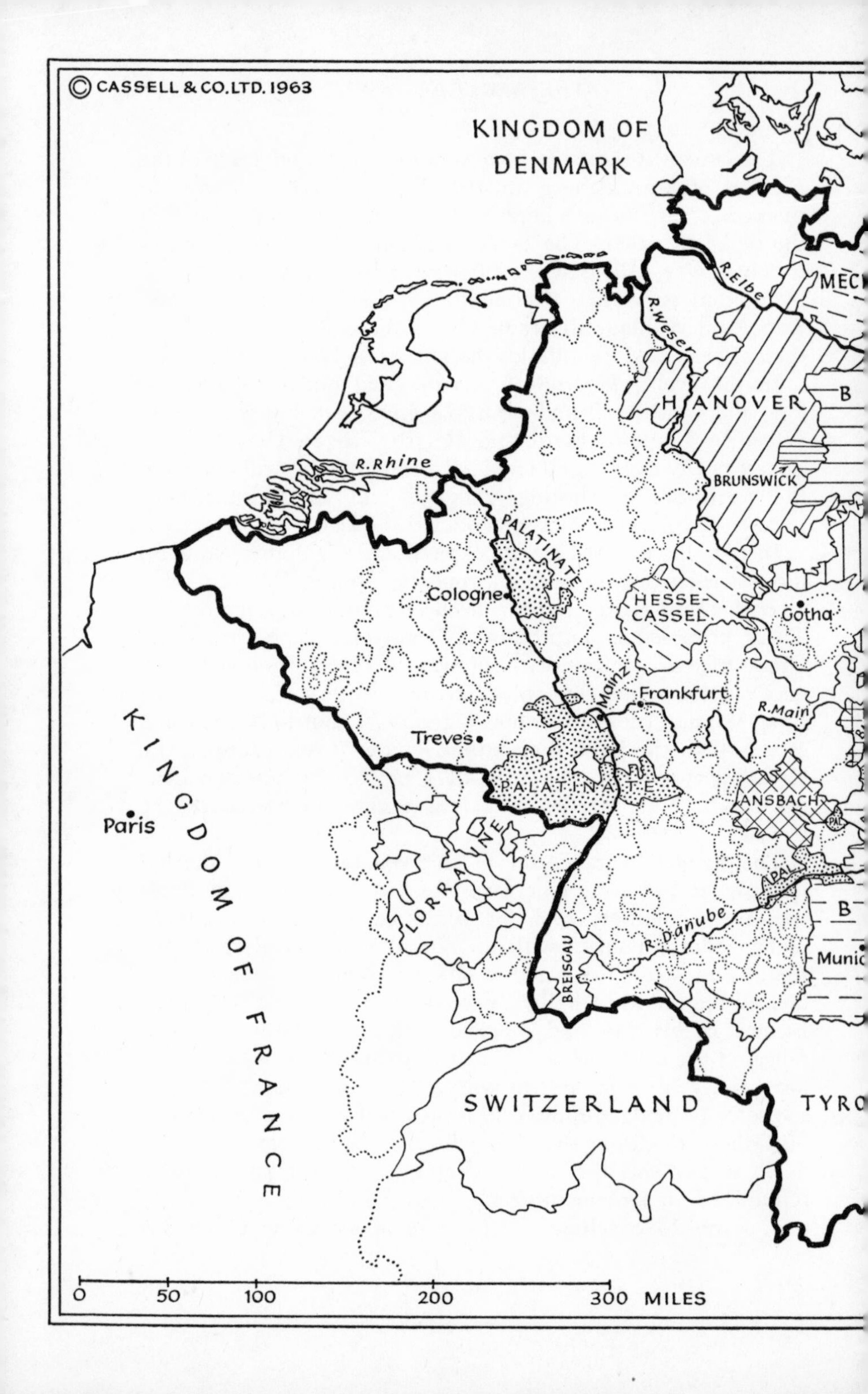

© CASSELL & CO. LTD. 1963
KINGDOM OF
DENMARK
R.Elbe
MEC
R.Weser
HANOVER
B
R.Rhine
BRUNSWICK
PALATINATE
Cologne
HESSE-
CASSEL
Gotha
Mainz
Frankfurt
R.Main
Treves
KINGDOM OF FRANCE
PALATINATE
ANSBACH
PAL
Paris
LORRAINE
PAL
B
R.Danube
BREISGAU
Munic
SWITZERLAND
TYRO
0
50
100
200
300 MILES

K. OF PRUSSIA
Stralsund
BURG
Stettin
KINGDOM OF POLAND
NDENBURG
Berlin
R. Spree
lle
AXONY
Dresden
R. Oder
SILESIA
BOHEMIA
MORAVIA
AUSTRIA
K OF HUNGARY
ARIA
Vienna
R. Danube
STYRIA
ALZBURG
CARINTHIA
CARNIOLA
THE HOLY ROMAN EMPIRE

father's death could be binding upon Brandenburg which had not then been his to bind. Again, he was not strong enough to hold out against the pressure brought to bear on him, and finally was compelled to let Schwiebus go. But forthwith he set down the following 'Instruction' to his progeny:

'I must . . . keep my own word. But my rights to Silesia, which I could not, and in these unjust circumstances do not, compromise, I leave intact for my descendants to prosecute . . . If God shall one day send the opportunity, those who come after me will know what they have to do.'

CHAPTER 3

MONBIJOU *v.* POTSDAM

Frederick William's Queen, Sophie Dorothee, was his cousin; Fiekchen, he called her, in his rough, dialect German. There is no documentary evidence as to how well she liked this; internal evidence to the contrary is strong. A nickname which she did like very much was Olympia.

That was what her courtiers were encouraged to call her, and the foreign envoys for whom she did her best to provide a congenial refuge from the austerities of her husband's aggressively homespun court, at her own little residence of Monbijou.

The King might frown at Monbijou, but that was as far as he could well go. Here, as in so many things, the great Elector had set the operative precedent, having given his first and much-loved consort her own palace of Oranienburg to play with; whereafter Frederick William's mother had duly received her Charlottenburg. Also, Frederick William's father-in-law cum uncle, the Elector of Hanover, on 10 August 1714 became King of England, which inevitably strengthened the daughter's position with her husband.

Not that Frederick William was at all inclined to knuckle under to his Hanoverian relations, whatever they might call themselves, 'conceited past bearing' on their new throne. The Court of Hanover, to which he had been taken as a child and which prided itself on being the most civilized in Europe next to Versailles, had never been to his taste. He had there disgraced his mother, rolling on the floor with Cousin George and bloodying Cousin George's nose—a contretemps which indelibly set the tone between the two future Kings; it being no emollient that Cousin George eventually married Frederick William's first love, the Princess Caroline of Ansbach.

Frederick William's uxorious ardour had, however, swiftly warmed to his Fiekchen-Olympia, a fine figure of a woman, queenly to her fingertips in deportment and tact. If with these regal qualities went an ambition to meddle in affairs as well as a host of cultivated affectations—why, so had the Great Elector's wife had her gardening and Frederick William's mother her Differential Calculus. If Sophie Dorothee evinced a not so tactful recoil from her husband's robust entertainments, it did not alter the fact that he was master.

It did not alter the fact, but it created a necessity of perpetual reassertion. The very existence of an enclave of refinement like Monbijou could not but undermine the integrity of the royal establishment as a whole, just as by the same token its frugality became imperfect. By degrees Court society grouped itself in two factions, the King's and the Queen's, and by degrees what had started as a division of cultures and tastes attained a clear-cut political character. The prevailing trend in the King's party was towards Austria; the Queen was for England.

England at that juncture was in alliance with France; France and Austria, though also no longer at war, remained in their perennial state of hostile vigilance. Yet by a curious confluence of circumstances this did not mean a clash of interests at Berlin. Rather, it meant that for once almost the whole of Europe endorsed the Prussian aspirations to major status—at least to the extent of some further Prussian territorial consolidation; so that for the present there was no apparent party issue between the parties of the King and the Queen.

France favoured Prussian expansion as being in principle against the Austrian interest; Austria must wish to prevent too-close Franco-Prussian rapprochement—which could only be done by satisfying some of Prussia's demands upon Austria. The Hanoverian newcomer to the English throne was not so securely settled there as to dispense with the windfall of French support or, for that matter, the advantages of his close connexion with Prussia, Hanover's next-door neighbour and potential protector—even though accretion of power to a next-door neighbour was in itself undesirable. Russia, manœuvring for leverage on German soil; Sweden and Holland, in constant maritime competition against each other as well as against England; Saxony-Poland, like Hanover-England coupling an Electorate with a foreign crown of problematical stability—all were similarly involved, to the temporary profit of Prussia.

This happy moment coincided with the opening of Frederick William's reign. Not many weeks after his accession the new King harvested the fruits of long previous negotiations under his 'feckless' father, in the shape of the district of Obergeldern, which nicely rounded off the Prussian possessions in Westphalia. Not long after that came the first transaction concluded entirely on his own account, by which access to the Baltic came at last within Prussia's reach and the Great Elector's gains in Pomerania appeared likely to be realized after all.

Altogether the new régime had got off to a good start. Land reclamation was accelerating, judicial and fiscal reforms were already in motion, also plans for new canal projects to extend the Kingdom's system of waterways which formed the only reliable means of transportation. So successfully had the administration been tightened up, that already here and there a little 'Plus' could be recorded, every spare Pfennig saved by infinite husbandry accruing to the benefit of the army.

Its army was the index of a country's standing in the world; the size and potency of a country's army stood in direct relation to its wealth. The growth of both went hand in hand, ad infinitum. Thus Frederick William reasoned. Yet there were aspects of his military preoccupation in which reason had no very distinctive part.

Where the army was concerned, his loquacious Christian conscience fell quite dumb. Here he was demoralized by something like the collector's zeal, something like the perfectionist's perpetual momentum; here was his weak spot, where he ceased to be incorruptible.

To put the King in a favourable humour it was necessary only to make him a present of a tall recruit suitable for his Giant Guard. He himself thought nothing of paying a sum equal to several times a cabinet minister's salary for a prospective Giant in good condition: his one extravagance as he admitted, which in the fullness of pre-Freudian innocence he likened to lesser men's addiction to women. Grooming, inspecting, exercising his 'Longfellows', the stumpy little monarch who still had to fight for recognition on all fronts, found the ideal docility he craved, in these looming, living, lethal, utterly obedient toys.

No traveller six feet tall or over was safe on Prussian soil, and not much safer in neighbouring countries. Tall men would be drugged, knocked on the head, tied up and sometimes suffocated in transit, regardless of who or what they were, and, once they had been incorporated in Frederick William's army, would be treated as deserters if they ran away. Only when the victim happened to be a foreign diplomat and international complications threatened, was he regretfully released.

International complications were not always avoided. The King could not put his entire male population under arms, much as he would have liked to, without prohibitive set-back to agriculture and trades which he wished to further. A fair proportion of Prussian peasantry, drawn from carefully worked-out cantons, made up the regimental nuclei, with a service term of twenty years and not ungenerous peacetime furloughs. Over and above this, the Prussian recruiting officers led busy lives and travelled far. Just as they did not confine themselves to hiring volunteers, they often seduced into the Prussian service soldiers already sworn to other sovereigns' colours. Although his worst enemy could not accuse Frederick William of having invented the press gang, or Prussia of holding the monopoly in this practice, under him military kidnapping was brought to a notorious art, often with serious enough repercussions.

But there were two specifically Prussian innovations, lynch-pins of a new type of military machine. One was the iron ramrod, supplanting the wooden, and giving greatly increased speed of fire. The second was the method of marching in step, extended to its ultimate conclusion, so that every movement, every breath, every particle of manœuvre were minutely synchronized, enabling troop formations to be handled indeed as one body. Both these originated with the Prince of Anhalt-Dessau—not strictly Prussian by birth, but eminently Prussian by association.

Dedicated to the profession of arms, Prince Leopold had trained himself for it from earliest youth, and become a colonel in the Prussian army at seventeen, the same year that he succeeded to his own principality, thereafter dividing his time, somewhat unequally, between the two. He had fought with great distinction and without a scratch under both Marlborough and Prince Eugene, was reputedly bullet-proof, now General Field-Marshal of Prussia and, though only twelve years older than his friend the second King, honorifically known as 'The Old Dessauer'. Fierce of visage, pitilessly brave, most absolute of disciplinarians, the Old Dessauer was feared as the devil and worshipped as morale incarnate in the army which, if not his child, was very much this martinet's special nursling.

At variance with the sort of character conjured up by these traits were an inventive brilliance smacking of the back-room rather than the battlefield, a total lack of that leavening of sentiment with which the tough professional soldier is usually credited, and questionable loyalty. Queen Sophie Dorothee fully believed that the bluff old warrior, given the chance, would cheerfully murder the whole royal family in their beds (to make room for his nephews of Schwedt); her son in after years endorsed this, adding that only the chance had been wanting, never the will. But the King himself remained indomitably blind to this view.

In one respect the Old Dessauer proved the rule of his unfeeling and unscrupulous nature by exemplary deviation. As a very young man he had fallen in love with a commoner, 'Mamsell' Anneliese Fos, daughter of an apothecary; he held fast to her and overcame every obstacle to make 'Mamsell' his legal wife, and they in truth lived most happily ever after. She often accompanied him on campaign, and later governed Anhalt for him during his absences at Berlin and Potsdam.

Potsdam, once a small fishing village in the pleasant lake district south-west of Berlin, had first taken the fancy of the Great Elector, who built himself a palace there. Frederick I, aged nine, wrote in his copybook of 1666, 'My father loves Potsdam very much. It certainly is a jolly place. I like being there and my brother does too,' and Frederick William there laid out his down-to-earth version of Marly, a combination of kitchen garden and pleasure ground. But the little town fast became something more than a jolly place as under Frederick I's practical-minded son its garrison functions were developed until Potsdam grew to be synonymous with model military training.

Two years after Frederick William's accession, the Prussian army was second to none and superior to most in equipment, discipline, and general health. Proportionately to population if not in actual size it was larger than any. In point of drill and uniformity it was unique. The latter, to promote esprit de corps and strike terror into the enemy, was carried so far that men of inadequate beard growth had the regulation moustache painted on. Frederick William's passion for order and the Old Dessauer's inspiration had come together at the to them most favourable point in time and space.

The Prussian service attracted other satellites of Brandenburg besides the Old Dessauer. Princes of Zerbst, of Köthen, of Brunswick were engaged in it at different times, though not always permanently: indicating not only their financial insolvency but also the functional anachronism residing in all these splinter-remnants of the feudal system, and, not least, the ever-irresistible pull of technical progress.

However, Frederick William's army had yet to pass the test of action.

War for the sake of war had no part in Frederick William's scheme, nor had conquest: 'God will prosper me, as I will act only in just cause,' he frequently reiterated. Yet the only accepted proof of martial power is in the fighting.

In all justice and equity the opportunity came with the spring of 1715.

CHAPTER 4

FREDERICK WILLIAM'S CAMPAIGN

The Prussian army mobilized. Berlin resounded with it, the famous arsenal—said not to have its like in Europe—disgorged its armaments, the mired streets sank under more traffic than would normally pass over them in years together. The bustle and din found a happy echo in the small Crown Prince. The court painter Pesne was directed to commemorate a promising incident, as follows: Frederick, aet. three, is shown still in skirts and feathered bonnet, but yet a budding soldier with his drum, as he strains in the direction of a distant grenadier, away from his sister and her girlish blandishments. 'As I am human and might die or be shot dead, I command you all to look after Fritz, and God will reward you,' the commander-in-chief wrote in valedictory instruction to the privy council; 'my wife to be consulted in all things,' meanwhile.

The seat of war was in Pomerania; the quickening cause of it had until very recently lain in Turkey: Charles XII of Sweden, without whom no gallery of great captains or eccentrics would be complete.

Charles XII was born in 1682 and inherited the Swedish Crown at the age of fourteen, without at first appearing in the least struck by the obligations of sovereign office. But his frivolous juvenile pursuits were abruptly broken off by the action of his neighbour the King of Denmark who, in concert with Augustus the Strong of Saxony and Peter the Great of Russia, deemed Sweden an easy prey to aggression under this boy king. They little knew what they were stirring up, and that the force thus brought into being would remain a source of unrelieved disquiet to the whole Continent as long as Charles was alive.

To begin with he was lucky, in that England and Holland could not stand idly by while a triple alliance of such magnitude took over the whole Scandinavian and Baltic complex. But Charles's thirst for vengeance grew even as he slaked it, and victory created its own appetite. From a defender of his own he turned into a crowned adventurer.

He beat the Danes, he beat the Saxons, he beat the Russians, and in the course of twelve years blazed a broad trail of fire and sword across Europe, which was halted only in the mid-Ukraine. Like Napoleon and Hitler after him, Charles XII immeasurably raised Russian prestige and pride by an ultimately unsuccessful invasion; like them he underestimated the galloping corrosion of defeat following on a run of ascendancy seeming resistless.

For the nonce Charles cut his losses and, leaving behind him all but a handful of attendants, fled to take refuge across the Turkish border.

He remained in Turkey for five years.

His asceticism and endurance bordered on the bizarre, his fearlessness and obstinacy on the maniacal, and it was during this period of exile that they displayed themselves at their most astounding.

The first three years he spent on friendly terms with his hosts and in relative quiescence, merely doing everything in his power to drag Turkey into war with Russia. The Turkish government then attempted to eject him, by a variety of methods not excluding siege and fire, all in vain. Even imprisonment could not persuade Charles to escape from his sorely tried gaolers. It is a measure of his force of character that the Porte did not solve the irksome problem by assassination, and that Charles, without a penny to his name but what was hospitably doled out to him, could thus blithely carry on his attempts to change the course of European politics, literally singlehanded.

Now, while Charles XII was thus in eclipse, the heir presumptive to the Swedish throne, Duke Karl Friedrich of Holstein-Gottorp, was attacked in his hereditary lands of

Holstein by the King of Denmark and asked the Prussian King for help. Frederick William was not unwilling, but, as picturesquely he put it, had a thorn in his foot dating from the Peace of Westphalia, which he needed to have pulled before he could march.

His meaning was clear; Holstein met the Prussian requirement with an offer of part of the Great Elector's conquests in Pomerania (notably the city of Stettin), which had gone to Sweden. The bargain was to take effect when the Duke became King of Sweden; meanwhile, it was pointed out, if Prussia would join with Holstein in guarding Hither Pomerania, and would furnish a part of the Stettin garrison, this would be more than half-way to possession, even now. The consent of the Swedish Crown was more or less taken for granted, since the addition of Holstein to Sweden would make up for what was ceded to Prussia.

The matter by no means ended there and then; but the eventual upshot was that Frederick William held Stettin in pawn, under sole occupation by Prussian troops, and with the blessing of most of the major powers.

At this the absentee King of Sweden decided to return. He sent his compliments to Constantinople and departed overnight, to travel incognito, improvising transport as he went along, barely pausing for sleep, so that he reached his town of Stralsund in Pomerania after a record journey of sixteen days. He was welcomed with an enthusiasm swiftly waning when it became clear to the burghers of Stralsund that he intended forthwith to start again where he had left off, with their town for his springboard and headquarters.

Charles's first objective was Stettin, being the key at once to the Baltic and to control of the River Oder. Nothing, no amount of international argument, blackmail, or attempted bribery, could dissuade him. After much heart-searching the Prussian King declared war on the Swedish and undertook to lead against him an allied force including Danish, Saxon, and Russian troops, with some token support by England who twelve years before had first helped turn the scales in Charles's favour.

The 'Iron Hero' of the North, who slept by preference on

the floor, never touched wine, and whose wardrobe consisted of one blue coat with brass buttons, was a man after Frederick William's heart: 'Why will the one King I admire force me to make war on him?' he mourned, but shouldered his historic duty and at the head of a combined army of nearly 40,000 proceeded to the siege of Stralsund.

The Swedish forces numbered 14,000. In the past Charles XII had triumphed against similar odds, but his opponents then had been mainly rabble; also, offensive not defensive warfare was his forte. Even so he gave them a run for their money: the siege went on till half-way through December—till, the defenders' last outwork fallen, Charles's officers begged him on their knees to give up, and till—tearing at the timber with bare hands—he was wounded in a last desperate charge against the Prussian palisades.

And even then he would not give the order for surrender. He could not bring himself to frame the words, only to mumble some cryptic phrase which his staff might interpret as they liked. However, he left them to it and fled, back to Sweden at last.

The Prussians, who had borne the brunt of the campaign, remained in possession of Stralsund and the island of Rügen, together with all Hither Pomerania up to the River Peene.

Frederick William was a happy man. His soldiers had done credit to the new method, and he had made good the spadework of the Great Elector. It was enough. He forbade any special victory celebrations at home—just as two years earlier he had saved the expense of a formal coronation: the coronation of the first King had cost enough to last for several generations.

Charles XII never saw his capital again. Early next year he staged the first of several attempts to annex Norway whence, in planned alliance with the Tzar so lately his foe, he would have launched an invasion of Scotland to restore the Stuarts and thus accomplish what most of the world now regarded as hopeless. But not two years later he died by a musket ball which pierced his head from eye to temple, in the trenches outside Fredrikshall, a Norwegian fortress he was then besieging. He was thirty-six years old at his death, and his country did not soon recover from the ravages of his exploits.

* * *

THE GREAT ELECTOR
Frederick William, eleventh Elector of Brandenburg

THE FIRST KING IN PRUSSIA
Frederick I, formerly Elector Frederick III of Brandenburg

THE SOLDIER KING
Frederick William I, a self-portrait
(signed, and marked 'original')

Frederick William, always looking ahead, had marked down three officers who had distinguished themselves before Stralsund as future tutors for his son. Two were professional soldiers of the Prussian nobility, Lieutenant-General Fink von Finkenstein and Lieutenant-Colonel von Kalkstein, appointed respectively Head Tutor and Sub-Tutor. The post of acting 'Informator' fell to a young man of Huguenot extraction, named Jaques Egid Duhan de Jandun, who had taken part in the Pomeranian expedition as a volunteer, though owning certain bookish interests.

The actual education of the Electoral and royal children usually was in the hands of Huguenot refugees or their descendants. It had been so ever since the Edict of Potsdam (1685), the Great Elector's answer to Louis XIV at the revocation of the Edict of Nantes, under which Protestant liberties had been guaranteed in France. By the Edict of Potsdam French Protestants were welcomed in Brandenburg with open arms, and a first wave of some 20,000 had immediately availed themselves of the invitation. As many of them were qualified to move in good society, as most of them arrived penniless, and as proficiency in the French language was the one indispensable accomplishment of princes, here was an obvious opening for Huguenot instructors.

So Frederick William had entrusted the early care of his children to his own childhood governess, Mme de Rocoulles, an emigrée widow greatly esteemed by his mother, the learned Sophie Charlotte. If, despite a lifetime in Brandenburg and a loyal attachment to the royal family, the entire outlook of the Frenchwoman remained true to her cultural origins, this caused the King no misgivings—after all, he himself had emerged from their association quite unfrenchified. (But the Prussian Soldier King, like his son after him, all his life spoke better French than German—albeit the antiquated, idiosyncratic emigré French.) He had no hesitation in exposing his son and heir to further French influence after Mme de Rocoulles' task was ended as regarded the elder children: Duhan de Jandun should take over when the Crown Prince was seven.

Already there were other influences at work upon the child. Before he had completed his fifth year, Fritzchen knew the whole fifty-four movements of the Prussian Drill and had begun to learn the German Catechism and the elements of arithmetic. ('The Prince learns but slowly,' a preceptor submits, 'like all fundamentally profound minds.') The King was proud of the little fellow who, the father's replica in everything but size, would attend troop reviews at his side, and drill and march his own cadet regiment to church on Sundays. The succession would be safe with him. In any case, another royal Prince had been born to Prussia in 1717 (after a pause in 1715 and a daughter in 1716).

The principle of primogeniture was yet far from being universally established. Even in countries where it was in force, it still had the flavour of an arbitrary invention rather than a law of nature. Here, too, the French monarchy, pioneer of centralization, had given the lead, which few of the German potentates had followed until it became an urgent necessity to do so. It was due to the older customs of inheritance, by which sons had each and every one the right to an equal share in the paternal estate, that the States of the Empire had multiplied beyond utility. Without keeping property intact by entail on the eldest son there could be no increase in territory, power, or wealth; allowing the time-honoured process of steady diminution to continue would set a limit to very survival. In Brandenburg the logical conclusion had been drawn only within living memory, by—whom else but the Great Elector? to the thus understandable chagrin of the descendants of his second marriage, the Margraves of Schwedt.

The whole subject and nature of succession had lately been thrown into particularly intense focus by the failure of heirs male to the House of Austria.

The Habsburg Emperor Charles VI after nearly a decade of childless marriage had got a son who died at six months, followed by a daughter one year later, 1717. His brother and predecessor also had left only daughters. With Spain having passed from the Habsburg possessions, it was of the greatest importance to safeguard the rest; and the entire Austrian-Imperial policy was becoming geared to this circumstance.

It raised the most varied hopes elsewhere. In the maternal breast of Sophie Dorothee these took the form of brilliant matrimonial possibilities: why should not her eldest son become the husband of the Emperor's daughter? The religious disparity could be adjusted; it would not be the first time in the Imperial family. On the other hand, a daughter of the Russian Tzar would be an equally good match for Fritzchen, if he did not follow in the footsteps of his father and grandfather and marry a cousin and daughter of England.

The Queen had an opportunity of closer acquaintance with the Muscovite kindred.

Tzar Peter paid a state visit to Brandenburg on his way back from France where, ostensibly on a mission of cultural enquiry, he had been negotiating fresh insurance against the resilience of Charles XII. The same dual purpose informed Peter's stay at Frederick William's court. He was no stranger there, but previously had made only brief appearances, in rather rough and ready fashion, and without entourage.

His entourage this time was vast. There was not sufficient accommodation at the Palace of Berlin, being mostly given over to the Administration (the royal dining-room served for audience chamber between meals). Monbijou had its uses. The Queen had a suite of apartments cleared of breakable objects and placed it at the disposal of the visitors.

The Russian visit forms one of the high spots in the memoirs of the eldest Prussian Princess, Wilhelmine, aged eight at the time. With great gusto she describes the Tzarina, by origin a Lithuanian peasant and one-time camp follower to Peter's army—she had saved the Tzar's life at one of the most serious Russian reverses during the Swedish invasion, and had been elevated to the throne in as nice an act of gratitude as royal annals can record. One would imagine that she had great beauty; but no, according to Wilhelmine she 'was a little stumpy body, very brown. . . . Her dress, you would have said, had been bought at a second-hand shop; all was out of fashion . . . loaded with silver and greasy dirt. The front of her bodice she had ornamented with jewels in a very singular pattern: a double-eagle . . . the plumes of it set with poor little diamonds—' Wilhelmine, like her grandfather, was a connoisseur of diamonds, even at an early age—'of the smallest possible carat and very ill mounted. All along the facing of her gown were Orders and little things of metal . . . and as many portraits of saints, relics and the like, so that when she walked, it was . . . as if you heard a mule with bells to its harness. . . . The Tzar, on the other hand, was very tall and might be called handsome . . .'

Nevertheless the little Princess cried rape and dishonour under the Tzar's smacking kisses, to his huge amusement. He was unaccustomed to such resistance: the nut-brown Tzarina's ladies (alias cooks, washerwomen, chambermaids, etc., as occasion recommended) 'nearly all' arrived with richly dressed babies in their arms, and monotonously answered polite enquiries as to these with, 'The Tzar did me the honour.' He scandalized the Western Ministers, as he would discuss the weightiest matters standing with an arm thrown round one of these maids of honour on each side, brazenly fondling them while he talked business. When Peter's favourite niece, the Duchess of Mecklenburg, came to pay her respects, the loving uncle with shouts of joy snatched her from the side of her husband the Duke and carried her off to an adjoining bed-chamber without so much as shutting the door: an incident reported by no less prosaic an eye-witness than Frederick William.

There were other trying moments, as when in the cabinet of curios belonging to the deceased King the Tzar unerringly discovered a small indecent statue—a Roman fertility charm, one gathers—which he forced the Tzarina to kiss with the threat of, 'Kopp ab!' in his broken German: head off! if she didn't. Frederick William was glad to make the Tzar a present of the horrid idol, together with the old King's collection of amber and his pleasure yacht—all equally redundant to his successor.

The two monarchs parted on excellent terms. Frederick William had the guests escorted as far as Potsdam, moreover stretching Prussian hospitality as far as the border of Mecklenburg, with secret orders to his stewards to 'see that it be done for 6,000 Thaler: not a penny more, understand that! but let it be given out that this has cost me thirty or forty thousand.'

Shortly after there arrived one hundred and fifty Giants whom the grateful Tzar had had rounded up in his dominions; and every year thereafter until Frederick William's death a hundred Russian Longfellows were shipped to him in kind remembrance. Frederick William for his part supplied the Tzar with Prussian artisans proficient in a number of essential trades as yet hardly known in Russia, as well as some experienced drill sergeants and other military specialists.

As for the Queen, she found that after four days of Russian occupation, the Monbijou guest apartments had to be redecorated from top to bottom.

* * *

The Russian visit in a manner marked the zenith of Frederick William's initial diplomatic headway. As an earnest of Russo-Prussian understanding, in which France also had a part, it radically altered the position which had previously brought him international encouragement. The reverse became the case, and he suddenly found himself hemmed in with obstructions, emanating especially from Dresden, London, and Vienna. It was the beginning of a nightmare for his simple consciousness with its absolutes of right and wrong. He could have got out of it only by turning his back on the diplomatic arena and devoting himself exclusively to internal affairs, where those absolutes remained reasonably applicable. But he did not feel able to delegate a single one of his many tasks, for which he alone was truly qualified by his sacrosanct office and personal virtue.

The time had come for the next stage in the training of his son—once more his only son: the Prince born 1717 had died in his second year, and 1719's child was again a daughter.

Fritz was now seven. The triple appointment made at the end of the Pomeranian campaign became effective; Count Finkenstein, Colonel Kalkstein, and Duhan de Jandun took over. The King reconsidered the programme in the light of contemporary medical opinion which held that too much sleep was bad for growing children. A plan of work was drawn up and annually amended, as ever in the King's own hand.

Here is an abridged version:

> Sunday. On Sunday he is to rise at 7, and as soon as he has got his slippers on, shall kneel down at his bedside and pray to

God, that all in the room shall hear. . . . After which the Our Father. Then rapidly and vigorously wash himself clean, dress and powder [his hair] and comb himself . . . prayer, with washing, breakfast [a cup of tea] and the rest to be done within 15 minutes precisely. This done, all his domestics then withdraw again, and Duhan reads with my son the Gospel of the Sunday, expounds it a little, adducing the main points of Christianity . . . questioning from Noltenius's Catechism . . . it will then be 9 o'clock. At 9 [Duhan] brings my son down to me, who goes to church and dines along with me [at 12 noon]. The rest of the day is then his own. At half past 9 in the evening, he shall come and bid me goodnight. Shall then directly go to his room; very rapidly get off his clothes, wash his hands, and as soon as this is done, Duhan says a prayer on his knees and sings a hymn [Fritz to accompany him 'lustily'], all the servants being again present. Instantly after which my son shall get into bed, shall be in bed at half past 10. . . .

Monday. On Monday as on all week days he is to be called at 6 . . . rise . . . without turning over in his bed . . . and say his prayers, the same as on Sunday morning . . . [The same routine of washing, dressing, etc, and worship follows: finished by 7 a.m.] From 7 till 9 Duhan takes him in History. At 9 comes Noltenius with the 'Christian Religion' till quarter to 11. Then Fritz rapidly washes his face with water, hands with soap and water; clean shirt, powder; coat on. About 11 comes to the King. Stays with the King till 2 . . . On the stroke of 2 goes back to his room. Duhan is there, *ready*, takes him upon the map and geography from 2 to 3, giving account of . . . the European kingdoms, their strength and weakness, size, wealth or otherwise of their towns. From 3 to 4 Duhan shall lecture on Morality, from 4 to 5 write German letters with him . . . About 5, Fritz shall wash his hands and go to the King. . . . ride out, divert himself, in the open air and not in his room; and do what he likes so long as it is not against God.

Tuesday, Wednesday, Thursday, Friday follow the same pattern, with some variation of subjects. On Saturday in addition to his lessons the Prince is examined in the presence of Finkenstein and Kalkstein. If it be seen that he has profited from the week's work, he may have the afternoon to himself. If not, 'he shall from 2 to 6 do revision and learn rightly what has not stuck.'

His further military education was not neglected. To spur Fritz on, the thoughtful father provided a unique and costly toy: a miniature arsenal exactly modelled on the unrivalled Berlin 'Zeughaus', possessing every tool of war in perfect working order though designed for the use of children. No child could fail to delight in such playthings; certainly the father was delighted with them.

It is not in human nature to doubt that what most interests ourselves must be equally interesting to everyone else, most of all to one's own children. Frederick William could not believe that his son might be different from himself, or that a child might be unable to appreciate the adult pleasures of hard work, which did not stop at play.

CHAPTER 5

'LOVE ME, SCUM!'

Fritz at seven was already overtaxed; at eleven he was showing overt signs of lapsing.

The amended paternal Instruction for 1723 has the postscript: 'You *must* accustom [Fritz] to get out of and into his clothes as fast as is *humanly possible*. You will also see that he learns to put on and take off his clothes himself, *without any help from others*, and that he shall be clean and neat and *not so dirty*. Frederick William.'*

Frederick William's personal cleanliness was excessive for his time. Behind his back he was mocked for washing himself as often as a mussulman. He changed his shirt daily, when changing it once a week would be considered over-fastidious, while combing one's hair regularly could only disturb coiffures that were built to last.

Frederick William himself had not been the most docile of children; perhaps he would have remembered, and more easily forgiven open headstrongness in his son. But his son merely went and did what he wanted on the quiet—seeing that almost everything he liked doing seemed to be classifiable as being 'against God', that is, contrary to the father's tastes. The father could not understand it.

The King's favourite recreations were tobacco and the chase.

* Translation will not do justice to the King's style: most of his personal writing reads like a bellow. So in an attempt to render the impatient tone, and the determination of a disillusioned parent not to leave the slenderest loophole for quibbling omission, the keywords have here been put in italics.

Every evening Frederick William and a company of stalwarts would foregather round a brazier in the 'red room' with their long clay pipes, a jar of tobacco, supplies of beer, cheese, and ham, and amid forthright jest and horseplay mull over the affairs of the day. During these sessions requests and suggestions could be submitted with which it might be neither wise nor feasible to approach the King at other times; also he would relax and think aloud. His Tabagie was the nearest thing to a Prussian Cabinet, the privy council being only a glorified secretariat, while even the most senior generals might not presume to advise their master as of right.

In the hunting season the Tabagie along with most of the court moved to the royal lodge at Wusterhausen, a place set in bleak, marshy wilderness. The rooms were damp, appointments primitive, the chimneys smoked, the furniture consisted in the main of barrels or planks laid across barrels; the company would cough 'like a flock of March sheep' (Fritz's description). As for the chief business of these holidays, hardened old warriors dropped out of the running long before the King would be ready to call a halt, and that after initial conveyance by *Wurstwagen*, i.e. sausage car, an instrument of torture made of a pole slung between four wheels, on which passengers sat astride, with merely a hand rope on either side to hold on to. Enormous quantities of game would be slaughtered. For the season of January 1729, admittedly a peak one, the total bag of wild boar alone was 3,602 head, '300 of uncommon magnitude', 450 killed on one and the same day. Waste not, want not: the neighbouring villages were constrained to buy up the carcases, to process and feed on, surely for months.

Fritz moped at Wusterhausen, had no stomach for strong drink or for tobacco fumes, and took no pains to hide that he found the King's cronies uncongenial. All he cared for—said the father—was effeminate dress after the French mode, vapid repartee, reading, and music-making. He got it from his mother, where else but at Monbijou; he and his sister were a pair, too much so.

That there was such an explanation and someone else to be held responsible for the Prince's disappointing progress could not lessen the King's exasperation nor the blame he attached to the son himself; particularly at a time when he was meeting with evasions and recalcitrance in all his sovereign business too. His diplomatic enterprises were no longer prospering, and although his subjects were beginning to feel the benefits of measures ranging from complete economic reorganization to compulsory schooling for all Prussian children, they did not show him gratitude.

On the contrary: they ran from his approach. The King's habit of patrolling the streets and buttonholing anyone he had a mind to question had long since taught the populace to flee and hide if possible. On one tragi-comic occasion the King caught someone who had not been quick enough, and, his inevitable rattan stick raised high, demanded to know the reason for the man's flight. The man, stammering and trembling, answered that he had been afraid. 'Afraid? Afraid?' the father of his country thundered, belabouring the captive with his stick. 'You are supposed to love me! Love me, scum!'

The combination of words and action characterizes Frederick William's entire, paternalist attitude as well as the frustration it was everywhere encountering.

The Queen, while taking the son's part against the father, was no more of an indulgent parent towards her daughters, whose daily life was ruled by strictness and tedium. Aside from a few obligatory accomplishments, the Princesses' education was largely left for themselves to pick up.

The eldest, Wilhelmine, was the only one appreciably to avail herself of her opportunities in this respect. Frederick in after days confirmed that without his sister's urging him on he might have frittered away his gifts and his time in haphazard dalliance. By default of outright prohibition, Wilhelmine not only joined but at first outdistanced her brother in his studies. She was his most intimate friend, confidante, and emotional mainstay. Together they read the classics, dressed up, played duets, versified, invented a code language, and exchanged satirical remarks over the heads of the uninitiated: Papa was not immune from their wit. They were forever scribbling notes to one another; and Wilhelmine had in her keeping Fritz's first novel, composed at the age of ten. If in nothing else, the father was wrong in calling him lazy.

But there was the rub: Fritz's precocious industry, vented along undesirable channels, did not count as such. One story Frederick liked to relate of his early youth was about a surprise visit of inspection by his father, catching the son out at a Latin lesson.

King: 'What are you doing with my son?'

Tutor: 'Sire, we are reading Auream Bulleam.'

King, roaring: 'I'll auream bulleam you, rascal!'

Amid kicks and blows, the tutor was dismissed on the spot.

This was not Duhan de Jandun but another, one might say sub-sub-tutor; happily for Fritz. For the person Frederick ultimately credited with having rescued his mind from 'the stupor of ignorance to which it would have been consigned', that person was Duhan.

From the point of view of his employer, Duhan betrayed a royal trust. Possessed of a genuine love of literature, and acting upon his belief that a future monarch would be the better for a more liberal education than what Frederick William's schedule provided, Duhan introduced the Prince to the banned Ancient and French authors, among other intellectual fare to feed a hungry, imaginative young mind.

The wonder is that the King did not put two and two together, whenever he discovered Fritz in forbidden occupations or in possession of forbidden fripperies; that he did not make a thorough investigation to find the confederate without whose co-operation the Prince could hardly have persevered in those courses.

How well Duhan discharged his authorized duties is open to question. The letter written to him by the Prince at their parting (not till 1727, when Fritz was fifteen), does small credit to the teacher as a teacher:

'Mon cher Duhan Je Vous promais que quand j'aurez mon propre argent en main, je Vous donneres enuelement [*annuellement*] 2,400 écu par an, et je vous aimerais toujour encor un peu plus qu'asteure [*qu'à cette heure*] s'il me l'est posible.'

One counts eleven mistakes in four lines; in other ways, however, the little note speaks for itself—the more as the writer honoured his promise as soon as he was able. Man and boy, Frederick never wavered in his affection for Duhan and

Mme de Rocoulles as long as these two comforters of his boyhood were alive.

His readiness to love was as eager as his father's yearning to be loved. It is strange, therefore, to read among his earliest independent jottings the reflection, 'One must not love too strongly.' Frederick was nine years old when he set this down. In an environment where love and duty were by decree identical, it seems unlikely that he echoed an adult proposition; yet what was wrong with loving, since all those of whom it is recorded that he loved them, loved him back? Can it have been that there was one person to whom the young Frederick offered love in vain—one person in whose eyes he vainly sought favour, constrained by his own pride (even as that other person would have been under answering constraint) to return indifference for antipathy?

The King's first public demonstration of his feelings towards the Crown Prince occurred at a dinner given by the Prussian war minister, Field-Marshal von Grumbkow. Holding forth over his wine, the King, with an arm thrown round the Crown Prince sitting next to him, began as though idly to underline his remarks with taps on his son's cheek. As he continued speaking, the taps increased in force, till the King for no apparent reason was fairly boxing his son's ears. The company, one is not surprised to learn, was in some embarrassment; the host, though otherwise no friend to the Crown Prince, worked hard to create a diversion.

The year was 1724. In 1722 Sophie Dorothee had given birth to another son, Augustus William, now entering his third year in good health. The succession no longer rested on the head of an only son such as must needs be the apple of a father's eye; the father of two sons was under no compulsion to love unselectively. Augustus William was the favourite: the current Baby, generically effulgent with the promise which older children, passing into a notoriously awkward age, seem to be wilfully betraying. Furthermore, the second son was not the father's designate successor and dispossessor. Others making much of him did not automatically place themselves under the suspicion of investing in the future.

The thought that people showing a regard for the Crown

Prince were in fact speculating on the present monarch's death had become a fixture among the irritants to the King's sensitivities. Allusions to it were constantly cropping up in his utterances. Like many men who pray aloud for death, Frederick William in fact could not bear the thought of it. Sincerely devout as he was, and undeservedly unloved as he believed himself, the thought maddened him not so much with the fear of extinction as such but with the prospect of others, as it were, dancing on his grave. He was already in the throes of an academic dilemma: which would he rather, after his own death, that his successor did well or that he did badly? Which would he rather, that his good work was undone or that another got the benefit of it—just as Frederick William himself had got the benefit of his own father's spadework at the outset of his reign? For the matter which, in the cause of Prussia's external increase, he had most at heart, the just acquisition of Jülich-Berg on the Lower Rhine, was progressing at the rate of two steps forward and one step back, when it was not, indeed, seething at a standstill. So near and yet so far, it began to look as if it might not be settled in his lifetime.

Allowing for the unavoidable falsifications of concise summary, Prussian foreign policy was determined by that issue. Perforce Frederick William swayed between the powers according as they now offered, now withdrew tentative guarantees of his succession to the Rhenish property. The principal alternatives were England and Austria. The rift between the King's and the Queen's parties at the court of Berlin had attained complete political import.

Yet the King, whilst being loosely credited with the leadership of one party, in reality was the objective of both.

Grumbkow and the Old Dessauer were the chief vehicles of Austrian influence, the Queen and her two elder children represented the English interest. Grumbkow was actually in the pay of Vienna, but as a leading member of the royal Tabagie enjoyed, like the Old Dessauer, the King's entire confidence. It was in the interests of both these men to play on the King's dissatisfaction with his heir; and as, the keener the King's dissatisfaction grew, the more surely one could please him by further whetting it, the majority of the Tabagie soon took their cue from the pair. The children, Fritz and Wilhelmine, were willing pawns in their mother's scheme, which hinged on an Anglo-Prussian marriage project, doubly to unite the rising generation: Wilhelmine with the eldest son of the Prince of Wales, Fritz with the latter's daughter, Princess Amelia.

Ambassadors reported abroad that the Prussian Crown Prince and Princess Royal were being used as their mother's spies in the father's camp, that the rugged court of Berlin was now to be classed as the most intrigue-ridden in all Europe, that the King seemed determined to work his heir to exhaustion ('The Prince looks pale and wan and moves wearily, like a veteran worn out by too many campaigns.'), and that much the same applied to the wonderful Prussian army: desertions were so frequent that the whole countryside was organized as a preventive grid, and the suicide rate in the Berlin garrison was two a month. So much for the Arch-Sandcaster's periodical sabre-rattling.

The consumption, not in Prussia alone, of paper, ink, and sand had gone up with the promulgation of the Pragmatic Sanction, also in the year 1724.

The Pragmatic Sanction had first been mooted in 1713: one year after Frederick's birth and four years before the birth of the Emperor's daughter Maria Theresa who was to become peculiarly associated with that Imperial instrument. By it Emperor Charles VI improved on an earlier Austrian 'House Law' extending the right of succession to females in default of males. This was a measure, long overdue, to knit the real possessions of the Austrian Habsburgs into one solid whole. Hitherto the so-called crown lands—including Bohemia and Hungary, the Milanese, Silesia, Moravia, Styria, Tyrol, Carinthia, Carniola, and portions of Flanders—had been held together only by the person of the reigning Archduke of Austria; in constant danger, thus, of piecemeal distribution among the collateral branches of the House in the event of the sovereign's death without heirs male. The primary significance of the Pragmatic Sanction rested in its asserting the indivisibility of the Austrian monarchy, rather than in its provision for female succession.

Such House regulations were always subject to ratification by the rest of Europe, as part of the universal bargaining that attended every slightest adjustment in the territorial pattern of the Continent and its network of alliances. Mutual recognition of terms of succession might involve anything from colonial claims to such trivial questions as to who should and who should not have the right to confer the Order of the Golden Fleece.

In this way for well over twenty years the Pragmatic Sanction was a dominant feature of the international scene, with the Imperial Government bent on collecting guarantees and discounting the scepticism of its doyen, famous Prince Eugene, who suggested that a few extra battalions added to the Austrian army would be worth more than any amount of parchment.

It took years for the new ruling to be endorsed even in the Habsburg crown lands, with the exception of the immediate Austrian core and the Kingdom of Bohemia which itself had first come to Austria by female inheritance. In trying to ensure the acquiescence of the Bourbon states a match was proposed between one of the young Austrian Archduchesses and a Prince of Spain. This proposition caused great alarm in Germany, where it was felt such a connexion would be tantamount to having the Pope himself for Emperor: in Spain the Catholic Church ruled with an anachronistic rigidity more Roman than that of Rome.

Brandenburg-Prussia accordingly gravitated more and more towards the anti-Imperial forces. Friendship with England was on the upgrade, with frequent family visits to and from Hanover whenever George I came over. The double-marriage project promised to thrive, for all that Frederick William's alertness to Hanoverian arrogance grew ever more poignant, while his children were intimidated by their grandfather's ceremonious manner—'positively Spanish', in Wilhelmine's words—together with their mother's hectic stage management to make them put their best foot forward.

With characteristic tardiness the Imperial Government, having of late consistently cold-shouldered Frederick William, now anxiously bethought itself how best to drive a wedge between the two Protestant royal Houses, without making greater concessions to Prussia than the Imperial equilibrium could afford.

To this end there was despatched from Vienna an old comrade-in-arms to Frederick William, the Imperial Ordnance Master Count von Seckendorf who had also fought in the Wars of the Spanish Succession and the halcyon Pomeranian campaign. With the connivance of Grumbkow a 'surprise' reunion was arranged: Seckendorf sauntered across the Palace esplanade of Berlin just as the King was at his window smoking his mid-day pipe. The King immediately sent for him and on learning that Seckendorf planned to stay only for a day or two, in transit to Scandinavia, importuned him to prolong his stay. Seckendorf allowed himself to be persuaded, till his stay became indefinite. He remained, a permanent Imperial envoy with unlimited Austrian funds at his disposal.

Seckendorf possessed a degree of cunning far above that of any other member of the Tabagie including its royal president, and a degree of stamina in which others, jaded by custom and imperfect in singlemindedness, could not equal him. He shirked nothing to make himself agreeable to the King who felt he had never had so truly kindred a soul at his beck and call, endlessly willing to listen to the King's repetitious anecdotes and sententious tirades which had long worn away the freshness of response in everybody else. In what time was left to him, Seckendorf studied the foibles of all who might conceivably become of use and played on them with eminent success, neglecting no one who was in the least venal, from the odd lackey to the Prussian Resident in London.

Thus Seckendorf's activities were an open secret to almost everyone except the King. The Queen, he reported to Vienna, so loathed the sight of him that he had the greatest trouble to get one word out of her even at table. Most of the courtiers cut him dead save when the King was by, and the Crown Prince and Princess Royal treated him with unveiled sarcasm—thus providing Seckendorf with useful ammunition against themselves in relation to their father. The Emperor's cause began freshly to flower at Berlin.

George I had died in June 1727, succeeded by Frederick William's boyhood antagonist, his cousin and brother-in-law,

THE ROYAL RESIDENCE OF BERLIN

OLYMPIA-FIEKCHEN
Queen Sophie Dorothee

THE OLD DESSAUER
Prince Leopold of Anhalt-Dessau

A SIDELIGHT ON FREDERICK WILLIAM'S POMERANIAN EXPEDITION (see p.33)
The Crown Prince and Princess Royal of Prussia, [illegible]

now apostrophized as 'My Brother, the Comedian', or 'My Brother, the Red Cabbage'—endearments which George II returned in kind, with 'My Brother, the Drill Sergeant', and so on. Like the Emperor before him, the King of England made the mistake of letting Frederick William see that one regarded him as a safe and therefore negligible ally, which Seckendorf lost no opportunity to rub in.

Matters were not improved when it came to Frederick William's notice that his son was heavily in debt and that the British envoy had been authorized to help him out. Seven thousand Thaler (two thousand of which had gone on musical scores) were owing to one Berlin banking house alone.

According to himself, the father took a most forbearing line with Fritz. 'I'll pay [your debts] with the greatest of pleasure, for I do not lack the means and care not *that* for money—just so long as you will mend your ways and show yourself an honest fellow in future: say but the word and you shall not want for money.' Thus Frederick William later transcribed what he had said to his son, a speech which could not well have been more charitable, or more unlikely.

Before ever that alleged speech was made, the situation between father and son had gone from bad to worse. The King was informed that Frederick had been heard to deplore the brutalities of army discipline and referred to the military uniform as 'the shroud'. He had found him out reading a book in the thickets of Wusterhausen when he was supposed to stalk deer; he had personally burnt Frederick's contraband dressing-gown and peruque, and given orders for a chamberlain to sleep beside the Prince to make sure he did not read at night.

It was as if the incident at Grumbkow's dinner had broached a dam; henceforth the King's feelings poured forth with ever-increasing abandon. Soon he did not care whom he told what he thought of his son, nor who was there to watch him abuse and chastise the object of his displeasure. Once he nearly strangled Frederick with a curtain cord, or at all events made as if to do so.

The mounting tension was arrested by an invitation to Dresden for the carnival season of 1728.

CHAPTER 6

THE VISIT TO DRESDEN

The Anglo-Prussian marriage project, now off, now on, and the intricate conjugations ceaselessly arising out of the Pragmatic Sanction, played their part in fraying Frederick William's temper. Besides, for the acting head of every existing government department, there was never any end of fiendishly interlinked problems, enough to daunt a mind more supple and detached than was this King's, calculated to disrupt the nerves of a less sensitive soul.

'I no longer understand anything about this world,' he wrote to the Old Dessauer, ever-willing repository of the royal depressions. 'May God make a blessed end [of me] soon, that there be an end to all vexations. Because it is past bearing.'

'Now I wish for nothing in this world so much as that I might go far away and find some lonely spot abroad to live in quiet seclusion. For that I am good for nothing in this world and everything annoys me.'

'The trouble is that, God knows, all my days I have been too gentle. Better I had been more choleric!'

Yet there were moments when the mist of self-pity cleared: moments in which Frederick William stated outright that the very, choleric propensities he disclaimed unfitted him for direct intercourse with the foreign envoys. Needless to say, he continued to treat with them in person.

The manic-depressive cycle became steadily more pronounced—never, to be sure, without good external reasons to justify the King's moods, which presently began to run to hypochondria and presentiments of assassination. He elaborated on his visions of retirement: he would be a farmer and till the soil, his wife would oversee the housekeeping, one daughter take charge of the linen, another do the shopping, and so on. Fritz might carry on the thankless burden of the Crown.

Count Seckendorf was seriously alarmed. With young Frederick on the throne, Prussia would come under English influence for good and all. The King must be coaxed into a happier frame of mind. So it was intimated to the Saxon Court that Austria would not be ungrateful if Frederick William were cured of the megrims amid the splendours and gaieties of Dresden; and this was the true object of the invitation.

Frederick William accepted; a rapprochement with Saxony was opportune. He wanted to put in a good word for the Pragmatic Sanction, which Saxony despite friendly enough relations with Austria had so far refused to recognize.

The Protestant Elector of Saxony, Augustus II, had in 1697 embraced the Catholic faith as a condition of his acquiring the Crown of Poland—an act which indirectly had helped to pave the way for the foundation of the Prussian Kingdom four years later, to right the disturbed balance of power within the Empire. Augustus, called the Strong, was a connexion by marriage of the Elector of Bavaria who was a Habsburg collateral and intended to claim the Austrian heritage on Emperor Charles VI's death, when therefore Saxony might hope for a share.

Though fifty-eight years old to Frederick William's forty, Augustus was a man of royal physique as yet showing little sign of the wear and tear which an in every sense active life might have wrought upon his person. His titular Strength applied also to his mental powers, and to a total ruthlessness in the pursuit of what he meant to get. But above all it was his sexual prowess which had caught the popular imagination. The final tally of his bastards came to 354.

This is the number cited in Wilhelmine's memoirs, to which we are indebted for so much of the information concerning her brother's early life.

Wilhelmine's memoirs have had their ups and downs in the regard of the historians. Some have accepted the material as it stands, others have dismissed it, while the majority have exercised individual discretion as to what is to be relied on and what adjudged false.

Where the Princess's writings touch on matters which were common knowledge, or to which other witnesses besides her testified, decision is easy enough—and it is usually in favour of her veracity. It is when dealing with events within the closed, inner circle of the family that she is most often charged with malice or invention. In other words, those of her stories which have been discounted at different times are the ones reflecting discredit on a family subsequently canonized, one might say, lock, stock, and barrel, for the sake of its most outstanding member.

Wilhelmine, it is true, wrote many years after the events described, at a time when ill-health, disappointment, and divers family unpleasantnesses might be assumed to have coloured her outlook; and doubtless like most people she preferred to make a good story of what she had to tell. She sometimes goes wrong in her details—enabling her critics to point out triumphantly that, say, a scene she may place on a Tuesday even if true could only have occurred on a Thursday and probably a year later than her date. Of malice certainly she cannot be exonerated; but it is writers themselves evincing the strongest counter-bias who most strongly denounce her want of detachment. A certain amount of hyperbole, too, one would be inclined to concede from the start: for example, the bevy of maids of honour to Peter the Great's Tzarina, 'nearly all' with baby bastards in their arms, perhaps might soberly be reduced to two or three in that position. As for the precise number of the bastards fathered by Augustus the Strong, some prodigious research programme may yet ascertain it; at all events, his illegitimate progeny was exceptionally numerous.

The Prussian royal visit to Dresden was recorded by other pens besides that of Wilhelmine*, whose general account agrees with theirs although she was not herself present.

* Count Jakob Heinrich von Flemming, Baron Karl Ludwig von Pöllnitz, etc.

Very nearly her brother had not been present either. Only at the eleventh hour did the King relent and allow the Crown Prince to accompany him. This was Frederick's first venture outside the family enclave. He was enraptured, and took to the glittering urbanities of Dresden like a duck to water.

'Fritz, Fritz, I fear you like it here, all too well,' his worried Papa expostulated; to which Fritz audaciously replied, 'If you did not want me to enjoy myself, why did you let me come?' One wonders.

Frederick took full advantage of his temporary liberation, caressed, indulged, applauded as other princes were all their lives, and feasting on the longed-for sweets of civilization. Augustus was a great collector and patron of the arts: compared with his host's style of living, Frederick William vowed, that of the first Prussian King had been as naught. Yet in spite of the prevailing emphasis on both culture and sensuality, Frederick William confessed himself agreeably surprised in some respects. Although the Dresden arsenal struck him as pitifully meagre, he enthused about Augustus's fortress of Königstein as well worth travelling a hundred miles to see, and found a number of Saxon regiments to commend. It but grieved him that here the military profession as such enjoyed small esteem, and he went out of his way to make much of every Saxon army officer he met.

The amorous temptations of Augustus's court Frederick William declared to have been very great, but, 'I am thankful to say I left as pure as I had come.' He took pathetic precautions to preserve the chastity of his son and heir—in vain, if Wilhelmine is to be trusted. On one occasion Augustus slyly sprang on the Prussian visitors a tableau vivant depicting Venus very lightly clad. Frederick William, with the greatest presence of mind, clapped his cocked hat over Fritz's eyes and propelled him out of the room.

All in all, however, Frederick William enjoyed himself too. Although his favourite dishes were of the simplest, like ribs of mutton boiled with cabbage, he could appreciate a fine gargantuan banquet; and practical jokes like Augustus's loving cup which fired a shot when tilted, could mellow him amazingly. He even took part in the dancing, split his uniform coat, and, as his waist measurement was well on the way to its ultimate 8 ft. 6 in.*, had to wait huddled in blankets for a replacement to be run up.

So on the surface the visit passed off well enough. But it may have had one rather more serious consequence than the generous exchange of pledges, decorations, and other empty amenities.

Shortly after father and son had returned to Berlin, Fritz fell sick. Regarding his symptoms the information is vague, loosely describing a state of general decline, which over a period of months reduced the Prince to 'a shadow' and wrought a transient change of heart upon the King.

'When one's children are well, one does not know that one loves them,' Frederick William wrote, unerringly revealing his anguish to the person least likely to share it—the Old Dessauer.

The theory, which has much circumstantial evidence in its favour, is that Frederick had contracted a venereal disease at Dresden, that this was either misdiagnosed, neglected, or wrongly treated, until his genitals were threatened with mortification, and that then an operation was performed which removed a portion of the penis—without, however, affecting the testicles and the hormone balance of an organism thus remaining wholly masculine though incapable of the sexual act. This would fit in well with the ensuing development of Frederick's personality and explain much that is otherwise enigmatic. But there is no incontrovertible proof. What has been adduced in support of this thesis, as well as how it first came to be stated, belongs in a later chapter of Frederick's life.

Certainly modern medical science was in its infancy, and the distinction between physician and quacksalver somewhat blurred—when, indeed, practitioners were available. The future Catherine the Great as a young child in rural Pomerania had to be doctored by the local hangman as the only person for miles around with any knowledge of anatomy and pharmaceutic lore. The incidence of venereal disease was high, and

* At the end of his life he weighed 19½ stone.

although standard treatments were in use, new supposed cures were constantly forthcoming.

It would be idle to pile speculation on speculation and try to gauge Frederick William's reactions to a calamity which (*a*) may or may not have happened, and (*b*) of which, if happen it did, he may or may not have been told. All we know is that he was deeply worried by Frederick's illness, and that his re-awakened love for his eldest son was of very short duration.

It almost seems as though during the abeyance of his dislike the feeling had gathered fresh strength, so that when once more he gave it rein, its manifestations broke the last rational bounds.

No doubt the double-marriage project had something to do with it. Relations with England were entering another stage. The unfortunate Princess of Ahlden, mother of Sophie Dorothee of Prussia and George II of England, had died and left considerable property, with the not unusual result of bitter wrangling among the heirs. Furthermore, Frederick William suspected George II of working against the Prussian succession to the Rhenish Duchies of Jülich-Berg, for which the Emperor had at last promised his unqualified support in return for Prussia's unqualified support of the Pragmatic Sanction.

By Frederick's analysis long after, Augustus the Strong also had an eye on Jülich-Berg, busily intriguing in all directions to bring the twin duchies into Saxon possession whilst pulling the wool over Frederick William's eyes in Dresden. But, says Frederick with dignity, 'The King of Prussia divined these ulterior motives and only despised the hypocrisy of the King of Poland.' This thumbnail sketch of silent contempt is in piquant contrast to the double portrait of the two Kings which commemorated Augustus's return visit to Berlin later in the spring, contrasting somewhat less amusingly with Frederick William's current behaviour at home.

No longer would he grant Fritz the benefit of the most slender doubt: at thirty paces, so he shouted, he could tell that his son's head was full of evil thoughts. He banished Fritz from his sight, except at meals, when the Prince was now relegated to the bottom of the table. It was the common talk that the Crown Prince of Prussia usually arose hungry, as dishes did not reach him until they were empty; his mother had to smuggle food parcels to him. He was still within easy reach of his father's ire, whether expressed verbally or by a soup plate hurling across. ('We ducked,' says Wilhelmine, 'and were not harmed.') Hardly a day went by without fearful scenes, reverberating far beyond the Palace; doubts of the King's sanity began to be voiced abroad.

The French Ambassador privately advised the Prince to cultivate his charm and show up his father's uncouth brutality the more, also to make a point of befriending other victims of the King. Frederick's humiliation can scarcely have been lessened by such sympathetic counsel.

He could not do right. If he stood up to the King's insults, he only swelled the flood; when he submitted without argument, the King accused him of dissembling. And of course he was dissembling.

Here is a famous sample of correspondence, dated some three months after the Prince had recovered sufficiently to resume his military duties:

Wusterhausen, 11 September 1728

My dear Papa,

I have not for a long while made so bold as to come to my dear Papa, partly because I had been discouraged from doing so, but mainly because I had reason to expect a still worse reception than usual, and for fear of provoking my dear Papa the more with my present request I have preferred making it in writing. I thus beg to ask my dear Papa to be gracious to me, and can assure him that after long reflection my conscience has not accused me of the least thing with which to reproach myself; if nevertheless without my knowledge and intention I have done anything to anger my dear Papa, I herewith most humbly crave his pardon, and hope that my dear Papa may relinquish the cruel hatred which I perceive in all his treatment of me; I could not otherwise resign myself to it, since I always used to think I had a gracious father, and now I have to see the contrary is the case. I now, therefore, trust confidently that my dear Papa will think over all this and will again be gracious to me, while I assure him that still I shall not wittingly transgress; and regardless of his disfavour am, with the most submissive and filial respect, my dear Papa's most faithful and obedient servant and son,

Frederick.

Frederick William replied, addressing his son in the third person singular—the form used towards strangers of inferior class:

> His obstinate wicked head, which does not love his father, for when one does do everything [i.e. everything required of one], particularly loving one's father, then one does what [that father] wishes, not only when [the father] is there to see it, but also when he is not there. Further, he knows full well that I can't abide an effeminate fellow who has no inclinations worthy to be called human, who disgraces himself being able neither to sit his horse properly nor hit his target, and who is withal offensive in his person, dresses his hair like a fool and will not get it cut; and have reprimanded him in all this a thousand times, but always in vain and without no improvement in nothin' (*keine Besserung in nits*). Furthermore, [the person under discussion] is conceited, haughty and proud, won't speak a word to anybody but for a few exceptions, and who makes no effort to be pleasant and affable, and who grimaces with his face like an idiot, and who don't do anything freely except he is forced, doing nothing from love and having no other wish than to follow his own stubborn head, which head is otherwise no use to himself or anybody else. This is the answer.
>
> Frederick William.

Both wrote in German, the son clearly after a good deal of thought and undoubtedly with help from somebody, whether Duhan or another person more at home than himself with grammar and spelling. The father's answer, dashed off at chronic white heat, is more like the spontaneous style natural to them both. They were of course staying under the same roof.

The son made one even more desperate attempt upon the father's heart, again at Wusterhausen where the King would be presumed in holiday mood ('Cross country chase yesterday, cross country chase today, cross country chase tomorrow,' Frederick listed the local entertainments in a note to Wilhelmine).

The occasion was a banquet celebrating the Day of St Hubertus, patron of the chase. The Crown Prince was seated opposite his parents and next to the Saxon Ambassador, Suhm. Contrary to habit, the Prince drank deep and often, and began to ply Suhm with details of the intolerable slavery of his existence. He begged the Ambassador to see what he could do with King Augustus, since possibly the latter's intercession might move Frederick William to let his son travel abroad, if only for a short spell. His voice grew louder and presently carried above the din of carousal. The Queen became uneasy and made signs to her son, which he did not heed. He went on dilating on his wretchedness, only interrupting himself with the periodical cry, '*But yet I love him!*'

The King called across to ask what Fritz was talking about. Suhm tried to put him off with the soothing remark that the Prince was intoxicated and did not know what he was saying. 'Oh, he is only shamming,' the King called back. 'I want to hear.'

The Queen abruptly rose to retire, beckoning Fritz to come with her. The son rose too, but only to demand the father's hand across the table and cover it with kisses. He then went round the table, threw himself on his father's lap, embracing the King and babbling that his enemies had been slandering him to turn his father's heart against him, that he had no wish but to love and obey his Papa; he fell on his knees and clasped the King's legs. There were tears in many eyes, some guests cried vivat to the Prince. Frederick William growled awkwardly, 'All right, all right, just see that you turn out an honest fellow.'

The Prince was then taken off to bed. The King was in unusually good humour for the remainder of the evening. Next day, however, the King became persuaded—by 'certain others', no names mentioned—that the Prince's outburst had been all calculated pretence.

If pretence it was, it seems oddly ill thought out, contradictory, badly managed. Frederick was an intelligent youth. Nor is it so unheard-of for the victim to love his tormentor.

Nevertheless, at about the same time as that chilling little scene took place and the abject letter above was written, Frederick stood in secret correspondence with his aunt, Queen Caroline of England, vowing eternal love and troth to his divine damsel the Princess Amelia and committing himself right and left as to the future, against present help.

When he was so rash as to speak of his feelings to his father, the King exploded as usual, 'How can one be in love with a person one does not know? Rubbish!'

CHAPTER 7

IN TORMENTIS . . .

Wilhelmine too had formed a strong imaginative attachment to her fiancé-elect the Prince of Wales, awaiting their union as she might—so the King once said in an access of unconscious penetration—the coming of the Saviour. To Frederick William's children, the English marriage spelt salvation. To himself it had become a symbol of all his besetting ills of office: for every time the matter looked as if it had been settled, either one way or the other, a consequent shifting in the international pattern caused the whole question to be reopened.

The conflict of interests between the Austrian compound monarchy and the established maritime powers of England and Holland, which had been steadily growing ever since the formation of an Imperial (Ostend) East India Company, was coming to a head. Spain had agreed to support the Pragmatic Sanction in return for the Emperor's pledge of active assistance in driving England out of Gibraltar and Minorca. In return for the Emperor's pledge to Prussia, at long last, to guarantee her succession to Jülich and Berg, Prussia was induced to withdraw from an alliance with England and France, thus leaving Hanover exposed to diversionary attack. Spain thereupon moved against Gibraltar, and Austria in behalf of Spain prepared for action in the North. Another all-European war was imminent.

The principals worked for all they were worth to bring in the remaining powers on their respective sides, not omitting

Prussia, once more in a key position. But so far from profiting by this as he had every right and reason to expect, the Prussian King saw himself taken for a fool, on both sides.

The Emperor found he might have a better use for Jülich-Berg than letting the twin duchies swell the strength of Prussia. He went back on his pledge and offered Frederick William compensation in Hanover—if Frederick William would defeat Hanover for him first. Against this, Hanover-England had the temerity, as Frederick William saw it, to offer only their Prince Fred and Princess Amelia whom, he was not slow to intimate, they could keep. He got a little of his own back at this stage by insisting that marriage was a purely private affair which he must refuse to discuss in political terms. As this refusal was itself a sound political move, he had some reason to be aggrieved that his nearest and dearest would not see anything but personal spite in it; yet he gave them plentiful cause for their interpretation, with rages and vituperation by way of argument.

Early in 1729 Frederick William had a severe attack of gout by which he suffered indescribable tortures, bringing his irascibility to boiling point.

Confined to bed, he tried to keep abreast of his paper work and to cheat his agony by painting pictures. A court artist would draw the outline and mix his colours for the royal amateur, the King signing their collective efforts as, 'in tormentis pinxit'. As soon as might be he was back on the prowl, albeit in a wheel chair, roaring and flourishing his cane as he chased his children round the table, still poking and lashing out at them when they hid underneath. In the presence of his wife he publicly proposed the toast, 'A scoundrel, anyone that is for Hanover!', addressed his love-lorn daughter as 'Hanoverian scum', and promised to exclude Frederick from the succession in favour of his darling second son (there was now a third, born 1726). He did not know what to do with himself, in constant pain and inner conflict: for he longed to be fully reunited with the Emperor, epitome of paternalism, yet could not, must not break with England until politically justified.

Every now and then the right moment appeared in sight. Hanover started meddling in yet another of Prussia's prospective preserves, the Duchy of Mecklenburg. Hanover protested against the abduction of ten Hanoverian subjects and arrested some Prussian recruiting sergeants. Hanoverian peasants garnered the hay mown by Prussian peasants in a debated meadow on the common frontier.

Ill-feeling between George II and Frederick William reached a pitch where the cousins seriously contemplated settling their differences in single combat. The duel was narrowly averted, but worse threatened as 44,000 Prussian troops massed by the frontier of Mecklenburg and Hanover. The Pope in Rome conjured Heaven to bring the quarrel between the two leading heretic powers to the proper climax; Prince Eugene pressingly offered himself for military adviser to the Prussian King; Grumbkow received round-about instructions from Vienna to 'keep treading on the Goodman's [i.e. Frederick William's] toes until he shall let rip [i.e. declare war].'

But the danger blew over. With the Treaty of Seville the Anglo-Spanish flare-up was doused for the nonce, and England and Prussia agreed to a settlement by arbitration. The double marriage project was resuscitated.

Monotonously the seesaw of negotiations went back into action. Now Frederick William in a glow of post-prandial contentment would drink to the marriage contract, suggesting that it was as good as signed; now he would not have a double marriage after all but only one, saying that a stuck-up English daughter-in-law undermining his authority in his own home was the last thing he wanted at Berlin. However, an alternative proposal, that his son should become Governor of Hanover and live there with his English bride, did not appeal to Frederick William either: what, have Fritz preening himself in splendour right next door—and as though his father were unable to provide for him? His father would rather endure the sight of Fritz's face at home for ever.

That this sight now galled him beyond endurance was common knowledge. The British Ambassador Dubourgay deposed as much, in so many words.

'The other day,' Dubourgay amplified, '[the King] asked the Prince, "Kalkstein* makes you English, does not he?"

* Frederick's official Sub-Tutor, now regarded as a partisan of the Queen.

To which the Prince answered, "I respect the English, because I know the people there love me;" upon which the King seized him by the collar [and] struck him fiercely with his cane. . . . There is a general apprehension of something tragical taking place before long.'

Frederick, describing the same incident, wrote to his mother: 'I am in the uttermost despair. . . . The King has entirely forgotten that I am his son. I am driven to extremity. I have too much honour to endure such treatment, and am resolved to put an end to it one way or another.'

As to this, the King was sceptical: 'Had I been treated so by my father, I would have put a bullet through my head: but you have not got it in you even to do that.' He rubbed salt into the wound: 'Let me tell you, the people who say to you that it will go better with you in time, are your enemies. For on the contrary, you'll find out I shall get harder every day.' Habitually labouring the point lest he fail to make himself quite clear, Frederick William added that any other officer who did not like the King's face could resign his commission: not so the King's son who had no choice but to stay put and take whatever was coming to him.

It was the King's expressed conviction that the more publicity attended reproach and correction, the more likely they were to be effective. Fritz got what was coming to him in front of his brother officers, in front of the generals, in front of the troops. Honour, Frederick William held, was the very stuff of the profession of arms; so he systematically set about punishing his son in that vital area. Yet Frederick by all accounts did his duty; he enjoyed sufficient regard in the army for rumour to attribute the King's persecution of him to envy of the Prince's popularity.

The happy family custom of lining up to kiss Papa goodnight led to another unbridled exhibition. Fritz, weary of his unvarying, bad reception, tried to shirk his turn. The King took him by the hair, threw him to the ground and forced him to kiss the father's boots. 'I treat you as my child, not as an officer.'

Frederick's secret store of books had been discovered, confiscated, and ordered to be sold out of hand. One wonders how it could have remained undiscovered long enough to grow to the number of some 3,700 volumes, including encyclopaedic works, a variety of scientific literature, manuals on rhetoric and rhyming, the classical authors in French translation, French and Italian poetry and prose, the novels of Cervantes, books on history, geography, philosophy, mysticism, and surprisingly many on theology: an ambitious programme of studies. The bookseller whom the King entrusted with the disposal of Frederick's library took the risk of keeping it together and secretly lending out the books as required to the former owner.

The King issued an 'Edict Against Money-Loans to Minors' with specific reference to the Crown Prince (though also to 'any other royal or margravely princes'), infringements carrying heavy penalties on life and limb. Needless to say, Frederick continued to find bankers willing to extend credit to the future sovereign. If nothing else, his nominal apanage—nominal in that he could touch only an infinitesimal fraction, otherwise perfectly real—was excellent collateral: Frederick William had just arranged to lend the King of Poland 300,000 Thaler of it.

Various further steps were taken to restrict the Crown Prince's liberty and keep him under supervision day and night. A new and unexpected danger had arisen which the King was grimly determined to put down. As witness his library catalogue, Frederick was developing an independent interest in theology. He was flirting with Calvinism, attracted by the doctrine of Predestination, which was anathema to Frederick William not only as a heresy but as over and above that providing a recalcitrant son with perfect metaphysical excuse for his misconduct. This, coming from the same youth whose confirmation had had to be postponed at the last minute because he did not know his catechism, was indeed an outrage. The King could not have been more upset had Frederick made to leave the Christian fold altogether; Frederick in this least frivolous of his defections showed an unwonted, candid firmness which smacked perilously of sincere conviction.

However, with the end of the black year, 1729, the hopes of Frederick William's family revived once more. Frederick's artless statement that he was loved in England had some foundation. English public opinion was in favour of the double marriage, partly for religious-political, partly for sentimental-moral reasons, it being considered high time Prince Fred (of Wales) settled down. In Government circles the matter was pursued as a safeguard to the Treaty of Seville. The only rub lay with Parliament which, taking a grave view of the royal family's expenditure as it was, balked at voting an appropriate increase in the Prince of Wales's income. But that was a minor obstacle compared with the changeable mind of the Prussian King.

In the hope of pinning him down at last once and for all, a special envoy with this exclusive mission was sent to Berlin. He was Sir Charles Hotham, a Yorkshireman of creditable lineage, military qualification, court experience, and the sort of address which would commend him to Frederick William: just such a man as might usefully have been sent years ago to counteract the influence of Seckendorf before it was too late.

Some little time ago, it had been discovered in London that the despatches to Berlin of the Prussian Ambassador Reichenbach were nothing but transcripts of what Grumbkow dictated to him *from* Berlin, as were also Reichenbach's communications to the English Crown and Cabinet. A dossier of these intercepted messages was prepared, for the attention of Grumbkow's and Reichenbach's too-trusting master.* It contained such gems as the following:†

> *Grumbkow to Reichenbach:* 'The time has now come when Reichenbach must play his game. . . . Let him write [to the King of Prussia] that the heads of the Opposition, who play Austria as a card in Parliament, are in consternation, Walpole having hinted to them that he was about to make friends with the King of Prussia . . . That [in London] they have already given out in the way of a rumour, how sure they are of the court of Berlin. . . . Make it known at [the English] Court that the purported illness of the Queen of Prussia is nothing but a feint, to work upon the King her brother. I have posted a couple of valets with Fatty

* Grumbkow and Reichenbach were both in receipt of sizeable pensions from Vienna.

† Under various dates.

[Frederick William] to keep on exciting him about his son. . . . Inform Fatty of his son's correspondence with England. . . . Have no fears: Fatty's heart is in my hands, I can do with him as I like . . .'

Reichenbach to Grumbkow: 'Reichenbach has told the King [of Prussia] today by courier . . . what amours the Prince of Wales has on hand at present with actresses and opera girls. The King of Prussia will undoubtedly be astonished. . . . If Grumbkow and Seckendorf have opportunity, they may tell his Prussian Majesty that the whole design of this [English] Court is to render his country a province dependent on England. . . . Singular enough, how these English are given to underestimate the Germans, whilst we in Germany overestimate them. . . . Inform his Majesty . . . that his Britannic Majesty is becoming from day to day more hated by the world, and that the Prince of Wales is no longer liked by the public. . . . That the Crown Prince of Prussia has given his written assurance to the Queen here, Never to marry anybody in the world except the Princess Amelia of England, happen what will . . . Lord Townshend is still at his place in the country, but it is said will soon come to town, having heard the great news that they have already got his Prussian Majesty by the nose. . . . Then as to Princess Amelia, [tell them in Berlin] she, who was always haughty, begins to give herself airs upon the Crown Prince of Prussia; she is as ill-tempered as her Father, and still more given to back-biting, and will greatly displease the Prussian Majesty. . . .'

Frederick William was somewhat taken aback when Dubourgay submitted these documents which, however, were only copies. Grumbkow at that evening's session of the Tabagie easily convinced him that the whole dossier was a clumsy English forgery. Great efforts were now made in London to get hold of an original letter in Grumbkow's hand, for the use of Sir Charles Hotham in case of need.

For a start, the special envoy got on very well with Frederick William. The pair were closeted in daily conferences, slowly making progress. But it was the Crown Prince with whom Hotham was most particularly taken; something of a friendship grew up between them.

Frederick, suppressed and supervised at every hand, was snatching every chance of furtive contact with the foreign representatives, at night and in holes and corners about the palace, or in the undergrowth of Wusterhausen. Following the example of his grandfather and great-grandfather in their time, he had started investigating possibilities of escape and asylum abroad. But his sister was in no better case at home than he, and more helpless.

'I am very sad to have things to say which I ought to conceal from all the earth,' he wrote to his 'dear friend' Hotham, who forwarded a copy of the letter to London. 'I am treated in an unheard-of manner by the King, and I know there are terrible things in preparation against me. . . . The real secret reason why the King will not consent to this marriage is that he wishes to keep me on a low footing and to have the power of driving me mad, whenever the whim takes him, as long as he lives; thus he will never give his consent. . . . I believe it would be better to conclude my sister's marriage in the first place, and not even to ask from the King any assurance in regard to mine; the more as he has no say in that: it is enough that I here reiterate the promises I have already made to the King my Uncle, never to take another wife than . . . the Princess Amelia. I am a person of my word. . . . I remain entirely yours, always.'

Possibly the seeming overtones of typical adolescent Weltschmerz, coupled with the naïve assertion that his word was his own, helped to discount Frederick's recommendation in London.

Hotham had arrived in April; in May the first wedding in the family took place. While the eldest daughter yet moped unpromised, the second of the six Prussian Princesses, Friederike Louise, not fully fifteen years old, was married to her cousin the Margrave of Ansbach ('Tell me, Louise, would you rather go to Ansbach now or stay with me?' 'Most gracious Papa, I will go to Ansbach!'), who had barely completed his seventeenth year—when Fritz, as the King had lately informed the Court of St. James, would not be ripe for marriage till twenty-seven at the earliest.*

* Queen Caroline's request to Frederick William for a portrait of Fritz was answered with the advice that any picture of a big long-tailed monkey would serve the purpose perfectly.

For the bride, the match was anything but a brilliant one. It is hard to see why it should have been concluded in such haste, or concluded at all; hard to avoid the inference that in truth the King's main purpose here was to intimidate his troublesome wife and elder children—especially as he had already dug up several similarly unenticing princelings to hold over Wilhelmine against her hopes of becoming Queen of England one day. By contemporary standards Wilhelmine was not young for an unmarried woman, already twenty. Underlining the possibility that Wilhelmine might even be left on the shelf altogether, the third daughter, aged thirteen, was betrothed to the heir apparent of Brunswick.

In June all questions of marrying and giving in marriage were adjourned for a month. Frederick William with his eldest son and a distinguished following repaired to Mühlberg, also called Radewitz, where King Augustus had arranged a spectacular entertainment for his friends and pseudo-friends. Though as skilled in diplomacy as Frederick William was maladroit, Augustus preferred whenever possible to advance his schemes by festivities rather than sedentary plodding.

As a setting for something like a modern pacific version of the mediaeval tournament, a sumptuous pleasure camp had been put up, covering some twelve square miles near the River Elbe, with tents, gilded pavilions, even temporary palaces having floors of wickerwork, admirable furniture, and flower gardens (for the King of Prussia there was ample provision of bath tubs). One neighbouring village served for slaughter-house, coping with herds of oxen daily, another for bakery, with 160 bakers working round the clock. Their pièce de résistance was a cake 14 ells long*, 6 ells broad, half an ell thick, and counting among its ingredients 5,000 eggs, which in the end was cut up by a carpenter under supervision by a high-ranking official of the Saxon Ministry of Works. Wines and beer flowed in commensurate streams. There were coffee houses, there were billiard tables, there were opera, ballet, and balls, as well as an impressive programme of military and naval displays, which the great ladies of the land adorned with their attendance.

* 1 ell = 45 inches.

At this camp, which caused great noise and wonder in the world but had no other memorable upshot, the Crown Prince of Prussia was thrashed by his father in front of thousands of onlookers of every degree. In full view of them all, the Crown Prince of Prussia, eighteen years old, had to limp off the parade ground with his hair pulled about his face and his clothes disordered. The limit of his endurance was reached.

Almost immediately after, it became clear that his last hope of reprieve from this sort of existence had collapsed.

Frederick William had decided to follow up the Mühlberg holiday with a round-trip through Germany, first returning to Potsdam for a few days. During those few days Hotham called to introduce Dubourgay's successor, Captain Guy Dickens, and improved the occasion by presenting the King with one of Grumbkow's compromising letters in the original.

Although, as Hotham wrote next day, 11 July 1730, to his immediate superior, Lord Harrington, 'the conduct of his Prussian Majesty has been such, for some time past, that one ought to be surprised at nothing he does', Frederick William managed to surpass himself. He took the proffered letter, and '*seeing it to be in Grumbkow's hand*', ejaculated furiously, 'Messieurs, j'ai eu assez de ces choses là!' Whereupon he cast the letter on the ground, turned his back on the two envoys, and rushed out slamming the door behind him. In the version which became generally current at the time, and to which Wilhelmine subscribed also, the King had first raised his foot as though to kick Hotham.

Hotham's account to Harrington makes no mention of this, though its length and repetitiousness otherwise are a measure of his shocked indignation, both on his own behalf and that of the King his master. To the magnitude of the departure from protocol, with or without kick, Frederick William's repeated attempts at placating Hotham also testify: the nearest thing to an apology ever to issue from this monarch. For the next twenty-four hours Hotham was bombarded with requests to forgive and forget. But he was not to be appeased and departed for England on 12 July, having barely acknowledged a beseeching note from his dear young friend the unfortunate Crown Prince who saw 'my happiness and my sister's' in ruins.

Frederick William's impulse of shame and desire to make up soon died a natural death. Such a breach, after all, was just what he had wanted, never mind what manner of figure he had cut in bringing it about. The most remarkable aspect of it all is his enviably incisive reaction to the evidence of Grumbkow's duplicity: the King cast it from him, leaving it for Hotham to pick up and take away again, thus literally declining to accept the unacceptable.

CHAPTER 8

THE RED COAT

The departure of the King of Prussia on his Empire tour was fixed for the following Saturday, 15 July. Frederick William had not at first intended to take his son with him. But, Frederick being unable to conceal his despair upon the final breakdown of the marriage negotiations, the King thought it wise to keep him under the paternal eye.

In the little time that was left, Frederick stole to meet Captain Dickens for some last midnight confabulations; but the news from London was not encouraging. King George counselled his nephew to do nothing rash and not to expect England to plunge Europe into war for his sake. Let Frederick possess himself with patience and bide his time, let him send in a full account of his debts and Uncle George would tide him over meanwhile. Frederick by return named a figure considerably higher than the actual amount (' . . . whereby you can see his excellent character,' Frederick William, when he found out about this later on, wrote bitterly to the Old Dessauer, 'God preserve all honest men from depraved offspring.').

Frederick needed cash. Nothing could now shake his resolution to run away. Though England did not want him and Saxony also warded him off, he had extracted a qualified promise of hospitality from the French Ambassador. His plan was to escape to France, lie low for a while, then perhaps make his way to Holland and when the time was ripe—as surely it would ripen—repair to England in the end. He had broached the idea to his mother and sister, and both of them had done their best to dissuade him. He now turned to the only source of assistance left to him, the friends of his own age in the Prussian officer corps.

These were by no means of the milksop breed which Frederick William held his son to exemplify. Only the wilder and more reckless of junior officers would so throw caution to the winds as to show open friendship for the King's eldest son. Neither had Frederick spent all his spare time sneaking away to read or play his beloved flute; with his intrepid comrades he had been indulging in the time-honoured relaxations of martial youth, such as roistering, gaming, and window-breaking. As a leading influence in these diversions, one Lieutenant Peter Christoph Karl von Keith had been transferred not long ago to a provincial regiment in the Rhenish backwater of Wesel. Since then Lieutenant Hans Hermann von Katte, grandson of two distinguished Field-Marshals of Prussia, had become Frederick's chief intimate.

Katte combined the qualities of a firebrand with higher interests, ranging from mathematics to the fine arts, and in education was superior to his fellows, not excluding the Crown Prince. He was eight years older than Frederick, and had originally trained for the Law at the University of Halle; he was witty, argumentative, mettlesome, and ardent, as dark of hair and complexion as Frederick was fair: at school, his heavy black eyebrows had inspired the jingle,

Wer solche Brauen hat
Wie der Ritter Katt',
Der endet am Galgen
Oder unterm Rad,

prophesying for him a sticky end at the hangman's hands, in conformity with a popular superstition. Wilhelmine in her memoirs adds that Katte's face was pockmarked, 'rendering him uglier still': Frederick's favourite sister seldom wrote gracefully about her rivals in his affection; but at the time she too liked Katte, what she had seen of him.

Katte himself believed that on first acquaintance Frederick had disliked him; however, after the removal of Keith, Katte more than took the former's place. Saving Duhan who belonged to the older generation, Katte was better equipped than anybody else within Frederick's reach to be sparring partner and boon companion to him. Just as they egged each other on in off-duty exuberance, the spark of intellectual curiosity flew back and forth in mutually stimulating give and take, so that soon neither could do without the other. When Frederick was tied down at Potsdam, Katte would make shift to break into the garrison sometimes at night in cloak and dagger fashion for an hour's conversation. They discussed like other young men before and since the nature of life and the universe, rediscovering for themselves all the speculations that eternally engage the human mind, exchanged titbits of their varied reading, enjoyed their kindred appreciation of the arts, and settled the subject of metaphysics.

Naturally it has been suggested that Katte's devotion was not of a disinterested kind, and he would not have been human had hopes of the future never entered his dreams; but God knows that apart from romantic and emotional satisfaction he got nothing out of the relationship but trouble. Another suggestion, equally a matter of course, is that their friendship was a homosexual one. So it may have been, and it is possible that such was Frederick William's suspicion, though gossip to this purport is not in evidence until after the débâcle.

Katte later told how in speaking of his lot the Prince sometimes would be overcome with weeping, so that he, Katte, wept too. 'I cannot deny that the great love I felt for him filled me so entirely that it was quite beyond me to refuse his entreaties for help.'

The charm which Frederick all his life exercised on everyone save those who had insuperable cause to hate him, coupled with the King's lunatic rigour, won the sympathy even of the guardian pair the King had now set specially to watch over the Crown Prince. One was a senior officer, the other still a subaltern: Colonel von Rochow and Lieutenant Keyserlingk, who on pain of death were never to let Frederick out of their sight. Rochow soon became aware of the friendship between the Prince and Katte, which the King was certain to disapprove; he dropped a word of warning to Katte, but otherwise held his peace.

With Katte Frederick now worked out a plan of action,

necessarily somewhat flexible as so much would depend on chance. Katte was not among those chosen to accompany the royal party; his hope was to apply for leave of absence on recruiting business and thus get away from Berlin, where he was stationed, after the King and Crown Prince were gone, to meet the latter somewhere en route to France, probably at Cannstatt near Stuttgart. For the time being Frederick consigned to Katte all his convertible worldly goods: a collection of rings and jewelled knicknacks, and what ready money he could lay his hands on. Also Katte was to take care of Frederick's papers, sealed in a portable desk; his books were to be sent secretly to Hamburg for storage as soon as the coast was clear.

The banishment of Keith now became a useful factor, since in Wesel he was half-way to France. He was to hold himself ready to join Frederick at Strasburg or possibly The Hague. A younger brother of Keith's travelled with the royal retinue as the King's page and was roped into the conspiracy. (The Keiths were Scotch nobles, descended from Jacobite immigrants long since settled in Pomerania; the name was pronounced *Kite* in German and spelled K-e-u-t, phonetically Koyt, by Frederick William, indicating the strongly dialect-flavoured vowels of the King's speech.)

The King's itinerary was: Potsdam, Wittenberg, Leipzig, Meuselwitz, Altenburg, Gera, Saalfeld, Coburg, Bamberg, Erlangen, Nuremberg, Ansbach, Donauwörth, Augsburg, Stuttgart, Ludwigsburg, Mannheim, Heidelberg, Darmstadt, Frankfurt-on-Main, Coblenz, Bonn, Cologne, Düsseldorf, Wesel, and home. In his way Frederick William was taking a leaf out of King Augustus's book and disguising business as pleasure: an ulterior object of the jaunt was to plead the cause of the Emperor's Pragmatic Sanction at as many sovereign courts as practicable. The party comprised some two score persons all told. The page Keith rode behind the King's coach. The Crown Prince travelled in a separate one, with his guardian trio, Colonels von Rochow and von Waldau and the aged General von Buddenbrock, who were to answer for him with their heads.

* * *

The roads of Germany were then so bad one marvels that communications were maintained at all and that communities survived where waterways did not provide immediate connexions. Travel was a serious undertaking even for private persons (except in that the pedestrian escaped some of the worst hazards of the road); a journey of a hundred miles was a major expedition. When princes went forth, engineering parties would be sent ahead to fill in holes up to the size of wild beast traps and bridge quagmires with tree trunks, sticks, and hurdles, to say nothing of elaborate arrangements for provender.

Here as in so many aspects of royal living Frederick William was the exception. He as it were ignored obstacles, and ignored discomfort. His bone-breaking speed of travel was notorious; it required great hardihood and stoicism to accompany him. For meals he liked to picnic under a tree in the fields; for the night he liked to take over a village barn and sleep on straw.

His visiting schedule would almost do credit to a present-day head of state with present-day facilities of transport. At most of his stations on this tour, if he spent a full twenty-four hours with a given host, he stayed long. Only for Ansbach, being the home of his newly married daughter, he had set aside so much as a whole week.

At Ansbach, therefore, the King found leisure to humiliate his son afresh, on the most trifling pretexts. Frederick cried out it were better to beg his bread than go on like this.

One difficulty in relating these events is the pile of later-than-last straws constantly heaped on Frederick, which time and again turns climax into anti-climax. It will scarcely stretch inference too far, to say Frederick must have felt something of this, himself. For after months of extreme caution, indecision, and minute weighing of every circumstance, from Ansbach onwards suddenly his actions show an element of flamboyance and foolhardiness.

At Ansbach he received word that Katte had been unable to get leave. A meeting at Cannstatt was now out of the question. As a deserter, Katte would not be safe in German territory, even outside Prussia; while with the hue and cry after him, his movements would betray Frederick at the outset. They would have to flee separately, one after the other, and

Katte had best make straight for France or Holland like the elder Keith.

It goes without saying that Katte could not write to Frederick direct, under the circumstances. He had a cousin stationed near Ansbach, a captain of horse named Hans Friedrich von Katte, acting Prussian recruiting officer in those parts. Frederick's friend used this cousin as a go-between, and Frederick rather took the Captain's sympathy for granted: when he if anyone should have known that ties of blood do not necessarily bespeak like-mindedness. Even as he relied on the mettle of the younger Keith, whom he hardly knew, so he straightway asked Katte's cousin to find him a pair of horses without telling anyone about it. Not unnaturally Captain Katte declined. Not unnaturally he was worried. He did not like to break trust with the Crown Prince, but neither did he wish to break his oath to the sovereign. He compromised, darkly enjoining Colonel von Rochow not to let the Crown Prince out of his sight for so much as an instant. Rochow, already under the most succinct royal orders to the same effect, forbore from mentioning the matter to his master.

Frederick had to think again. He and his confederate agreed that they must take what they needed whenever an opportunity might present itself; meanwhile it would be well to see about civilian clothes to disguise themselves. At Augsburg, where the King delayed, sightseeing, Keith went about this errand and eventually procured two coats of French cut—were they not bound for France?—one blue, for himself, the other bright red: a colour well-known to act on the King as on the proverbial bull, besides being the most conspicuous in the spectrum. For the present Frederick hid it in his luggage.

On 3 August the Prussian party reached the turning point of the tour, and headed for Württemberg and the Rhine. On the other side of the Rhine lay France. The intending fugitives planned to make a crossing near Speyer, meantime observing the greatest circumspection. So what did Frederick do in his circumspection? As soon as his carriage had started from Ludwigsburg, he pulled out his brilliant-hued coat and put it on. No doubt he felt a dire need to create even a small sensation. He had already written to Katte in Berlin, unburdening himself as to the most recent humiliations; but he must have been bursting to show the witnesses of his continual abasement that after all he had some spirit left.

Colonel von Rochow quickly recovered from his surprise and contented himself with remarking that the Prince had best be careful not to let the King catch sight of him in that coat. Frederick, saying he had only brought it because he was cold, took the coat off again and pushed it under the seat.

Mannheim, the King's next port of call, at his pace was only a few hours' drive distant. For once the King decided to take it easy. The journey was broken earlier in the evening than usual, at a village called Steinsfurt on the Sinsheim-Mannheim road. The King chose a barn for himself and his attendants, including Seckendorf, allotted another, opposite, to Frederick and his guardians, quartered the remainder of the company round about, and gave orders to start at five o'clock next morning instead of at three o'clock as was his wont. Rochow's valet was bedded by Frederick's side.

The Rhine ferry to Speyer was a mere three hours' ride away. The opportunity was too good to miss since, so soon after the shortest night of the year, the King was unwittingly allowing his son a full two hours of reasonable light for his escape.

Frederick and the page Keith had managed to exchange the few words necessary, before retiring. A little after two o'clock Frederick stealthily rose and began to dress. Instantly Rochow's deputy sat up and asked what his Royal Highness were doing. 'I'm getting up: don't ask silly questions,' Frederick replied, sensibly enough—and got into his red coat, its pockets jingling with all the specie he had by him. Rochow's valet reminded him that the coat was supposed to be kept out of sight. 'Well, I feel like putting it on,' said Frederick and walked out of the barn.

The valet hastened to arouse his master. Rochow hurried after the Prince and found him leaning pensively against one of the carriages on the green, waiting for Keith to keep their appointment at three. Rochow cheerfully bade him good morning and held him in conversation, so that Frederick could do nothing to warn his confederate. Presently Keith appeared, leading two horses, ready saddled. Upon Rochow's enquiry Keith explained that the horses belonged to himself and another page, and that he had just got them ready for the customary hour of starting. Rochow pointed out that today's departure had been fixed for five, and ordered Keith to take the horses back to the stable. Keith obeyed.

Waldau and Buddenbrock had now joined the group; suddenly Seckendorf emerged from the barn opposite. Rochow did his best to save the situation, implying that the Crown Prince was but amusing himself, by parading his red coat in peace and quiet; he jokingly asked Seckendorf how he liked the Prince in his coat 'which his Majesty of course must never see'. (Frederick William apparently slept through all this.) The guardian trio then took Frederick back to their barn, got him out of the coat and into his carriage—which was heavier and therefore slower than the King's—and left word that they were driving on ahead.

We do not know what passed between Frederick and his guardians that day, 4 August 1730. The blank is the more tantalizing as the King, setting out one hour after his son and fully expecting to catch him up in Heidelberg at the latest, reached Mannheim three and a half hours before him.

Wondering what had become of his son, Frederick William hardly talked of anything else to his host, the Elector Palatine; finally the latter sent out an equerry to look for the Prince's carriage which was found duly approaching Mannheim and was brought in by half past eleven. Whatever excuses were made must have satisfied the King, for no altercation followed, and the Crown Prince accompanied his father visiting the local places of interest.

Frederick had not yet given up. He slipped a pencilled note to Keith directing him to hire post horses in the town.

But the young Keith was breaking under the strain. Divine service next morning, Sunday, so worked upon his conscience that on their return from church he fell at the King's feet in tears and confessed Frederick's plan.

There was little Frederick William could do then and there, especially as the Prussian visitors were expected to dine with the Elector Palatine immediately. He laid hold of Rochow on the way in to dinner, drew him into a window embrasure and said, he gathered Fritz had been scheming to desert: why had not the King been told of the occurrence at Steinsfurt? Rochow, Waldau, and Buddenbrock, he would herewith remind them, should pay with their heads if they did not bring the Crown Prince back into Prussia, 'alive or dead'. Rochow assured the King that the Prince should not escape and in any case never would have cheated their vigilance.

Later in the day the party left, for Darmstadt. Even yet the King said nothing to his son, save to express sarcastic surprise on seeing him at Darmstadt: he had quite thought, he said, that Fritz would have reached Paris by now. The Prince retorted flippantly that was precisely where he would be, had he wished to go.

The general assumption is that Frederick did not know Keith had betrayed him: though one might suppose Rochow would have warned him. The King himself had said nothing further to anybody meanwhile. They left Darmstadt the first thing next morning, Monday, and arrived at Frankfurt about 7 a.m. An express mail package was waiting for the King, from Captain Katte.

In his last note to Katte Frederick had instructed his friend to betake himself to The Hague directly he heard that the Crown Prince had made good his escape, to bring with him Frederick's valuables, and ask for the Comte d'Alberville, the alias Frederick meant to adopt. It is not clear how this letter fell into Captain Katte's hands: whether Frederick had meant to send it through him or whether he had omitted to include 'Berlin' in the address so that it was misdelivered. In either case, present-day psychology would tend to attribute some subconscious responsibility to Frederick in the miscarriage of his escape.

Whatever the circumstances by which he got the letter, Captain Katte had opened and read it, and had seen no other way but to send it straight on to the King.

Frederick William's behaviour at this point was as unusual as Frederick's bravado. With an amazing degree of control he kept his information and his feelings to himself. He gave orders that the Prince was not to enter the town with him, but to be taken on board one of the royal yachts waiting at anchor to convey them to the river junction at Mainz and thence down the Rhine to Wesel. Then according to programme he spent his two hours in the ancient Imperial city, inspected the Golden Bull in the original, played his set part in the sedate farewells, and shortly after 9 a.m. boarded his yacht.

But then the storm broke. Raging, the King flew at his son and belaboured him with the handle of his cane till the blood ran down Frederick's face and General Buddenbrock bodily intervened. Frederick was then transferred to another vessel, closely guarded as the page Keith was also. Nevertheless Frederick succeeded in preparing further pencilled warnings, one to the elder Keith at Wesel ('Sauvez-vous, tout est découvert!') and one to Katte, and to get them posted, it is not known how, probably at Bonn, where the party stayed the night at the residence of the Bishop-Elector of Cologne.

There Frederick contrived to get a secret interview with Seckendorf, reduced to invoking his old antagonist's influence with the King: 'Help me in this labyrinth—nothing will ever so oblige me as help now.' He admitted he had meant to run away: he could not, at his age, bear the indignities showered on him, any longer; he would have gone long since, had he not feared for his mother and sister; and he would still go if the King did not stop ill-using him. For his own life, which was not worth living, he cared little: but he feared greatly for the friends who had helped him. If only Seckendorf could bring the King to pardon Frederick's friends, Frederick would make a full confession.

Seckendorf knew his Frederick William and was afraid of some too-impolitic aberration of the royal temper; he may even have pitied the Prince, though it is more likely that he bore in mind Frederick was still the heir to the Prussian throne.

But Frederick William, brooding on deck in a fog of solitary tobacco smoke, had convinced himself that there was more behind the affair than met the eye: namely, an English-inspired plot to overthrow and murder him and place the

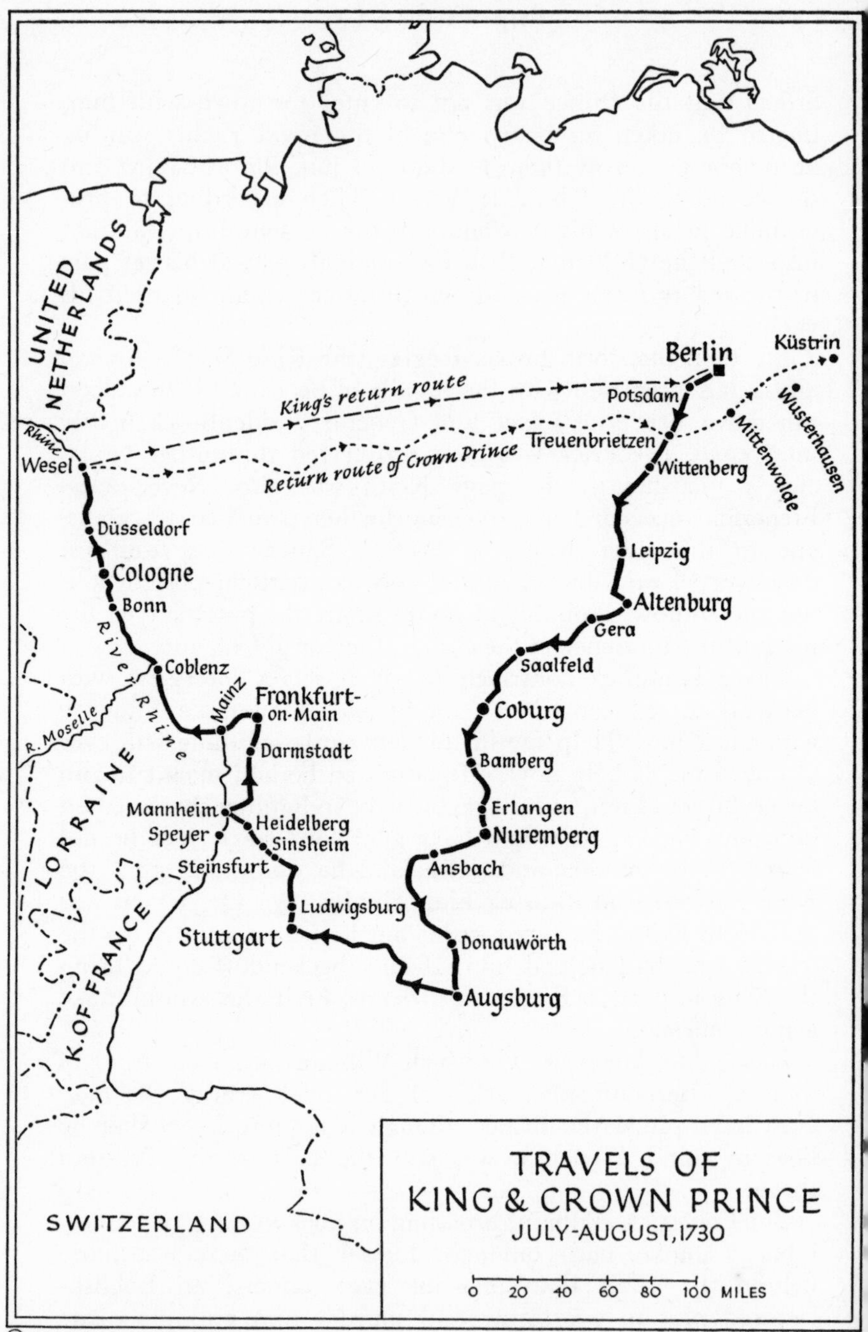
UNITED NETHERLANDS
King's return route
Return route of Crown Prince
Berlin
Küstrin
Potsdam
Wusterhausen
Mittenwalde
Treuenbrietzen
Wittenberg
Rhine
Wesel
Düsseldorf
Cologne
Bonn
River Rhine
Leipzig
Altenburg
Gera
Saalfeld
Coblenz
R. Moselle
Mainz
Frankfurt-on-Main
Darmstadt
Coburg
Bamberg
LORRAINE
Mannheim
Speyer
Heidelberg
Sinsheim
Steinsfurt
Erlangen
Nuremberg
Ansbach
Ludwigsburg
Stuttgart
Donauwörth
Augsburg
K. OF FRANCE
SWITZERLAND
TRAVELS OF
KING & CROWN PRINCE
JULY-AUGUST, 1730
0 20 40 60 80 100 MILES

bloodstained crown on Frederick's wicked head. The more he thought on it, the more ramified the plot grew in his mind: no doubt the French were in it too with who knew how many of his German neighbours waiting to applaud the coup; no doubt his homeward route was beset with skulking foreign soldiery ready to snatch Frederick from the grasp of justice. Seckendorf's attempted intercession only sharpened the King's sense of persecution. His transcendent urge to punish his son became identified with the plausible necessity of learning the whole truth.

Late on the evening of 12 August the King made his entry into the fortress of Wesel and in the presence of the commandant subjected Frederick to his first official examination. The record states merely that the King 'most earnestly called upon the Prince to do God and his father so much honour as to confess freely every circumstance pertaining to his intended desertion . . .' and that the Prince admitted his intent and confirmed the identities of his two chief helpers whom he believed to be safely out of the country by this time. A more elaborate account, given also by Wilhelmine, instances the following dialogue—which when onc compares it with similar, attested exchanges between father and son, rings fairly true:

The King: 'Why were you going to desert?'

The Prince: 'Because you have been treating me not as a son but as a slave.'

The King: 'Then you are nothing but a mean-spirited deserter who has not a shred of honour in him.'

The Prince: 'I have as much honour as you; I have done nothing but what you had told me a hundred times you would do in my place.'

At this, the narrative proceeds, the King drew his sword and would have run his son through, had not the commandant thrown himself in front of Frederick, with the words, 'Kill me, Sire, but spare your son.' In the commotion Frederick was spirited out of the room, and Frederick William was prevailed upon to let others handle future interrogations.

That this was done is a fact, also that the King said he had no wish to see his son again. He drew up a questionnaire for the guidance of his deputy inquisitor, one Colonel von Derschau, who was a valued member of the Tabagie and notoriously ill-disposed towards the Crown Prince.

Frederick, having no such thing to confess, had failed to confess to the complicity of England or any other foreign power: a confession which the King was determined to get out of him.

CHAPTER 9

A MOST UNHAPPY FATHER

Frederick was placed under formal arrest and guarded day and night by two soldiers with fixed bayonets. A warrant was issued for the arrest of Katte in Berlin, against hope: news of the elder Keith's having got clean away to England had reached Wesel on 15 August. Derschau began the interrogation of the Crown Prince.

The eighteen-year-old prisoner, thrown entirely on his own resources and having the whole weight of his father's machine pitted against him, now bore himself with the most impressive coolness. The red coat had served its turn; all the world would soon know that he had shown fight at last. There was no more theatrical defiance, no more scatterbrained improvisation, not one noticeable tremor of forgivable hysteria. Firm and sober, Frederick faced the inquisitor, admitted his fault, reiterated his motives and the details of his plan of escape, side-stepped every attempt to trap him into incriminating his mother and sister or the British Government, and steadfastly denied any designs upon his father's life or crown.

It at once occurred to him to cite the extenuating precedents of his grandfather and great-grandfather. Frederick William was furious and parried with, more or less, the classic rejoinder of 'That was different,' the difference being that, he said, both Frederick I and the Great Elector had had good reason to go into exile for a time, whereas Frederick had had no reason to flee save his own wickedness. Though the charge of plotting with his father's enemies had not yet been brought home, Fritz already stood convicted as a deserter from the armed forces. Against this, Fritz had the effrontery to argue that placing one's self out of reach of ill-treatment which in filial piety there was no resisting, was an entirely different matter from desertion. The King, who had gone back to Berlin, fell from one paroxysm of rage into another as Derschau's reports came in.

September had come; word of the Crown Prince's attempt and arrest had spread through Europe. The King was informed that there were machinations afoot at the courts of Hesse-Cassel, Saxe-Gotha, and in Hanover, to rescue the unhappy Prince. Arrangements were made to place him out of rescue's way at Küstrin, a small, dismal, isolated town in the remote south-east of Prussia, by a circuitous route swerving away from all border country. The date of Frederick's departure from Wesel was kept secret, and he was bundled into a shuttered carriage at dead of night, with a strong guard who had strict orders to kill the prisoner sooner than let him go: care was taken that Frederick knew of this. For the journey the King laid down in writing that there was to be no stopping on the way, even for the prisoner to satisfy the calls of nature, save only in open fields 'without shelter of bush, tree, ditch, or hump'. Thus Frederick William surpassed himself in his celebrated attention to detail.

The grim cavalcade travelled day and night till a brief halt was made at Mittenwalde not far from the happy hunting-grounds of Wusterhausen. Here Frederick was questioned once again, having first been softened up by a blow as heavy as it was unexpected. He learned that Katte had been a prisoner in Berlin since 16 August.

* * *

The behaviour of Katte after Frederick's abortive flight is even harder to explain in straightforward, surface terms than that of Frederick in the act. Although Frederick's note from Bonn never reached him, it is clear that Katte had received some warning. Though nothing definite was as yet known in Berlin, the town was full of awful rumours; and Katte through a lady known to him at court sent the sealed casket containing Frederick's jewels, ducats, and papers to the Queen. Moreover, he took steps to make himself scarce—albeit in an incomprehensibly dilatory manner. As late as 15 August his commanding officer met him in the street and blurted, 'What, you still here?' to which Katte replied composedly that he was off tonight. Even then he delayed until the officer charged with the King's warrant could no longer put off taking Katte into custody.

The King was still away, but 15 August was his birthday, in celebration of which the Queen gave a ball. In the middle of this a letter from her husband was brought to her—rendering her 'pale as death'. The letter was not preserved, but is substantiated by one which Frederick William wrote at the same time to the Mistress of Ceremonies, Frau von Kamecke:

'My dear Madame de Kamke, I have unfortunately the misfortune that my son wanted to desert with the page Keut, I have had him arrested, I have written to my wife, you must break it to her in a round-about way even if it takes a few days so she won't get ill [the Queen was pregnant]. Meanwhile pity an unhappy father, remaining your ever devoted friend, Fr. William.'

There was no chance of breaking it gently to the Queen, as Frederick's casket had arrived at the Palace. Nor was the King's expressed solicitude borne out when he returned in person on the afternoon of 27 August.

To receive him the Queen had repaired to the apartment of the King, who from afar greeted her with the words, 'Your worthless son is no more, he is dead.' 'What,' cried the Queen, 'you have had the barbarity to kill him?' 'Just so,' said the King, 'but what I want now is that sealed desk of his you've got.'

Trembling, half-fainting, continually exclaiming under her breath, 'My God, my son!' the Queen went to fetch it. The King tore it out of her hands, broke it open and took the papers to look them over by himself. Presently he came back, in an even greater fury than before. He had not found a jot of evidence against his son, his wife, his daughter, or their presumed English accomplices.

The reason was simple, and was precisely what he suspected. The royal ladies had had nearly a fortnight to manufacture some six or seven hundred harmless letters, which had been substituted for a similar number of extremely compromising ones ('enough to be our death, several times over,' says Wilhelmine): they had of course opened the desk right away to see what was in it. By unbelievable good luck they had then got hold of a seal almost identical with the one used by Frederick, and resealed the desk afterwards so that it appeared untouched.

The manual labour alone of writing six or seven hundred letters in ten days, even when shared between two, was very heavy. Yet for all their fatigue and panic, Sophie Dorothee and her daughter had proceeded with no little ingenuity, even careful to unearth specimens of the right type of stationery as used in the royal household at given times. In case of leakages, they meticulously reproduced the dates of the originals, also alluding to the occasions which had given rise to those. Letters of other authorship than their own were merely destroyed with the rest; but Wilhelmine saved some of the first-fruits of Frederick's poetic talent.

Realizing that he could not prove his suspicions, the King now was quite beside himself. In the interval his family had been told that the Crown Prince was not dead after all, and the assembled children down to four-year-old Prince Henry fell to kissing Papa's hands and imploring mercy for their eldest brother. The King brushed them aside and fastened on Wilhelmine.

'He became black in the face, his eyes sparkled with fury, he foamed at the mouth. "Infamous scum," he said to me, "do you indeed dare to show yourself before me? Go, keep your scoundrel of a brother company!" So saying, he seized me with one hand and with the other struck my face several blows with his fist. . . . I lay senseless. The King in a frenzy was for striking me with his foot, had not those who were present prevented him. . . . The Queen kept shrieking . . . she wrung her hands and ran in despair up and down the room. The King's face was so disfigured with rage, it was frightful to look upon. The little ones were on their knees begging for me. . . .'

All this took place in a lower room facing the open courtyard, presumably with the windows open too; for the guard turned out at the appalling noise and crowds began to collect outside.

'The King had now changed his tune; he admitted that my brother was still alive, but vowed horribly he would put him to death and lay me fast within four walls for the rest of my life. He accused me of being the Prince's accomplice, whose crime was high treason; also of having an intrigue of love with Katte, to whom, he said, I had borne several children. My governess was unable to keep silent at these insults and had the courage to reply, "That is not true, and whoever may have told your Majesty such things, lies." . . . I saw Katte crossing the esplanade; four soldiers were conducting him . . . some sealed trunks belonging to him and my brother came on behind. Pale and downcast, he took off his hat to salute me. . . . The King . . . went out exclaiming, "Now I shall soon have proof about the scoundrel Fritz and the scum Wilhelmine, enough to cut off their heads." '

Madame von Kamecke and a second lady went after the King, remonstrating; the Mistress of Ceremonies told her 'ever-devoted' royal correspondent that, it having hitherto been his pride to be a just and God-fearing King, Heaven's blessing had attended him: if now, however, he would scout the divine commandments, let him beware the wrath of the Lord, and remember Philip II of Spain and Peter the Great of Russia, who had each shed the blood of a son and heir, and died, leaving their thrones orphaned, their countries laid waste by war, their names an abomination to humankind.

When she had done, the King gazed at her in silence for a moment and at length dismissed her, conceding that she meant well—and would she now go and look after his wife. He himself went on his way, stick in hand, to confront Katte. The public executioner had been notified: other means of persuasion failing, it would not be Frederick William's fault if one had to resort to torture.

Throughout these sorry proceedings, protestations absolving himself from blame and invocations of the ideal of Justice, were forever on Frederick William's lips and flowing from his pen. Throughout he declared himself a helpless victim of circumstances, circumstances compounded of other people's wickedness on the one hand and the demands of sacred principle on the other.

'I have done everything,' he lamented, as so often, to the Old Dessauer, 'I left nothing undone. . . . I tried kindness and sternness, precept and example, I verily crawled to my son to win his love. . . . All to no avail. . . .'

Katte's father, who was Lieutenant-General of Königsberg, wrote asking for clemency, and received the lugubrious answer, 'Your son is a scoundrel, so is mine: so what can we poor fathers do?'

Frederick William's stick obtained no more satisfactory results from Katte than it had done with his son. Katte, like Frederick, admitted everything factual that there was to admit —with the proviso that he for his part had never intended to go through with the escape plan. He felt sure, he said, that Frederick too had never been really serious about it: once he had got away, he would soon have come back of his own accord; in any case, he would not have got very far without his valuables.

The King impatiently dismissed this: if Frederick *had* escaped to England, what would Katte have done? Why, then, Katte had to answer, he would indeed have followed. No; neither the Queen nor the Princess Royal had been party to the scheme. Yes; Katte had occasionally carried messages between the Crown Prince and the British Embassy: but the Prince's sole intent had been to remove himself from the King's disfavour; there had never been any question of conspiracy against the throne or the sacrosanct person of the monarch.

Katte was not to be shaken. He was told that he would be questioned again on the morrow, probably on the rack, and had to exchange his military coat for the linen smock of delinquency before he was marched back through the streets to prison. Between 28 and 31 August he was subjected to four further interrogations; a fifth was to follow after Frederick had been re-examined at Küstrin. Each time the threat of torture was renewed and everything was ready to carry it out; already the King talked of applying it to Frederick too: evidently one would never get at the truth by anything less drastic. The prisoners had Seckendorf's alarmed foresight and eloquence to thank for it that finally the hangman was told to pack away his tools.

* * *

Frederick for the first time since his arrest broke down when he was told that Katte had been taken and would certainly pay with his life. Wildly he besought the inquisitors to impress upon the King that he, Frederick, alone was guilty, and that he would never know an hour's peace were he to be the cause of another's death. He did not change his testimony. He was taken the rest of the way to Küstrin.

On arrival he was immured in a room of Küstrin's fortress, which had one single window, high up, and no furniture other than some wooden stools. The door was secured with double locks and bolts; guards were stationed outside it and at every conceivable vantage point about the adjoining passages, stairs, and landings. His sword had been taken from him at Wesel; now he had to give up the last exterior marks of rank and dignity in donning prison dress. He was permitted neither knife and fork nor paper and ink. His flute of course had been impounded. Nobody was allowed to speak to him, no one to be with him for longer than exactly four minutes together, not even the two officers who came to search his cell every morning and supervise his defecations three times a day. He was allowed one tallow candle, extinguished daily on the stroke of 7 p.m., and reading matter in the shape of the prayer book.

After nearly two weeks of solitary confinement, he was taken before a special commission of enquiry furnished by the King with a new list of 185 questions—framed in such a way that the prisoner could hardly help convicting himself out of his own mouth, as the leading commissioner protested, fruitlessly. Frederick again managed to extricate himself, by means of indirect if not evasive replies:

Question: 'What punishment would the Prince consider fitting for his crime?'
Answer: 'The Prince would throw himself on the King's mercy.'
Question: 'What in the Prince's opinion are the deserts of one who has trodden honour underfoot and plotted desertion?'
Answer: 'The Prince does not think he had acted dishonourably.'
Question: 'Is such a one as he fit to rule?'
Answer: 'The Prince could not undertake to be his own judge.'

Question: 'Does the Prince wish to have his life spared or not?'

Answer: 'The Prince would submit himself to the King's mercy and will.'

Question: 'Having rendered himself unfit to rule by reason of his breach of honour, would the Prince renounce the succession, so as to save his life?'

Answer: 'The Prince does not hold his life so very dear, but trusts his Majesty will not so utterly reject him.'

However, on reading over the record, Frederick was suddenly struck by the inference that the King intended life imprisonment for him. In great agitation he applied for another hearing. The request was granted, in the belief that he would now divulge the desired evidence involving England. But Frederick only wished to declare that sooner than endure perpetual prison he would prefer to die or else abjure his rights—and whichever the King's decision, his son would ever love and reverence him.

After this two further padlocks were fastened on Frederick's door and the King appointed a Court Martial to try the case at Köpenick near Berlin towards the end of October.

CHAPTER 10

'SHOULD JUSTICE PERISH?'

The tribunal was composed of three Captains (Itzenplitz, Podewils, Jeetze), three Majors (Lüderitz, Einsiedel, Lestwitz), three Lieutenant-Colonels (Weyher, Schenck, Milagsheim), three Colonels (Stedingk, Wachholz, Derschau), three Major-Generals (Schwerin, Dönhof, Linger), and one Lieutenant-General (Schulenburg) acting as president. They were in no doubt as to the onerous nature of their task. One thing they were agreed on from the first was that in their capacity of vassals and subjects they were not competent to judge what was (*a*) an affair of state, and (*b*) a private, family matter; while (*c*) as a Prince and functionary of the Empire—e.g. heir apparent to the Brandenburg Electorate and thereby holder of certain traditional offices under the Imperial Crown—Frederick was immune from any jurisdiction save the Emperor's. Lastly, the Prussian Military Code contained no articles applicable to the case as the King wished to have it tried, since the defendant 'deserter' had never in fact encompassed the crime of which he was accused.

Frederick William made no bones about his wishes. Before the report on the successive interrogations of Frederick went to the Court Martial, the King altered and amended it with frank intent to ensure a conviction. In his own words, he 'spoke very seriously' to Commissioner Mylius (the one who had raised legal objections to the 185 questions), bungling author of a summary on the basis of which 'half the assessors might say, the King is in the right: yet the other half, or more, might well side with the Crown Prince.' Mylius must understand that would not do. As always, the King must see to everything himself to get it done rightly. He set down detailed editorial directives for Mylius to rewrite the report, with nice artistic changes, such as substituting throughout 'the Delinquent' or 'the run-away Lieutenant Fritz' for 'His Royal Highness'.

He was at that time contemplating having the report printed for publication. Already, to allay a plague of world-wide, fantastic rumours, the King had been obliged to issue a circular letter acquainting the courts of Europe with the facts; for home consumption there sufficed an edict under which persons spreading idle talk about His Majesty's domestic trouble were liable to have their tongues torn out.

Meanwhile the Prussian court was purged of pro-English sympathizers. The Minister Knyphausen, last of the few who had held out against Grumbkow and Seckendorf, was directed to resign; his post went to Grumbkow's son-in-law Heinrich von Podewils (the same who also sat on the Court Martial). Court officials of both sexes, friendly to the Crown Prince, the Princess Royal, or the Queen, were banished to the darkest hinterlands of the country; likewise Duhan de Jandun, who had ceased to act as Frederick's tutor three years earlier, and the bookseller Hanau or Hauen, who had been taking care of Frederick's library. The Queen was called upon to drink to the downfall of England in public. Wilhelmine was locked up in her room, on a purposely execrable diet, and with sentries guarding every exit.

Grumbkow was instructed to tell Frederick of all this, with the addition that already Frederick was 'quite forgotten', that his mother too had turned against him, and that she would not even have his name mentioned. Frederick replied meekly he hoped the King would put in a good word for him with his mother.

The prisoner was in much-heightened spirits. While he did not know of the flood of intercession pouring into Berlin from every corner of the Continent, he was benefiting by the sympathy of others closer to. His cell was directly under the apartments occupied by the head of the Küstrin administration, President von Münchow, who had a hole bored through the ceiling, to talk to the Prince and enquire how one might serve him. Frederick asked for books, fresh fruit, and cutlery. A son of Münchow's, seven or eight years old (and small for his age, one imagines), was put back into long clothes, with a row of deep pockets sewn into his petticoat, which were stuffed with fruit and dainties. The guards outside Frederick's door could not believe that the King's prohibition of visitors would extend to a lisping infant, and let the boy in to divert the prisoner a little from time to time. Next, Münchow brought off an even better trick and had the prisoner's close-stool replaced by one specially constructed with secret compartments wherein books and cutlery could be hidden. How much his kindness meant to Frederick can be gauged by the fact that many years and many happenings later he still spoke of the President as 'my benefactor Münchow'.

But Münchow was not alone. The Old Dessauer also did his bit to temper the prisoner's lot, seeing to it that a certain Captain Fouqué, who knew and liked the Prince of old, was transferred for duty with the Küstrin garrison; Fouqué spent many hours keeping Frederick company.

The Old Dessauer was no sentimentalist; his contribution was a straw in the new wind that was blowing from the quarter of Seckendorf and Grumbkow. Their victory was too complete for the comfort of these two. The King showed every determination to over-reach himself. Also his rages now were such that, in conjunction with his girth and apoplectic flush, he looked like bringing a fatal stroke upon himself at any moment. At any moment, then, the prisoner of Küstrin might reappear in very different guise.

The Court Martial went into session. It took two days to read the revised report, and four days to deliberate. The resulting verdict emphasized again the judges' incompetence regarding the Crown Prince who, with some grace notes of scriptural quotation, was commended to 'his Royal Majesty's most supreme and paternal mercy'. 'The former Lieutenant Katte' was sentenced to imprisonment for life—or rather, as Frederick William construed it, for the duration of the present King's life only.

The verdict was unacceptable.

Frederick William changed it.

'... While his Majesty is not in the habit of increasing sentences as a rule, but rather, usually reduces such whenever possible, [the fact is that] this Katte is not only an officer of my army, but an officer of the *Garde Gens d'Armes*, therefore owing me an especial, personal loyalty over and above the ordinary. Since, however, this Katte had [on the contrary] been in conspiracy with the rising sun*, and intrigued with foreign Ministers and Ambassadors in the matter of [Frederick's and Katte's proposed] desertion, and since it was not his job to plot with the Crown Prince, but on the contrary he should have informed his Majesty ..., his Majesty cannot see on what possible basis the Court Martial can have failed to pronounce sentence of death. Thus [i.e. if matters were to be handled in this way] his Majesty would never be able to rely on any officer or servant bound to him by oath and duty. Any [future] miscreants would feel encouraged by Katte's having got off so lightly. His Majesty in his time had some schooling too, so that he knows the Latin proverb: *Fiat iustitia et pereat mundus*. Will you, therefore, give out in all due form that, although by rights Katte for his *Crimen laesae majestatis* deserves to die by tearing with red-hot pincers and hanging, he shall nevertheless, in consideration of his family, be put to death by the sword. When the Court Martial acquaints Katte with this sentence, they shall tell him that his Majesty is very sorry, but that it is better he shall die than that Justice should perish from the earth.'

No longer was sternness dictated solely by emotion. There was growing unrest among the Prussian nobility, and the outside world was more and more importunate with its unsolicited advice. The King of Prussia had to show he brooked no interference.

The monarchs of the eighteenth century were haunted by the memory of the Fronde—the bloody revolt of the nobles of France against the Crown, in the reign of Louis XIV—precisely as the monarchs of the nineteenth century were to be haunted by the memory of the French Revolution. In Prussia there were no great families other than the royal; the power of aristocracy had long ago been broken, so that the nobles

* A phrase Frederick William was fond of using in the context of his heir.

formed merely a level upper stratum of servants to the Crown. But they were up in arms now, no less on Katte's behalf than for the Crown Prince—as yet only metaphorically. The movement must be quelled before it went further.

With reference to the world at large, Frederick William knew full well what was said about his army: half of it would run away in the event of war. Now by his own obstinate interpretation the world had been told that the King's own son had tried to desert from the Prussian forces. A demonstration was required, of discipline upheld.

In repudiating foreign intercession for his son, the King echoed the Court Martial of Köpenick, stressing the entirely private character of the case. With the Court Martial itself, however, he again insisted that the Prince's crime was a perfectly clear-cut military one, on which the Law set the death penalty and nothing else. So the Court Martial had better try again.

While the renewed proceedings against Frederick were being got under way, Katte on Sunday, 5 November, was abruptly told that a carriage stood waiting to take him to Küstrin where he should die. 'To soften Fritz's hardened heart,' his accomplice was to be executed in front of his eyes; 'Should there not be room enough outside his window, take him to another place where he shall have a good view.'

Frederick knew nothing of this until he was roused from his sleep at five o'clock next morning with the news. Katte had just arrived at Küstrin and was to die in two hours' time. The reaction upon Frederick's heart left nothing to be desired. He wept, lamented, prayed for death, prayed for a stay of execution: let them only give him time to send a messenger to Wusterhausen and offer to renounce his rights, his liberty, his life in exchange for Katte's. But the King had in advance forbidden the slightest postponement by any cause whatsoever.

Katte showed more fortitude: calm, uncomplaining, punctilious alike in religious observance and farewells to his family and friends. By order of the King he was dressed in the brown prison habit, like the Prince who was at his compulsory observation post in time to see the mound of sand prepared which was to soak up his friend's blood.

The guard of 150 men took up position in a circle round the scaffold, without obscuring Frederick's view from the second-storey room to which he had been taken by the fortress commandant and President Münchow. The drums began to sound and Katte appeared, flanked by two chaplains who had travelled with him from Berlin. Frederick cried out loudly, kissing his hand to Katte and asking his friend's pardon. Katte returned the salutation and called up to the window, 'La mort est douce pour un si aimable prince.'

The sentence was read. Katte took leave of his brother officers. He himself removed his neckerchief. He refused a cloth to bind his eyes, knelt down and prayed aloud, and thus received the death stroke. The severed head was then re-arranged in position with the body, which by the King's command was left to lie till two in the afternoon, albeit covered with a black cloth.

Frederick had not seen the head fall; he had fainted. The Chaplain sent to work upon his softened heart had to defer this, as the Prince when he came to was in no condition to take in anything that was said to him. He could not be got away from the window, staring at the bloody sand heap and the black-covered body, until a detachment of townspeople came with a coffin and took Katte's remains off for burial.

Not very surprisingly, 'The Prince took no nourishment, either at mid-day or in the evening.' In the night they heard him pacing up and down and raving; he ran a fever and then mercifully lost consciousness again for a time. The Chaplain, an officer of the garrison, and a servant took turns at watching by his bed. By morning the delirium abated and Frederick returned to full awareness, though still manifestly in a state of shock.

'The King thinks he has taken Katte from me,' he said, 'but I see him all the time.'

THE 'IRON HERO'
Charles XII of Sweden,
'Gothorum et Vandalorum Rex'

PETER THE GREAT OF RUSSIA

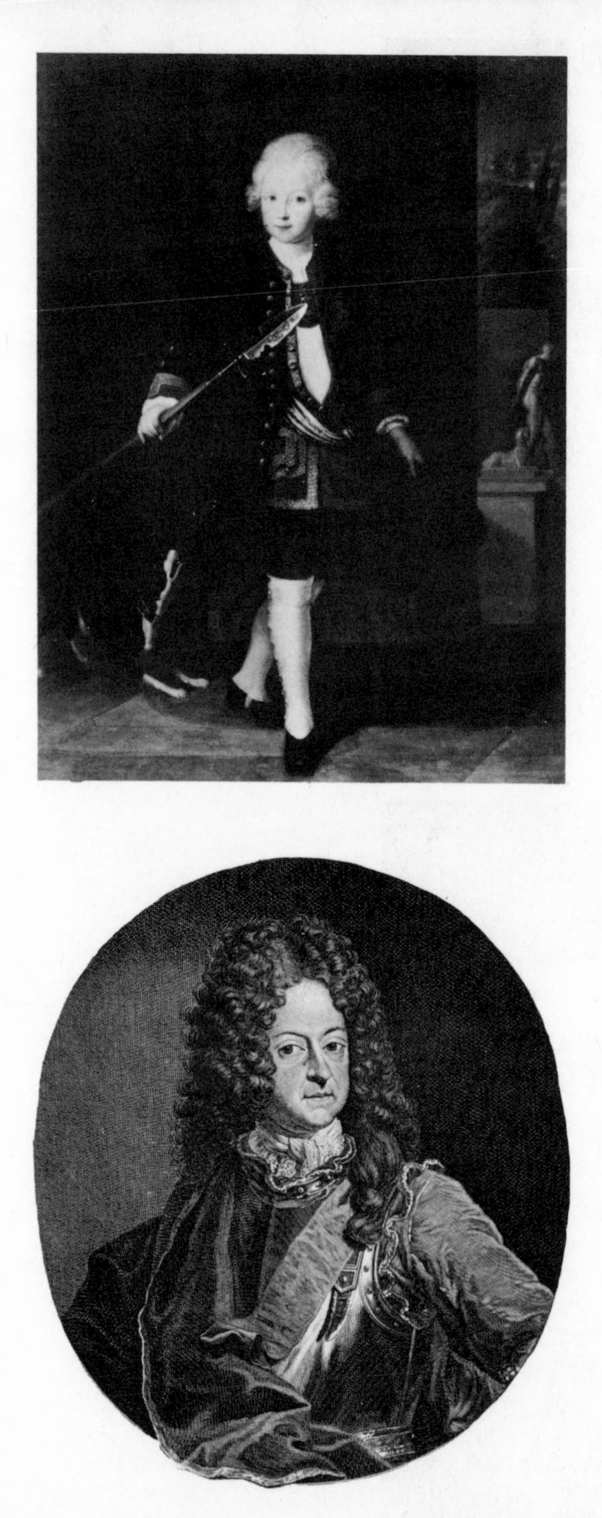

FREDERICK AS A BOY

THE FIRST HANOVERIAN
George I of England

CHAPTER 11

THE QUALITY OF MERCY

Apologists for Frederick William have averred that the execution did not in fact take place in front of Frederick, who only saw Katte as he was led past, Münchow and the commandant having taken it upon themselves to go against the King's orders (which were preserved, so that there is no getting round them). While it is difficult to see how contravention of those orders may be used in the King's favour, it nevertheless appears from various exact topographical descriptions, as well as by eye-witness accounts such as the Chaplain's, that the orders were obeyed.

Chaplain Müller was attached to the Garde Gens d'Armes, and his spiritual ministrations to the condemned Katte had been so fruitful that the King desired him to stay on at Küstrin and wean Frederick from his Calvinist error, to true and orthodox repentance.

Frederick on recognizing in him the priest who had escorted Katte to the scaffold, misunderstood the situation. Instantly his hopeless grief turned into naked terror: he thought the Chaplain had come to prepare him for death likewise. The Chaplain had the utmost difficulty in soothing him.

Together they read Katte's last message to the Prince, which indeed testified to a most remarkable change of disposition in the former freethinking worldling, being full of pious and self-lacerating admonitions. Frederick was deeply moved. All the same he yet clung firmly to his intellectual belief in the unchangeable design of God, from the beginning of time apportioning to some men everlasting happiness and everlasting misery to others: more than ever the only terms on which he could reconcile experience with Faith, at all.

A prolonged bout of theological wrestling ensued. Day after day, for hours at a time, often from six o'clock in the morning by Frederick's request, the disputation went on. However, as early as 8 November Chaplain Müller was able to write the King that Frederick's contrition was entire, wherefore assuredly the time had come to vouchsafe him a ray of hope to warm his shuddering soul and raise up his broken spirit lest it go under in incurable melancholia: to which end he, Müller, would pray All-merciful God to guide the King's heart.

The King's heart was then a difficult thing to penetrate. Nobody knew quite what to make of it; and his true intentions at that juncture have been debated ever since. He had won his point; the Court Martial at last had yielded the required verdict on Frederick, with a strong recommendation to mercy. It was hoped that he might be satisfied with the principle, and forgo exacting the death penalty in actual fact; but as yet he gave no sign. He too was wrestling, albeit only with himself; should he show Christian clemency, or would that be construed as giving in? For once the absolute certitude of his righteousness failed him.

He too was having nightmares. He suffered from insomnia and brought in half the Tabagie to sit up smoking with him of nights. When he did get to sleep, he would start up again in anguish and roam the empty corridors or go for comfort to his wife. For a month, according to Captain Dickens, he never went to bed sober. One would like to know the substance of the dreams that plagued him.

During daylight hours, he was the target of unremitting attempts to influence his decision, coming from the courts of England, Austria, Russia, Poland, Sweden and Germany, from family and friends, from the chiefs of the army. Seckendorf, Grumbkow, the Old Dessauer, everyone sufficiently distinguished to speak out with impunity, pleaded for Frederick; old General Buddenbrock went to the length of tearing open his tunic and baring his breast: 'If your Majesty must have blood, take mine: but that other blood you shall not have so long as I have voice to speak.' They only made it harder for Frederick William to know what he really wanted and what would be truly right and good, by stimulating his resistance and hypersensitive amour propre. Perhaps also he was wishing to stimulate a consensus of petition of sufficient weight to overbear him without loss of dignity. Sophie Dorothee, who knew him well, was convinced that only the intervention of the Emperor could now save her son. She trod pride underfoot and made her peace with Seckendorf, in order to obtain this.

Frederick's humiliation was the most complete he had yet undergone, since coming from within: survival, bare survival had become his only aim. The only form his struggle for life could take was the theological discussions with Chaplain Müller, who was moreover his only channel of communication. Little by little he seemed to relinquish his heresy; the Chaplain was filled with ever-waxing admiration of Frederick's cognitive and dialectical faculties, and with ever-waxing compassion, the more assiduous as the King remained unimpressed by all his good reports.

However, the King had finally decided on reprieve—whether or not it was the Emperor's autograph appeal which turned the balance. At all events he did himself the honour of granting more than had been asked of him.

Not only was Frederick's life to be spared, but he was provisionally reinstated to rank and title and freedom—freedom, at least, from prison. A full pardon he had yet to earn ('I hope he won't end on the gallows yet,' Frederick William wrote, as if he himself had nothing to do with that, to Grumbkow, 'though I doubt it myself.'), first by serving a penitential term in the Küstrin Administration, and further, 'if war breaks out, he shall be among the first to go over the top . . . then, provided he does it all with a good grace and goes on that way, there'll be pardon.'

In the same event, too, 'I shall cleave to the Emperor, never mind if everything goes to the devil over it. I will with pleasure give my army, my money and my blood, to bring about the destruction of England.' War between Austria and England was now expected before the end of the year.

Though having made his choice, the King's feelings were

unchanged. Unappeased wrath sounds through his letter authorizing Chaplain Müller to apprise the Prince of the good news. Frederick would have to take a fresh oath of allegiance to his father, 'loud and clear: no muttering or anything like that, and as for mental reservations, if he has anything like that in mind—for I know his wicked heart—we don't recognize that sort of thing here.' Neither would the King consent to see his son again for the present.

He tied up the last loose ends of the case. The elder Keith was condemned to death *in absentia* and hanged and quartered in effigy; the younger got off with banishment to Wesel. Rochow's valet—who ought to have gone straight to the King at Steinsfurt instead of reporting merely to his master—was laid in irons at Spandau prison. One young subaltern, who had several times helped Katte to see Frederick secretly at Potsdam, was cashiered and also sent to Spandau, for three years; another, having done so only once, got six months. Duhan's father, to whom no responsibility attached save in that he had begotten Frederick's one-time tutor, lost the small government post he had held and with it his pension. The same happened to another minor functionary, the Potsdam precentor Ritter. This man's crime also was one of paternity. He was the father of Dorothea Ritter.

Doris Ritter was sixteen years old and fond of music. Frederick somehow had struck up a friendship with her, innocent enough since an army surgeon and a midwife whom the King sent to examine her found the girl's virginity intact. The fact remained that the two young people had met a few times when Doris's father was from home, and she had received presents from the Prince, such as a bunch of silk ribbons, a song sheet or two, and the like. For this Doris Ritter was arrested and publicly whipped, 'first in front of her father's house, and after at every street corner in the town,' as a prelude to penal servitude for life in the hemp spinneries of Spandau.*

* * *

A royal commission headed by Grumbkow went to Küstrin to superintend Frederick's release. The day before, Grumbkow

* She was, however, released after three years.

had a long, private interview with the Prince in which the pair came to an understanding. Henceforth Frederick would ask Grumbkow's advice on all things touching his relations with the King, and Grumbkow would promote Frederick's interests in that quarter.

On the second Sunday after Katte's death, 19 November, Frederick took the oath of allegiance, 'loud and clear' as stipulated, received back his sword, and was discharged from his prison. He was then taken straight to church where 'all Küstrin' attended with him to a sermon on the text of Psalm 77, verse 10, full of allusive force in Luther's translation: 'I have to suffer even thus; the right hand of the Most High can alter all,' under which the Prince and many of the congregation broke down in tears. After that he was conducted to a small house in the town, furnished strictly to the King's specifications, and sat down to write to his father.

> Most illustrious and most merciful father, Your Majesty my most gracious father has rightly conceived a just wrath and repugnance against me for my disobedience as His Majesty's subject and soldier as well as for my recalcitrance as His Majesty's son. With the utmost subservience and respect I now submit myself to the mercy of my most gracious father and beg him most graciously to pardon me, since it is not so much the loss of my liberty . . . as my own reflections which have brought me to see reason in regard to my . . . iniquities. I remain with the most perfectly submissive respect and humility, to the end of my days. . . . etc, etc.

It looks as if Grumbkow had already entered upon his office of private adviser.

Although the King had pointed out that Frederick's service in the Administration was not to be regarded by him as a punishment only, but as an indispensable part of monarchical training, he took care that the punitive aspect should be unmistakable. Frederick was not allowed to set foot outside the little moorland town; the sentries must not salute let alone present arms to him. The only books permitted him were the German Bible and Hymnal and Arndt's *Treatise on True Christianity*; a well-meaning suggestion that these might be supplemented by such light literature as some textbooks on taxation, police organization, geometry, and engineering, was promptly vetoed as vapid and frivolous. Frederick's flute remained confiscated and he was forbidden to hear secular music of any kind. He was also forbidden to write to anybody, except for duty-letters at prescribed intervals to the King and to the Queen.

On Monday Frederick started work. The King had sent precise instructions as to the furniture and position his son was to occupy in the Administrative Chamber—a small table and chair placed at the foot of the Councillors' board—and warned the Council to be alert against the noxious and deceitful character of the trainee. His hours were 7–11.30 a.m. and 3–5 p.m. His function was to listen and learn, undertake occasional clerical donkeywork, and to append his signature in a separate space well below the others, on documents promulgating the Council's decisions, in which he had no vote. On Sundays he was to attend three church services and meditate upon them in the intervals. Social amusements of even the most staid and humdrum kind were banned; a request by the Governor of Küstrin that the Prince might be permitted to come to his daughter's wedding was turned down: 'A person under arrest stays locked up.'

Frederick gave no sign of distress; more, soon he appeared positively cheerful. Doubtless Frederick William was not far wrong in commenting, ay, he dared say Fritz *was* happy at Küstrin—because there he was far away from his Papa. But also it was made abundantly clear to the penitent that most people were on his side. Frederick's supposedly Spartan larder overflowed with charitable offerings of oysters, capons, and champagne, and tacit moral encouragement was not lacking.

But there was no pleasing his father. Again the King discounted all the good reports, predicting that as soon as people got to know Fritz better they would see there was no good in 'that holy saint of yours—but for his tongue: there's never anything wrong with that!' When Frederick began to show an interest in his work and drew up a little survey on the local linen industry, the King refused to believe that he was the author—and anyway, the Prince should keep off 'projects and wind-making' and confine himself to copying and listening.

The set hours of dry, theoretical instruction became as tedious for the teachers as for the pupil. Director (of the Chamber) Hille penned a graphic account of how the talk would dry up by degrees till 'one sits around yawning, desultorily pushing the quill, reduced to playing chess or doing nothing at all'. Frederick, however, had something else to exercise his mind.

The King's contemptuous snarl about 'that holy saint', his son, was no random invective. The holy saint, after having apparently seen the error of his ways under Chaplain Müller's guidance, all at once refused to make a formal recantation of his Calvinist convictions. The father who believed he had finally crushed his son, had to see him raise his head again, powerless now to strike it off. The King who had just reprieved the deserter could not punish him for being steadfast in faith. The Christian who subscribed to the Lutheran axiom that 'the Calvinist dragon is pregnant with all the horrors of Mohammedanism', had his hands tied by circumstances so that he could only rail, not pierce the monster rearing in his own house. And Frederick made the most of his morally impregnable position.

One almost has the impression that both were to some extent using the issue, as it were, to sanctify their conflict in the eyes of the world—for both sought to give it every publicity. Such a view may be grossly unfair, facile, anachronistic; certainly the narrow mind of Frederick William must always absolve him from conscious hypocrisy, and Frederick never entirely relinquished sympathy with the dogma of Predestination. But in after days religion was never an important part of Frederick's life; and now, after holding out for a month or two, he finally abjured his heresy, with a verbal shrug—saying he had no intention of making a martyr of himself.

Reluctance had enhanced the value of surrender, and Frederick William, having got his price, at last yielded to the universal entreaties to grant his son an interview. More than a year after they had last met, the King arrived at Küstrin on his birthday, 15 August 1731. Grumbkow and Derschau were with him.

The inhabitants turned out in strength and trailed the royal carriage to the Governor's house. The Prince was sent for and brought in by three attendants. The King 'immediately turned round and looked at his son', Grumbkow thought it necessary to note. Frederick fell at his father's feet. The King told him to get up and launched into a prolonged recapitulation of his faults, sprinkled with equally redundant assurances that Frederick could not hope to get the better of him. In lurid colours he painted the fate of Frederick's mother and sister as it would have been had Frederick escaped to England, and the fate of Hanover too, which the injured father would have ravaged, 'ay, and if it had cost me life, land, and people!'

Frederick said what one could say to this, which was not much, fell on his knees again and kissed his father's feet. The King demanded to hear from the son's own lips whether Frederick or Katte had instigated their conspiracy. Frederick answered, 'It was I,' and the King said grudgingly, 'Nice to hear you tell the truth for once.' Next he fired off a really awkward question: 'Well, how do you like life at Küstrin? Have you still as much aversion as ever to Wusterhausen and to *the shroud*, as you used to call it?' Frederick being at a loss for an answer, the King resumed in full spate: 'Likely enough my company does not suit you. I have no French manners and cannot spout bon-mots in the petit-maître way. . . I am a German prince and mean to live and die as such. But you can see what you have got by your waywardness, hating everything that I liked, and if I distinguished anyone, despising him—while when anyone was out of favour with me you went out of your way to make yourself agreeable to him. Your real friends, who intended your good, you hated and spoke ill of; those that flattered you and encouraged you in your infamy, you caressed. You see what it has all come to. In Berlin, in all Prussia for some time past, nobody so much as asks after you. Nobody cares whether you are in the world or not; and were it not for one or the other coming from Küstrin with news of your playing tennis or wearing French hairbags, nobody would know whether you were alive or dead.' One can see the direction of his broodings over the past year, and incidentally register the fact that the King employed the sort of shafts which would have hurt himself most sorely, had he been in Frederick's place.

Lastly, having got Frederick to affirm over again his return to doctrinal orthodoxy, and further improving the occasion at some length, the King said he forgave the son his past misdeeds and hoped 'the future will show fruits'. Sobbing, Frederick once more kissed his father's feet; the King's eyes were *not dry*, says Grumbkow, and everybody else likewise was much affected.

In the presence of several hundred spectators, Frederick saw the King to his carriage, kissed his feet for the third time, and in return was himself embraced—at which, again in Grumbkow's words, the Prince was thrown into such transports of bliss as no pen could describe. Küstrin rejoiced with him. Following the King's departure, the town notables vied in giving banquets for the Prince, who shone among the younger guests with smashing of wine glasses and breaking of windows.

This was premature. The revised Instructions for Frederick's curriculum, eagerly awaited by all, fell far short of expectation. As yet his liberty was nothing like restored, although he might now venture outside the town on brief visits of inspection to estates and factories nearby, always provided he had a pass from the Governor and returned before dark. Provided 'girls and females' were strictly excluded, he might even enjoy some social life. But no date was fixed for a reunion with his mother and sister, nor for his readmission to the army. To gain these objectives would be the next step in Frederick's slow ascent to rehabilitation.

It was also the next step in the King's strategy to subdue his family for good.

* * *

To see his mother and sister might be an emotional necessity, but to be in uniform was a prime condition of existence for the heir to the throne of Prussia. Without that he would always be a freak, an outcast from a society where almost every normal male of quality had some military rank and the greenest ensign took precedence over the hoariest councillor. Frederick, ranking below the meanest councillor—where did that leave him? Under the Soldier King, a civilian Crown Prince of Prussia had no social reality. Also, Frederick was after all his father's son, imbued from infancy with the superiority of the profession of arms and bred to that profession from the cradle. No matter how fiercely he might have resented it before, with deprivation came nostalgia. His father's taunting reference to 'the shroud' had been shrewdly aimed. Frederick now would give almost anything to don that shroud again.

* * *

The King intimated to Wilhelmine that it was up to her whether Frederick should be granted a full reconciliation. The British, anticipating their future reputation of obtuseness to defeat, had been putting out new feelers in respect of her marriage to the Prince of Wales. Once she was safely married off elsewhere, they would perforce take no for an answer and stop pestering him.

Consciously magnanimous, the King offered his daughter complete freedom of choice—between three selected suitors. Tentative proposals on behalf of the heirs to the thrones of Sweden and Russia had long since been squashed. The three favoured candidates were the titular Duke of Weissenfels, a connexion of Augustus the Strong, middle-aged, penniless, and lacking other distinction; Margrave Frederick William of Schwedt, the Old Dessauer's nephew; and Frederick of Brandenburg-Kulmbach, Hereditary Prince and future Margrave of Bayreuth, of whom at least it could be said that he had made the Grand Tour.

Sophie Dorothee, seeing her dearest hope about to vanish, tried to force her daughter to swear a solemn oath that she would never marry anybody but the Prince of Wales. But Wilhelmine was afraid of on the one hand perjuring herself or on the other swearing away her life and Frederick's chances. Still under house arrest and weak from lack of food, she was regaled with threats and abuse by both her parents every day. She must marry, or she would be immured somewhere in the country like her grandmother, the Princess of Ahlden, while Fritz would remain a semi-prisoner at Küstrin. She must not marry, or be accursed of her mother.

Wilhelmine exercised her right of choice in favour of the Prince of Bayreuth, being the least unattractive of the three, as he was nearest to her in age and education; also, she had never met him whereas she knew and disliked the other two. The Queen raged at her daughter: it was the King and Frederick all over again. But the King wept tears of joy, took her into his arms, and told her *probably* Fritz would be allowed to come to the wedding.

The wedding, which took place on 20 November 1731, was celebrated with a generous magnificence such as Frederick William had not displayed since the funeral of his father. The bride derived sufficient pleasure from the nuptial splendours to list them carefully even years later; though Mama was yet unrelenting and, we gather, saw to it that Wilhelmine was hideously over-dressed, her hair done in 'twenty-four locks the size of your arm' and hanging all over her face, in addition to a gown of cloth of silver trimmed with Spanish gold lace and so heavy that she staggered under it.

The festivities went on for several days. On the third evening there was a court ball, 'seven hundred couples, persons of quality all', the future Margravine of Bayreuth was to remember proudly. Wilhelmine loved to dance, and led off the quadrille with all her noted grace and animation.

Suddenly, 'Grumbkow came up to me and said, "Eh! Mon Dieu, Madame, it looks as if you had been stung by the tarantula! Have you not noticed those strangers who have just come in?" I stopped at once and gazed round to all sides; I then saw a young man in grey, indeed unknown to me. "Go on then, go and embrace the Crown Prince: there he is!" All my blood boiled up with joy. O Heaven, my brother! I cried; but I can't see him, where is he? Show him to me, in the name of God! Grumbkow led me to him. Coming closer, I began to recognize him, though with difficulty. He had grown much stouter, shorter in the neck, his face not so beautiful as it had been. I threw myself upon his neck; I was quite incoherent; I wept, I laughed, as one out of her senses. In all my life I have never felt so lively a joy. I then went to throw myself at the feet of the King, who said, "Well, are you pleased with me? You see I have kept my word." I took my brother by the hand and begged the King to restore his friendship to him. The scene was so affecting that it drew tears from the whole assembly.'

The King himself presented Frederick to the Queen: 'There you are, Madame, here's our Fritz back again.' But the Queen was cool, and Frederick well-nigh icy.

'My mother,' Wilhelmine analysed the situation, 'had in fact no love for her children save insofar as they could serve her ambitions. It was painful to her that I and not she should have been the cause of the reconciliation.'

As for Frederick, who 'wore a proud air and seemed to look down on everybody', answered in monosyllables and treated his sister's young husband with mute incivility—his behaviour Wilhelmine could not make out at all. Even when next day she told him of all she had endured for his sake, 'he returned thanks for the obligation I had laid on him, with some caresses which clearly did not come from the heart.' It is singular that Wilhelmine should have found so puzzling what her own words make only too plain. Who in Frederick's place would have been at his ease under the King's showmanship; who would have relished being told in so many words that his pardon had been purchased by a sister's sacrifice?

When the newly married pair left for Bayreuth, the King and his daughter were on terms of utmost tenderness; his parting words were: 'I am too sad of heart to take leave of you. Embrace your husband for me: I am so overcome I cannot see him.' (However, 'The King took no further notice of me afterwards, and all the wonderful benefits he had promised me went up in smoke.')

The Crown Prince appearing with the King at a troop review was greeted by popular ovations. Later the generals of Prussia, headed by the Old Dessauer, in a body waited on the King with the earnest prayer to restore Frederick to the army, which was granted.

CHAPTER 12

FREDERICK'S MARRIAGE

For the time being Frederick returned to complete his apprenticeship at Küstrin. In February 1732 he was to resume 'the shroud' as colonel to an infantry regiment cantoned in Ruppin and Nauen, some distance from Berlin—which competent opinion judged to be just as well, if the good relations between the King and his son were to last. Frederick William himself remarked, touchingly, in this way it would always be something of a treat for them both, to meet.

Most of the special restrictions upon Frederick were rescinded; the remainder gradually lapsed in the observance. Books reappeared in the Crown Prince's household, and so did the flute, an instrument as necessary to his relaxation as the pen. Able to move more freely about the countryside, he found his grasp of administrative problems benefiting by concrete acquaintance with what hitherto had been presented to him only in the form of statistics.

He was not cut out to do anything by halves, he wrote to a friend: whatever he took up he had to plunge into headlong. 'I am up to my ears in Silesian Trade at present, which makes me so absent-minded that if I am asked whether I want mustard with my beef, I am perfectly capable of answering: look it up in the new customs register.'

Director Hille substantiated this, up to a point. In his final assessment, Frederick liked work and evinced both understanding and initiative, though tending to be more interested in large issues and general principles than in day-to-day matters and practical detail. Also the Prince set too much store by verbal elegancies and sophisticated conceits: present the soundest viewpoint to him plain and unadorned, and he would dismiss it; but season it with Attic salt and Gallic sauce, and he would lap it up; compliment him on his own wit, and he was yours heart and soul. Then, he had a regrettable penchant for making others look ridiculous. Yet on the other hand he was punctilious in courtesy towards inferiors, and more liable to be led astray by misplaced compassion than to err in the opposite direction. If God would but grant his Majesty a few more years of life, the chances were that the Crown Prince would mature into an outstanding ruler.

While one might suspect such a prediction of being the obligatory sugaring to a critical report, Hille was an earnest, upright man who, the Prince complained, was often very rude to him and a republican at heart. (The Director of the Küstrin Chamber was a commoner, and Frederick in a thoughtless moment once remarked to him that it was odd to see the landed nobility having to render account to persons of low degree. Director Hille replied: too true, but then the world was a very odd sort of place altogether, as witness especially the phenomenon of brainless princes expecting to be in authority over sensible people.) Others who did not, like Hille, observe Frederick in working hours or study his large, spare-time output of essays and draft projects, were less optimistic in their judgment of him at that time. To a good many people the young man who, no longer to be pitied, was putting on flesh and exuberance, was 'not so beautiful as he had been', to borrow his sister's significant phrase.

But Frederick was not out of the wood, by a long way. Although the King had fixed the date when his son might cast off the last shackles of his 'galley' of Küstrin, there was no question that he would let him go until he had settled him in life, like Wilhelmine. The subject of marriage for Frederick had been broached during his stay at Berlin, and in his heart he must have known that was that; but yet he hoped to stave it off, or at least win some concessions as to choice.

He was winning some reputation as a rake. His yearly allowance was 6,000 Thaler—so small that Grumbkow called it an absurdity. Seckendorf, who had seen to it that after his release the Prince had written a letter of thanks to the Emperor, took the opportunity to lay the Crown Prince of Prussia under added obligation. Vienna offered Frederick a supplementary income of 2,500 Ducats, payable in instalments so that the King would not notice. (Austrian money presents, in the same cause, went also to Wilhelmine and to Frederick's exiled tutor Duhan, both of whom were in financial straits.) Discussing the Crown Prince's expenses, Seckendorf opined that women accounted for the greater part: 'But it is said that the flesh is weaker in him than the sinful spirit, from which it would seem to follow that the Crown Prince seeks a vain renown rather than satisfaction.'

Frederick's own remarks on this point do nothing to clarify it: sometimes he would disclaim the prowess with which he was credited, at other times he talked like a confirmed debauchee.

His only documented love affair of this period was, indeed, so much a matter of correspondence as to exude its own fog of ink.

His beloved was Luise Eleonore von Wreech, wife of the lord of Tamsel, a country estate in the vicinity of Küstrin. She was twenty-three years old to Frederick's nineteen, and according to him a paragon of all imaginable graces. 'That little wonder of Nature,' he was to recall, '. . . wished to teach me both poetry and love. I made out well enough in love, but not so well in poetry.' Though the latter was ever a cherished ambition with him, he had no illusions about his ability; to Tamsel he sent notice of a 'mass invasion by certain winged things, more menacing than locusts, many-footed, with sharp teeth and long-extended bodies, named *verse* and hailing straight from Parnassus, whence Good Taste expelled them.' He also wrote her reams of closely scrawled prose epistles in which amorous protestations mingled with digressions on literature, philosophy, and the arts, and an abundance of sardonic pen portraits of the worthies among whom he served his term.

Frederick had entered on a path of systematic calculation, which, to be safely sustained, required that his real thoughts must always have an outlet somewhere. As he had been suppressed in the past, so he would now suppress himself on purpose to promote his advantage; he had been so shamed, by his own moral collapse in face of death no less than by ill-usage, that there was nothing left to make him blush—except that he permitted nobody to see him naked, to the end of his life. It is a familiar psychological stratagem to camouflage a secret with apparent incontinence of candour. At all events, relentless frankness and self-revelation, side by side with expedient deceit, had become a compulsive necessity with Frederick; and he opened his heart to Frau von Wreech as to no other woman besides his sister Wilhelmine. She must have been a little wonder indeed, for Frederick's demands as to looks, elegance, cultivation, repartee, and sensibility were very high, modelled on his idealized conception of the French which he had drawn from his reading.

Grumbkow presently announced to Seckendorf: 'The King tells me in confidence that Wreech, the Colonel's wife, is with child to the Crown Prince and that Wreech vows he will not own it for his. And his Majesty in secret is rather pleased.'

However, when the time came Colonel von Wreech did not disown the infant*, nor were relations between him and his wife noticeably disturbed. Frederick's parting sonnet to the lady, on his leaving Küstrin, was elegiac, but no more than conventionally so. In a note accompanying a gift of his portrait he asked Frau von Wreech to remember him as 'a good boy at bottom though a bit of a nuisance, as he used to make me very angry sometimes with his importunate love'; and that was the end of the interlude, for ever.

Whether or not what Grumbkow said about the King was true, Frederick William now pressed on the matter of the Crown Prince's marriage. Frederick had expected to be given a choice of three, like Wilhelmine, and had sworn he would never take a pig in a poke.†

He was given no choice at all; but there was no pig in a poke. Frederick heard all about his bride. Not even the ambassadorial marriage brokers, usually so glib, were able to build up Frederick William's pick as attractive and intelligent. 'Not handsome and not ugly', and 'pious and shy', were the

* A daughter, who lived only a few months.
† The expression Frederick used was, 'Die Katze im Sack'—the exact German equivalent.

IMPERIAL ENVOY
Count Louis Henry von Seckendorf

PRUSSIAN MINISTER
Frederick William von Grumbkow

FRIENDSHIP
Augustus the Strong and
Frederick William I

'MY BROTHER, THE RED CABBAGE'
George II of England

best adjectives they could find for Elizabeth Christine of Bevern-Brunswick, a niece of the Empress and the only Protestant princess so connected with the House of Habsburg, but possessing neither fortune nor education.

Impossible! cried Frederick, in open desperation—open, that is, with his only potential helper, Grumbkow. The King must be made to see reason, and to take warning from the example of poor young Louise in Ansbach whose marriage had turned out most unhappy. Surely the King could be brought to understand that one must at least be able to *talk* with one's wife? Tactless in his agitation, Frederick assured Grumbkow he would rather marry 'Fräulein Jette', Grumbkow's daughter, without a penny, or any common wench of Berlin, than be saddled with a bigoted imbecile like the Princess of Bevern. Misfortune dogged him, that appeared to be his ordained fate; but sooner than go on reaping misery upon misery like this he would shoot himself: and omniscient God would not condemn him for it.

Grumbkow rebuked him sharply for his want of fortitude and extravagance of expression, and declined to make any attempt at arguing with the King. 'Do you want to plunge me and my family into absolute ruin? The shirt is nearer to the skin than is the coat!'* There being no alternative, Frederick gave in.

The King expressed himself no less extravagantly than his son, when he learned that he had won again. *He burst into tears of joy and vowed this was the happiest moment of his life.* One might have thought that the proposed match spelled salvation to his House and country, when materially speaking it was at most a courtesy gesture towards Austria. But no doubt Frederick's capitulation did give him the most satisfying moment of his life as a family man.

Tears, also, were seen in Frederick's eyes during the betrothal ceremony—tears of joy again, said the sycophants of the King. Directly it was done Frederick turned away from his betrothed and talked to a lady of the court, said to be the latest object of his addresses. Seckendorf wrote to Prince Eugene in Vienna

* i.e. my own welfare is more important to me than yours.

that a few dancing lessons and some general instruction doubtless would improve the Princess of Bevern so that Frederick would be surprised when next they met (Frederick had been overheard to say Elizabeth Christine waddled like a goose): also, once her few trifling pimples went and her pockmarks faded and her throat grew less scrawny, she would be quite a beauty.

'I am sorry for the poor soul,' Frederick wrote to Grumbkow. 'There is going to be one unhappy princess more in the world.' And to Wilhelmine: 'She is a decent sort and I wish her no ill, but I can never love her.'

It is difficult to decide what the luckless bride really looked like and whether she was in truth so stupid, or merely excessively shy.

This is what the Queen told her other children at table, in front of the servants: 'Your brother is in despair, and he has every reason. She is a veritable goose. Ask her what questions you will, she only answers yes or no, simpering idiotically so that it makes you sick. Her teeth are bad and quite black.' Her daughter Charlotte chimed in: 'Oh, but you don't know the whole of her charms! One morning I attended her at her toilet. I was nearly asphyxiated. She stinks like the pest. I think she must have ten or eleven fistulas, for this is unnatural. Besides I noticed that she is crooked . . . one hip higher than the other . . . quantities of padding . . .' and so forth.

Yet, another letter of Frederick's to Wilhelmine, written some time later, says, 'I do not hate her so much as I pretend. I affect complete dislike, that the King may value my obedience more. She is pretty, complexion lily-and-rose, features delicate, face altogether that of a beautiful person. True, she has no breeding and dresses very badly, but I flatter myself . . . you will have the goodness to take her in hand. I recommend her to you and beg your protection for her.'

Having gone through with the betrothal, Frederick got his reward and was discharged from Küstrin to take up his independence at Ruppin and Nauen. He threw himself into his military part, reporting regularly to the King with a cloying enthusiasm for which he compensated himself in other letters charged with heavy irony concerning the enthralling fascinations of drill and the rarefied subtlety of regimental business. He still had his worries.

'My God,' he wrote to Count Hacke, a former enemy like Grumbkow and Derschau, 'how am I supposed to put in another thirty men, without any money? I've applied to Brandenburg but they won't let me have any extra. I'd like nothing better than to produce Longfellows for the King, like old man Dessauer . . . that's easy enough if you're flush. . . .But I, poor devil, can't even borrow. . . . If I don't get some help, I'll have exactly one recruit to show the King at next year's review, and my regiment will come out bottom. . . . Please help.'

The King did not think that Frederick wrote often enough to his betrothed. 'The idea is,' Frederick explained, 'to beat love into me with a stick. . . . What am I to write to her?' But orders were orders; well-pleased with the augmented correspondence, the King proclaimed, 'The lovers are thoroughly in love.'

The wedding had been fixed for 12 June 1733.

* * *

On 1 February 1733 the European constellation altered again. Augustus the Strong, Elector of Saxony and King of Poland, died at Warsaw—having intimated his decease at Berlin by there appearing in phantom shape to Grumbkow.

The crown of Poland was elective; in theory its bestowal rested with the Polish magnates, who in practice were divided in subservience to the respective interests of Austria and France: huge sums were set aside for them each year in Paris and Vienna.

While Augustus the Strong was yet alive, Russia and Prussia had been drawn into an engagement with Austria to ensure the exclusion, in future, of Saxon princes from the throne of Poland. But Augustus's son, now succeeding him under the style of Elector Augustus III, offered to recognize the Pragmatic Sanction in return for the Emperor's sponsorship, a bargain to which the Emperor agreed forthwith.

The French candidate was Stanislas Leszczynski, a Polish grandee who had transiently occupied the throne under the aegis of his friend Charles XII of Sweden, then at the height of his ascendancy; who had since become father-in-law to Louis XV; and whom previously the King of Prussia, in concert with the Emperor, had also undertaken to support. When now the Emperor, without so much as having consulted Frederick William first, suddenly demanded his support for the very personage who was to have been unconditionally disqualified, Frederick William felt deeply affronted and stuck to Stanislas.

France declared she would defend 'the freedom of the Polish elections' by force of arms if driven to it; Austria was resolved to prevent the election of Stanislas at any price. But if that price were to be war, Austria had to have the material and active support of England. England in consideration of present Bourbon expansion also at long last accepted the Pragmatic Sanction; but her price for supporting Austria in support of Augustus III was the marriage of the Crown Prince of Prussia with an English Princess—partly to help guard Britain's continental base of Hanover, and partly because the betrothal of Frederick to the Empress's niece was to be regarded as a move towards isolating England.

So late in the day, then, the buried Anglo-Prussian marriage project was resurrected. After well-nigh twenty years of labouring to sunder the Houses of Hanover and Brandenburg, Austria suddenly wished to press for their union.

Seckendorf had his doubts about putting it to Frederick William, thus badly and abruptly; but time was getting short and Vienna insisted. Grumbkow had no relish either for the task, but as a long-standing pensioner of the Emperor had no more choice than Seckendorf. The two were instructed to bring out the old trump card again, pretty dog-eared by now, of Jülich-Berg, and try a piece of last-minute bribery on the King of Prussia.

The King of Prussia was thunderstruck. He could not believe his ears. He gasped, he stood petrified, he exploded. 'It crushes my heart! This, from people who ought to know me! That they should think to make a scoundrel out of me: me! me! To make me into a villain! They have killed me, for this will be my death; they twist a dagger in my heart.' All who witnessed the scene said that never in his life had he been seen in such a rage—which, as we know, was saying much.

Of course it was not merely the brazen imposition of the Austrian volte face as such, but the inescapable inference of the Emperor's contempt for that inferior dolt the King of Prussia, which so exercised Frederick William. Perhaps a shade of repentance tinged his fury, or at least regret: for had not his entire family life gone to pieces over his pro-Austrian policy, as it now seemed needlessly?

It was a month before he could bear to speak to Seckendorf again. Grumbkow, who had not ventured quite as far into the open, retired in tolerable order and refused to have anything further to do with the matter.

For in Vienna the matter still was not considered closed. On the contrary, the most extraordinary passage in that whole, extraordinary, blundering enterprise was to come.

* * *

It was 11 June 1733. The wedding of the Crown Prince of Prussia and the Princess of Bevern-Brunswick was tomorrow. The King and Queen of Prussia with their son, the relations of the bride, and all other wedding guests were already assembled at the palace of Salzdahlum where the old Duke of Wolfenbüttel, Elizabeth Christine's grandfather, wished to stage her nuptials. It was nine o'clock in the morning. Frederick William, for once taking his ease as he was from home, was still in bed, when Seckendorf asked to see him.

Seckendorf had just received a courier from Vienna with urgent orders, dated 5 June, to break off the marriage which like everyone else Seckendorf was here to help celebrate.

It is impossible not to feel for the man who had been the evil genius of the Prussian court, but who could not, like Grumbkow, extricate himself from this last, preposterous errand. He smiled, he tells us, as he said what he had to say.

The King in his bed kept calm this time, even when Seckendorf suggested that *a* wedding could still take place on the morrow, though not of Frederick and Elizabeth Christine: why not marry the latter's brother Karl to Frederick's sister Charlotte instead?*

* In fairness it has to be stated that these two were about to be affianced.

The King replied with abnormal composure, 'If I did not know you so well . . . I would think you were dreaming. Three months ago I might have let myself be talked round to this, for love of his Imperial Majesty and even against my own interests. . . . But now, when we are all here for the wedding and the whole of Europe knows it is tomorrow—! This is nothing but another English trick, to represent me to the world as a fickle person who knows not how to keep his honour and his word.'

Frederick William was not so unmoved as he pretended. The thought of an English trick to discredit him, on the instant revived all his old suspicions of his son. Only when Frederick swore at last that only death should part him from his bride, would the King allow himself to be convinced that his son had known nothing of the grotesque proposal.

After that Frederick changed into peasant costume for the wedding-eve theatricals, in which he took the part of a lovesick shepherd and at the hands of Apollo received 'first prize for flute-playing': clearly the author of the piece could not think of any other noteworthy quality in the bridegroom.

The marriage was solemnized next day as arranged.

By midnight the newly-wed husband was writing to Wilhelmine, 'Thank God, it is all over.' He spent one hour in the bridal bed, then dressed again and showed himself in the pleasure gardens of the palace.

This time it took Frederick William several months to forgive Seckendorf.

CHAPTER 13
BUCEPHALUS AND PEGASUS

As customary, the courts of Europe were notified of the marriage; but England was omitted. A double family alliance was concluded right enough, but not with England: Frederick's fourth sister and his wife's brother, the heir apparent of Brunswick, were united in Berlin less than a week after the first couple's bridal entry. There was sarcastic comment in the British press.

Wilhelmine met the new Crown Princess. 'She was much heated and dépoudrée*, her hair coming down. I went with her to her room. My brother, introducing me, said to her, "This is a sister I adore and to whom I am under infinite obligation . . . I wish you to respect her even beyond the King and Queen, and not to take the least step without her advice: do you understand?" I embraced the Crown Princess and gave her every assurance of my affection, but she remained like a statue, not answering a word. Her people not being come, I repowdered her myself and adjusted her dress, without the least sign of thanks from her. . . . My brother got impatient at last and said, "Devil take the blockhead: thank my sister, can't you?" She then made me a curtsy . . . I took her back to the Queen's apartment, little edified by such a display of talent. . . .'

As soon as the festivities were over, Frederick went back to

* After a gala troop review which started at 4 a.m. and lasted for several hours on a scorching day, the ladies having had no breakfast nor a wink of sleep the night before.

his regiment and left his wife in the bosom of his family. The King in acceding mood also gave his consent to Frederick's desire for a fitting crown-princely residence at Rheinsberg, an estate near Ruppin with a decayed chateau which under royal licence was to be rebuilt for him. Meanwhile the provident father gave his attention to moulding Elizabeth Christine into a more suitable companion to her husband, even to denying his own principles: for in addition to dancing lessons she received a short course in philosophy and classical literature. More, Frederick William spent a small fortune on fine, foreign clothes and jewellery to beautify this dull and gentle daughter-in-law and give her pleasure.

Nobody else thought to give her pleasure. The Queen treated the unoffending instrument of her disappointment as its cause, and the Princesses took their cue from her. Frederick, it is true, made some effort at civil compunction. Only a fiend, he said, could fail to appreciate her touching endeavours to please him; in some private letters he even dilated commendingly on her sexual equipment; but in effect he kept away from her as much as he could. Nor did he at the best of times—or what Elizabeth Christine would look back on as their best time—address to her so much as two lines of verse: a negative distinction in which she stands alone among his personal correspondents.

His fertility in this respect was amazing, and could range from horrible doggerel to quite respectable compositions. Versifying had the same effect on him as music, refreshing his spirit and winding up his mind again when it ran down. Altogether, he must read and write as he must eat and breathe: 'If I can't, I am like the snuff addict without his box, dying of restlessness, his hand forever darting into his pocket.' But, more than a drug, literary activity also was his signal channel of acquiring and digesting information. In every field that came within his province, his capacity of both intake and output seemed unlimited.

Although at the same time he appeared to be enjoying life to the full of his bent as well—some hunger, some discontent, some unalleviable pain are generally found at the bottom of such inordinate industry: it is happiness which makes for indolence. Frederick had as much to deaden as to attain. He caused some amusement to various phlegmatic persons by trying to pretend (they said) that 'the year 1730 had been rubbed out of the calendar'. Yes: Frederick who talked about everything and anything, discouraged conversation on the events of that year—strange, was it not?

Only some extraordinary exploit would truly expunge the events of that year from the memory of the world.

There were two roads to glory as he saw it. The one was art, more especially the articulate art of literature, and the other was war. Which was more desirable, to create great works of literature, or to provide a great theme for such? The question was insoluble; why should one not do both, each in its season? For age was no hindrance to literary pursuits, whereas in war it was imperative to win one's spurs young.

Frederick had not been married many months when his chance came.

In August and September 1733 the Polish Diet exercised its proud privilege and elected a King—under protective custody by an Austrian army gathered on the Silesian border and a Russian army on the Lithuanian one. Disguised as a merchant, Stanislas Leszczynski slipped through the cordon, and was elected by unanimous vote. Ten days later he was in full flight from the advancing Russians.

France thereupon invaded the Imperial dependency of Lorraine and thence crossed into Germany. Sardinia and Spain followed suit, threatening the Austrian possessions in Italy, while England and Holland answered the Emperor's call for help with polite evasions. So the Emperor had only the Empire to fall back on and rallied the statutory contingents to be furnished by the States of Germany, to augment the inadequate forces of Austria.

The Brandenburg contingent was fixed at 10,000 men, a fraction of Frederick William's army. Under a treaty of 1728, Prussia and Austria were to have been equal allies in any forthcoming defensive enterprise against France. Frederick William was only too willing to come in on these terms now, with everything he had. But the Emperor declined with thanks: 10,000 Prussians was all he wanted. One did not have to be hypersensitive to see the reasons plainly: first, Prussia was to be kept in a subordinate position; second, large concentrations of Prussian troops in the Rhineland, that is, near Jülich-Berg, were to be prevented at all cost.

At first the King of Prussia reacted more in sorrow than in anger. 'Tell me,' he wrote to the Old Dessauer, 'would you have thought we'd live to see a French war, with Prussia left out in the cold? I would never have believed it: so all is for nothing in this world!' He soon warmed up; to Seckendorf he wrote: 'I for my part have every reverence for Imperial Majesty, but after my death the House of Brandenburg will abandon the Emperor and join the opposition, because the House of Brandenburg has been so injured, so that Prussia sits like a parrot in its cage: which is something the House of Brandenburg is going to even the score for.' Further, to Frederick for future guidance: 'That is the sort of thanks one gets . . . you can see it's no good sacrificing oneself for the Emperor. So long as they need one, they are all flattery; but as soon as they think they can get along without one, off comes the mask, and they remember nothing. The reflections which cannot but occur to you in this connexion may help you . . . in similar cases . . .'

No doubt 'reflections' of many kinds crossed Frederick's mind; but for the moment they could not cool his ardour to see battle, and that under Prince Eugene, a living legend, identified with seventeen famous victories. In summer 1734 the King let him go, loaded with paternal instructions how best to profit from the practical lessons in store for him.

For a start Frederick wrote two poems, one about the glories and one about the horrors of war. All too soon he noted, 'No laurels to be got here, only plenty of mud.' However, Prussian influence made itself felt: 'The drill-demon has now infected Prince Eugene, he keeps at his people worse than us, whereat his army curse us so that it is cruel to hear!' Two things impressed him: 'The rank confusion permeating the Imperial Army,' and the heroic stature, coupled with heroic modesty, of the septuagenarian commander-in-chief.

The siege of Philipsburg, which was the action Frederick took part in, was a desultory and indecisive affair; but at least he got his baptism of fire. Riding on reconnaissance with a number of others, and passing through a spinney raked by cannon shot from the lines, the Prince (it was recounted in a number of letters, not his own) continued his conversation without halt or tremor though trees splintered and crashed right beside him.

Among the many distinguished visitors to the Imperial camp was the King of Prussia, who spent a month with his contingent, under canvas, in spite of Prince Eugene's repeated invitation to share a dry, solid roof at headquarters. In consequence he nearly got his death. (Some said, however, that he had worried himself sick over the bad state of the Imperial Army.)

For some time past Frederick William's health had not been good; now on the way home he collapsed, with severe symptoms of gout, catarrh, and dropsy. The campaigning season was nearly over, and Frederick was delegated to oversee the transfer of the Prussian troops to winter quarters. It took four weeks to get the King to Potsdam. He was so ill that nobody believed he could survive. People's behaviour towards the Crown Prince underwent a perceptible change.

Frederick himself was racked with ambiguous feelings. On the one hand he was tense with expectancy; on the other he found out that, in fact, he did not want his father to die. Seckendorf reported that Frederick's eyes filled uncontrollably with tears at any mention of his father's illness. 'If only he would let me live my own life,' he burst out, 'I would give an arm to prolong his life by twenty years.'

The doctors gave Frederick William a fortnight to live, which perhaps was all he needed to be told, to mend. And as soon as the danger was past, his son sank into unambiguous gloom. He tried to make light of it: 'Some parents, knowing the tender hearts of their children, in their charity drive those children to desperation in their lifetime, so as to obviate the final pain of their demise,' he wrote to Wilhelmine, whose father-in-law passed on shortly after; 'The Duke of Brunswick, like a man of honour, has had the decency to die, unlike some.'

With the King's recovery, everything went back to the old tenor. As always when coming face to face with extinction, all the father's grudge rose reinvigorated against his heir. The only difference was that he no longer laid hand on Frederick.

Even so Frederick William could still surprise his son. Spring had come and with it the resumption of the Rhine campaign: and Frederick William, who as far back as Frederick could remember had done everything to make a soldier of him, absolutely refused his passionate entreaties to let him go back to the front. Frederick argued, cajoled, humbled himself, for weeks; the King was adamant and fobbed him off with 'secret reasons'—so secret, said Frederick, that Papa did not know them himself.

Papa's only conscious reason was that he feared Frederick might become too attached to the Imperial cause, which, Frederick's admiration of Prince Eugene notwithstanding, was the last thing to be apprehended.

* * *

Frederick's memory was not so short, or not so malleable as Frederick William's. His rancour could lose its edge, but it would not be switched. All he wanted was to see some real fighting and gain experience.

Great possibilities were churning in his brain. During the winter pause and while as it was thought Frederick William lay dying, the Crown Prince had entered into secret negotiations with the French Ambassador (the Kingdom of Prussia as such, of course, was not at war with France). He let it be known that on stepping into his father's shoes he would not be averse from donning also the mantle of Charles XII of Sweden, who had made Stanislas Leszczynski King of Poland the first time, and reinstating Louis XV's father-in-law by force of Prussian arms, at a suitable price. (Stanislas had come to rest at Königsberg, where under Frederick William's loyal hospitality he set up a shadow court of fellow-exiles.)

The negotiations went slowly; France was playing Frederick along whilst waiting to see what would happen. For one thing Cardinal Fleury, Louis's former tutor who ruled France, in general favoured an anti-war policy; for another, there was no reason for anybody besides Frederick himself to suppose that he had the stuff of a Charles XII in him. And as soon as his father recovered, the Crown Prince of Prussia drew in his horns again.

Then, after a brief repeat of last year's sparring on the Rhine, France suddenly dropped the war, left Stanislas to his own devices for the nonce, and made peace with Austria. The resulting settlement was that the Polish Crown might rest on the head of Augustus III, who had meanwhile put it on with Russian aid, while Stanislas retained royal title and the enjoyment for life of the revenues of Lorraine, which conquered province should revert entire to France at his death. The young Duke of Lorraine, prospective husband of the Emperor's eldest daughter, would in due course be indemnified with the Duchy of Tuscany. Sardinia finally got the Milanese and the Spanish Bourbons kept their hold on the two Sicilies, a double blow to Austria which was, however, palliated by France's consenting to guarantee the Pragmatic Sanction.

All in all, there have been worse settlements, and more cynical; Prussia on the face of it lost nothing thereby: indeed, Frederick William's chief grievance in this context was that the Emperor had not troubled to notify him formally that the war was over. But the Crown Prince of Prussia, feeling that he too had now been made a fool of, hotly indicted Fleury's perfidy. That was what he called it to Grumbkow, who urbanely tried to represent this as a useful object lesson in political realism. Nobody in Berlin had any inkling that already France and Austria were cementing their new friendship with a plan to place Jülich-Berg forever out of Prussia's reach.

Just as Frederick William inveighed against the Emperor, with tears in his eyes yet without ever quite taking the logical step of cutting loose—even so, whatever he might say about Cardinal Fleury, Frederick's heart remained tied up with France: France, if not as a political entity, as a conceptual Elysium of mankind and the humanities.

* * *

Other influences apart, language itself had done much to condition Frederick's fidelity to that ideal. The bounded logic, precision, and, therefore, predictable perfectibility of expression, of the French language had come to form not only the medium but the very nature of Frederick's thought, thus also determining his aesthetic-moral judgment. Conversely the German language, which his upbringing had taught him to identify with bigotry, harshness, and literary ineptitude, repelled both his comprehension and his standards. In an element so alien to his mentality, Frederick was incapable of discerning such virtues as stylistic flexibility and imaginative iconoclasm. All he could see therein was barbaric confusion, opacity, and—forgetting that naturalism is a late stage of evolution in art—a vile bondage to reality, which would always inhibit artistic creation.

Much the same applied to English, with which Frederick had even less familiarity, and which as a language seemed to wallow on an even more primitive level than German. Thus the English spirit, benighted like the German in its own semantic chaos, was equally beyond attaining the intellectual kingdom of heaven. From this viewpoint, Frederick's dismissal of the works of Shakespeare as fit for consumption by the Redskins of America, becomes less incomprehensible; from it, too, sprang his denial of any indigenous German literature deserving the name.

Like every rule, this was not disproved by the exception; like every principle, it stood undemolished by the occasional contradiction. In the realm of philosophy, the leading trends of the day, to which Frederick subscribed, emanated from England; while in Germany they were being developed into a variant thesis of peculiar attractiveness to Frederick. It was another paradox that the whole tendency of contemporary Advanced Thought went in the direction of reality, away from metaphysical exclusiveness, and thus counter to that formalizing classicism which to Frederick and those like him constituted the whole nature of Art.

The nature of Nature was become the dominant quest of intellect. A universe more and more of which was opening up to human apprehension wanted to be *reasoned* into alignment with a supernatural order. An ultimate supernatural order had to be maintained if those prerequisites of society, ethical absolutes and the value of the individual, were not to fall to the ground; the sad determinism of Matter somehow must be reconciled with autonomous existence of the Spirit.

Descartes' grand design to elevate Doubt itself into the

highest instrument of Faith, reinforced by the neo-pantheism of Spinoza by which the identity of Godhead with every particle of Creation was restated in modern terms, received at the hands of Locke and Newton a fresh empirical twist, affording a technique, as it were, to show that persistent enquiry could be compatible with both absolute good and absolute toleration, hitherto mutually exclusive. God the serene mathematician had superseded God the capricious dabbler in clay.

That concept was again enriched, principally by the new Deist epoch's most famous and most versatile man of letters, Voltaire, with the sub-divisions of God-Geometer and God-Artist. In the immanence especially of the latter, all consciousness was held to be resident, capable thereby of sustaining the dignity of free will though at the same time forfeiting personal immortality in the transitory individual tenant.

This last was the only shortcoming of an otherwise irresistible theory, in Frederick's eyes. His philosophical system must have a place for Predestination*, and preferably for immortality of the soul, also. A system covering both was devised by Christian Wolff, late professor of mathematics and natural philosophy at the University of Halle.

This disciple of Leibniz, who simultaneously diluted and systematized fin de siècle rationalist theology, and who is remembered chiefly as the founder of a workable vernacular terminology, was regarded as a very Antichrist by Frederick William. For, having linked the doctrine of Predestination with the belief that the whole Creation was centred on the benefit of Man, Wolff had been represented to the King of Prussia as the would-be destroyer of all secular fealty and obedience. In 1723 he had been ordered to leave Prussia at forty-eight hours' notice and on pain of hanging. As sometimes happens, victimization was the making of the victim. His case became a cause célèbre throughout Germany and he won a nation-wide following. As Wolff's writings were the first of their kind to be entirely in German, the Crown Prince of Prussia had to have

* It is perhaps worth noting that Frederick repeatedly and gratuitously protested he had *no personal reasons whatsoever* for his stubborn adherence to the tenet.

French translations made for him by Wolffian friends. He longed to enter into communication with Voltaire and bring the Wolffian arguments to his attention. But yet he did not feel himself to be in any position to approach so dazzling a celebrity.

Voltaire was the intellectual's dream, made flesh: thinker, poet, rebel, reformer, wit, and international best-seller. Had Frederick William but known it, his son's recent martial ambitions without a doubt owed something to the anathematized French 'Schwarzscheisser'. Among Frederick's confiscated books there had been two copies of Voltaire's *Henriade.*

This work had burst upon the contemporary public as a pioneer effort in heroic portraiture, after the antique but of a modern subject. While the figure of Henri IV of France was among Kings what Voltaire was among writers—possessing every perennially popular trait of royalty—his career incidentally presented Frederick with a number of interesting parallels. Henri IV might have been the pattern on which the latter-day sovereigns of Brandenburg modelled themselves, their forerunner in his economic policy, in soldierly example, and in gradual antagonism to Austria, which strange to say had reached its peak in an earlier issue connected with Jülich-Berg. Meanwhile, moreover, Voltaire had published an account of Charles XII of Sweden. *Les grands sujets* fit for that admirable pen were rapidly advancing nearer home in Time.

* * *

Frederick waited until he could feel himself arrived at his princely majority, so to speak, with a court of his own. After three years' work his residence at Rheinsberg was, if not completed, ready to serve. A housewarming was held on 6 August 1736—somewhat under picnic conditions. Exactly two days later Frederick sat down and wrote to Voltaire, a long and ardent, typical fan letter, enclosing an introduction to the philosophy of Wolff.

The great man replied by return, most flatteringly. Apart from avoiding to commit himself on the subject of Wolff and the possibility of a visit to Prussia, Voltaire more than matched Frederick's effusiveness, writing to his unknown, untried young admirer, 'You shall be my judge, you shall stand me in lieu of the public. . . . Your instruction shall be my reward: a prize few sovereigns can give. . . . We go to Rome to see churches, pictures, ruins, sculptures. A prince like yourself is far more deserving of pilgrimage, being a most marvellous rarety . . .'

The keynote was set for a relationship which continued altogether over forty-two years. Because to modern ears it has a fulsome ring, there has been a tendency to regard the correspondence as a kind of ballet of insincerity. The dividing line between tact and hypocrisy, praise and flattery, fluctuates restlessly according to time, place, and class; the one separating admiration and cupidity can never be distinctly drawn. Naturally each man saw what he could get out of the other, but their potential profit was not therefore ipso facto of a base order—unless hero-worship be denied its rights or vanity declared a rare and abnormal adjunct of human character. Frederick's delight in a tame genius, and Voltaire's delight in his tame royalty, were nothing if not sincere.

CHAPTER 14

RHEINSBERG

In a rather idiosyncratic piece of mathematics, Voltaire calculated as follows: 90 men out of 100 are imbeciles; so at about 20,000,000 men to 1 monarch, the chances are 18,000,000 to 2 that a King will be an unmitigated blockhead. At that rate a King having Frederick's intelligent enthusiasms, trained in the school of Voltaire, would be a prodigy indeed, of incalculable value to the world. Voltaire, therefore, slid gracefully into the part which Frederick wished him to play: teaching Frederick the French of France (as opposed to the French of Berlin) and teaching him to be a poet.

In his hope that the first could be acquired, by dint of superior tuition and hard work, Frederick was not deceived; as to the second, his misconception after all has been honoured in our day with university courses. He was not so deluded that he failed to realize 'at least three quarters' had to be subtracted from the heavy sugar coating of Voltaire's constructive criticism (e.g. 'Anyone seeing my letters would say: Here is a complete pedant, prosing away about long and short vowels to a prince full of genius!'), or to see through the pedagogic intention of extravagancies like, 'You think like Trajan, you write like Pliny, and your French is equal to that of our best writers. Louis XIV . . . did not express himself as civilizedly as you . . . etc etc.' For Frederick replied with exemplary modesty, 'You draw the portrait of an accomplished prince, wherein I do not recognize myself. It is a lesson dressed up in the most ingenious and most obliging fashion, in short, a trick to insinuate timid truth into a prince's ear. I will take this portrait as my model.'

Voltaire was not the only one to see himself as moulding the King of the future. Each of the friends whom at Rheinsberg Frederick could now assemble round himself, cherished such a happy conviction. With some his friendship dated back to before 1730, some he had met during the Küstrin period, others were of no older standing than the court of the Philosopher Prince which had attracted them. The most prominent were Charles Étienne Jordan, Huguenot by birth, theologian by training, bel-esprit by avocation, acting as Frederick's secretary and literary adviser-in-ordinary; Baron Dietrich Keyserlingk ('Caesarion'), once paired with Rochow in supervision of the Crown Prince before his attempted flight; Heinrich August de La Motte-Fouqué (who had visited Frederick in prison), ornament of Rheinsberg's amateur stage; another relic of Küstrin, young von Münchow, not so long ago dressed up in petticoats to smuggle comforts to the Prince; Georg Wenzel von Knobelsdorff, formerly a captain of the army, now painter and chief architect of Rheinsberg; and one or two favoured officers of the Ruppin garrison. Of these cavaliers a new Order of Chivalry was formed, its transactions recorded in an approximation to archaic French, and perpetuating a fanciful conceit that 'Rheinsberg' was really 'Remusberg', since, according to a certain seventeenth-century savant, the dispossessed brother of Romulus had here found another home in days gone by.

Of such was built an everlasting pastoral symposium, set in a limpid scene which combined in close natural grouping every characteristic feature of the landscape of Brandenburg having power to charm and soothe: placid water, soft sand, pine and grasses, groves of silver birch and beech and oak.

The chateau stood on the shore of a lake which almost lapped against the colonnaded terrace of the former ruin, modernized to suit one of the most appealing of architectural epochs. What with the limited expenditure allowed, necessity here had indeed proved the mother of invention and achieved a synthesis of refinement and simplicity: Rheinsberg was eminently a *country* palace. Funds apart, Frederick had been given a free hand; all the interior decoration emphasized that here he would lead the civilized life as it should be lived. But it was also made graphically clear that he was biding his time, among frescoes pointedly hailing the dawn that must surely come: Aurora parting the clouds; Phoebus in his chariot; the rising sun—that Rising Sun of Frederick William's invective!—driving out the demons of darkness; Fame announcing the future. (The allusions must have been lost on the King, for when he came to take a look at Rheinsberg, he passed them over unremarked.)

The ideal court could hardly be a monastery, for all that Frederick sometimes called Rheinsberg his convent. 'The fair sex lends an indescribable charm to everyday life,' he discovered. 'Even without regard to the delights of love, women are quite indispensable to social existence; without them every entertainment is insipid.'

Youth, beauty, liveliness, wit, it seems, abounded in the ladies of the Crown Princess, who now at last shared a home with her husband. Already rumour was busy guessing at the identity of the future royal mistress. Yet Elizabeth Christine was happy too. Her passive, unassuming nature derived as much pleasure from the sparkling gaieties of Rheinsberg as did those who contributed to them more conspicuously; and Frederick, she said, was kind to her. For his part, he summed up his first twelve months at Rheinsberg, 'If I had to compose my epitaph today, it would run: Here lies one who had a year of life.'

But Frederick would not have thought himself living without that quasi-snuff of his, reading and writing; several hours, every day, were inviolably set aside for concentrated study, ranging widely. His other constant need, of a private safety valve against the pressures of his public existence, was also served. He had found it in his valet, Michael Gabriel Fredersdorf, a man possessing the rare gift of accepting total familiarity without repayment in contempt. Frederick, thirsting to become a hero in the eyes of the world, did not want and did not have to be a hero to his valet.

Fredersdorf, who was four years older than his master, had been a private in the regiment of General Schwerin,

Frederick's and Katte's irrepressible supporter on the Köpenick Court Martial. Noticing the man to be an excellent flautist, Schwerin had sent him to Frederick at Küstrin; and Fredersdorf had stayed with Frederick ever since, more and more closely attached to him both in professional service and personal confidence. The confidence, if not the service, was mutual; there grew to be a strangely equal interchange between the two, of mutually extended protectiveness and received security. Their understanding was so complete that the risk of taking advantage did not enter into it on either side and the hiatus of education, rank, and pursuits might be conceded without being felt. Fredersdorf is described as tall, handsome, quiet and well-mannered, intelligent and resourceful; subsequent imputations of a homosexual tie derive no evidence from the voluminous correspondence between master and servant, most of which was not discovered until the present century and which is distinguished, startlingly so, by over-explicitness rather than reserve.

With no other person was Frederick able so entirely to relax his guard; not with his adored Jordan or Keyserlingk, not with the enchanting nymphs of Rheinsberg, not with his wife, not even with his sister, not with the idol Voltaire. With all of them there always remained some part for him to act; and even the best of them always had, if not an axe to grind, some little trumpet of their own to blow, be it never so delicately.

The 'race of artists', with whom he lavishly surrounded himself at Rheinsberg, disappointed on closer acquaintance. 'It takes more finesse to govern them than is often needed in governing States. . . . As soon as your artist can display the least bit of dexterity, pride and temper form a threesome with his artistry, to the detriment of his employer. . . . To these charming traits add the inevitable grain of base jealousy, preening itself under the resounding title of noble competition, which results in instant war at the merest suspicion of rivalry. You can, for a time at least, limit the conflagration, but you cannot extinguish it; sooner or later there is nothing for it but to part company.' But for a superior facility of expression, one might momentarily fancy hearing the voice of Frederick William.

The wonder is that Frederick William tolerated Rheinsberg as he did. Even though it is possible that on the few occasions of his visits attempts were made to damp the Rheinsberg tone somewhat—without shrouding the whole place in dust sheets and emptying it of most of its normal occupants, the Crown Prince's establishment could hardly be made to conform to the King's tastes.

True, Frederick continued to work hard to please his father in all other respects; punctilious in his regimental duties, even to reading Sunday sermons to the garrison, with an eloquence and dramatic delivery 'that would not have disgraced a Fénélon'; acquitting himself unexceptionably on tours of inspection of the more outlying Prussian territories to which he was now sent from time to time. He promised to do his best in the way of procreation, and ignored no immediate means of ingratiating himself: 'I have received orders to go to Berlin on Thursday. My regiment is full of blandishments 6 feet high. If it be true that by the dumb intercession of giants anyone can make his fortune at Berlin, mine ought to be assured.' Frederick's debts were catching up with him again. 'I have a Dutchman of 6 ft. 9 in. who shines as brilliantly as a comet with a tail.'

But relations between father and son had deteriorated again, along with the King's health and the latest turn of the political screw, as so often coinciding. Frederick said, every time the King's messenger arrived bidding him report at Berlin, 'that place of ill-omen', it was like a foretaste of death. To see his mother was no anodyne. Frederick had taken Grumbkow's advice, not to show more than dutiful respect to the Queen, for her own sake as much as for Frederick's; but Sophie Dorothee was very far from appreciating this form of consideration. With regard to Grumbkow himself, Frederick was caught in a trap, as he knew full well. Grumbkow was his advocate with the King; but Grumbkow also saw to it that his good offices continued necessary.

There was a curious situation now prevailing at the court of Berlin, showing the contradictions of human nature affecting even the most straightforward opportunism. Although the state of the King's health made it improbable that he would live much longer and although, therefore, every speculative interest must focus on the Crown Prince—nonetheless in Frederick William's immediate environment his personality was still so dominant as to over-ride the long-term view. There were many who, to curry favour with the King—perhaps also to direct his chronic irascibility away from everybody else into one channel—continually baited him with scandal about his son. There were others, some of them in foreign pay, provoking Frederick William in sheer levity: at the courts of Europe the King of Prussia had become something of an unwitting buffoon, a golden goose of ridiculous anecdote, who must not be allowed to stop laying.

The goose was infallibly prolific on titbits of Frederick, and never more so than under the goad of physical pain and intimations of death; though the yield was not always comic. 'The smallest false step, the slightest incaution, the merest bubble of inflated nothing, would suffice to destroy me,' Frederick soberly assessed his danger. Frederick William, too, was not entirely blind to what went on around him: 'Ah yes, there's a fortune to be made when I die, by whoever rides fast enough to be first with the good news to my son!' And: 'People will say, good riddance to the old slavedriver! but you tell them this: the one who will come after me is going to send them all to the devil, that's what they will get out of it!'

Frederick observed wrily that no artist had ever expressed himself with such modesty about his work as the King about his son. Yet from time to time the mood would veer again, for the King to point dramatically to Frederick as his future 'avenger'.

The agreement had now become known, by which France and Austria guaranteed to each other the exclusion of Prussia from Jülich-Berg. Even after twenty-five years in harness, conversant with some centuries of past Imperial double-dealing towards Brandenburg, Frederick William found it hard to credit so bare-faced a breach of faith, and harder still to swallow.

A sick man, sufficiently troubled about the internal future of his realm, he was herewith forced to reconsider and if possible reverse the foreign policy of a lifetime—more: of generations of his dynasty—or aquiesce in the inexorable reduction of Prussia to insignificance, which in the end could only lead to national extinction. For England and Holland were in process of forming a new four-power alliance with Austria and France, which, leaving Prussia completely isolated, was bound sooner or later to attack her.

Heroically Frederick William roused himself to seek a last-minute understanding with France. Having little hope, he met with an agreeable surprise. Cardinal Fleury, whose ways often seemed inscrutable as those of Providence, immediately affirmed that France was very willing to reconsider the question of Jülich-Berg, provided negotiations were conducted in unbroken secrecy and on neutral territory.

The explanation was that Austria had become involved in another war with Turkey, at the same time as a fresh outbreak of Anglo-Spanish hostilities threatened: the value of the Imperial ally on the one hand, and continued harmony between England and France on the other, thus being rendered problematical. Furthermore, now that almost the whole of Europe had accepted the Pragmatic Sanction, statesmen were beginning to ponder how best to undermine it.

For Frederick, the unexpected rapprochement caused his first set-back as an author, at least as regards seeing himself in print. To avert the catastrophe of Prussian isolation under French leadership, the heir to the throne had conceived the enterprising notion of turning pamphleteer. The aim of his polemic, entitled *Considérations sur l'état present du corps politique de l'Europe*, was to open the eyes of the Maritime Powers to their own danger in abetting France's ulterior pretensions to supremacy in Europe. Naturally the author's identity must not be disclosed: Frederick wrote in the guise of an Englishman, asking the reader's indulgence in case, as the son of a free people, he were expressing himself with a degree of frankness 'unknown among the majority of mankind'. The idea was to have the text translated into English and to have it printed in England first, whereafter Frederick's original version should appear in Holland as a French translation.

Frederick William would have been astonished at his son's powers of analysis and exposition, though Frederick's classical analogies and his philosophical arguments, with echoes of both

Montesquieu and Wolff, were unlikely to have won his approval. Voltaire, to whom Frederick submitted the manuscript as soon as it was finished, was generous with his praise, evincing only a modicum of patriotic sensitivity, and agreed to help with the round-about publication. But owing to the sudden friendship with France the whole scheme had of course to be dropped.

Nevertheless, the *Considérations* had done something for the author, in point of self-respect as well as literary assurance. Not having been put to the final test, meanwhile it had done nothing to shake his sustaining belief that men can be swayed and the course of history influenced, by rational persuasion.

CHAPTER 15
CHANGES

Seckendorf had gone from Berlin during the Rhine Campaign, recalled to active service at his post of Imperial Ordnance Master, after seven years of quite other occupation. The Old Dessauer's fixedly pro-Imperial influence had waned, partly owing to a discord with Grumbkow which was only superficially resolved, partly as a concomitant of the Imperial affronts dealt out to Frederick William. Grumbkow's position was more adaptable, his Viennese pension notwithstanding, because at bottom he had no loyalties, except to himself, and no ulterior purpose beyond feathering his nest: 'The shirt is nearest to the skin,' might have been his armorial device. So, paradoxically, he was able to maintain a hold on Frederick William because he cared nothing about the great issues he was using to promote his own security. In spite of occasional hitches and alarms, Grumbkow's simple scheme of keeping in Frederick William's good graces by feeding the King's antipathy to his son, and ensuring the future ruler's gratitude by pouring oil on the thus-troubled waters, continued to work. But in the middle of it he died, on 18 March 1739.

'His death,' Frederick wrote to Wilhelmine, 'is the greatest imaginable gain for me. I dare hope now we shall begin to breathe again.' Three months later he was able to confirm the forecast. 'Since Grumbkow's death everything is changed in Berlin; his passing has brought us peace. Heaven be thanked, I now stand as well as conceivably possible with the King.'

At twenty-seven, Frederick could still respond with childlike eagerness to the boon of paternal affection. Suddenly he was

Frederick William's 'Fritzchen' again, as if two intervening decades had been wiped out; without Grumbkow's single-minded leadership, the smear campaign against the Crown Prince in the Tabagie had lost its force. 'I cannot say enough about the King's kindness. His behaviour towards me is everything I always wished for.' He could not say enough, he had to tell everybody to whom he had occasion to write, he must boast of the virtues of his partner in this late-flowering 'brotherly friendship' like a lover discovering his beloved.

These things are mutual, and cumulative. The more the King relented, the more ready his son became to see all the good that there was to be seen; the more Frederick William found himself appreciated, the better he loved his son.

There was a great deal that was admirable, to be appreciated. Frederick William's bullying cantankerousness and the failures of his foreign policy ('I was not cut out for the higher state-craft: in this I am no use to man or beast.') were sufficiently spectacular to distract the general view from his immense achievements in the internal affairs of his country. Therein he had never looked back, had proved himself altogether the 'rocher de bronze' of his quaint imagery, and had gone from strength to exemplary strength. He rightly boasted that he was the only solvent sovereign in Europe; his state was free of debts, with an income of seven million Thaler and an army of more than eighty thousand (to a population of two and a quarter million), a comprehensively centralized administration, trade and industries flourishing, colonization steeply on the upgrade; the formerly private estates of the King turned into Crown domains in which serfdom was abolished while heavy inroads had been made into feudal privilege throughout the realm, and with continually extending provisions for public welfare, not to mention universal education, in which Prussia was far ahead of other European nations. There is no question that most of the basic measures leading to this overall result had been conceived and drawn up by the King in person.

Father and son went on a joint tour of the East Prussian provinces, and Frederick was moved to communicate his enthusiasm to Voltaire—Voltaire the tireless champion of humanity, not hitherto remarkable for an especially good opinion of the King of Prussia (compared with whom, Voltaire had said, the Grand Turk was a prodigy of liberalism).

> Here we are, in Lithuania, which I must describe as the Non plus ultra of the civilized world. It is a country deserving to be made better-known to Europe as entirely the creation of the King my father. Now the richest and most prosperous of our provinces, Lithuania at the beginning of the present century was a desert, laid waste by pestilence and hunger . . . coupled with the indifference of a government which did nothing to examine or alleviate the prevailing misery.
>
> Frederick I died and was buried, together with his false and empty magnificence. . . . My father came and was moved by the . . . appalling conditions. He went to see with his own eyes . . . the devastation brought upon the land by disease and want and the filthy greed of local administrators. He found twelve or fifteen deserted towns, between four and five hundred uninhabited villages, fields everywhere reverting to wilderness. Far from being intimidated by the dreadful spectacle . . . he resolved to bring back human life and trades to a land which had lost every trace of cultivation. He spared no expense to carry out his salutary intentions. . . . He built up what was broken down, he brought in thousands of colonists from all over Europe. . . .
>
> Today Lithuania has more than half a million inhabitants, more towns and more and larger herds of cattle than ever before, while fertility and abundance reign as nowhere else in Germany. And all this is solely due to the King, who not only made the appropriate decrees but personally watched over their execution, who is alone responsible for the design as well as the fulfilment, who spared neither thought nor incalculable treasure to secure life and happiness for half a million thinking beings: to him alone they owe both. . . . The King's great-hearted and indefatigable industry seems to me something so heroic, I feel you too will see it thus. . . .*

* Voltaire incorporated the information almost verbatim, in his *Précis du Siècle de Louis XV*, published ca. twenty years later: 'La Prusse n'était encore qu'un vaste désert; mais Frédéric-Guillaume II (*sic*), son second roi, qui avait une politique différente de celle des princes de son temps, dépensa près de vingt-cinq millions de notre monnaie à faire défrècher ces terres, à bâtir des villages, et à les peupler: il y fit venir des familles de Souabe et de Francoine; il y attira plus de seize mille émigrans de Saltzbourg, leur fournissant à tous de quoi s'établir et de quoi travailler.'

Frederick returned from the journey the richer by an annual revenue of 12,000 Thaler, as the King with unprecedented generosity made over to him the great royal stud-farm of Trakehnen. Frederick William, however—travelling at his usual break-neck pace, embracing rather than eschewing every discomfort of terrain and climate, begrudging himself all but the barest minimum of repose and warmth—returned in a state of physical bankruptcy.

Since 1734, it had been said, he had lived only by the grace of his physicians. From autumn 1739 onwards his body slipped with increasing rapidity beyond control by medical artifice. He was in almost constant pain—and by all accounts the symptoms of gout are among the most excruciating known to suffering humanity: Leibniz in his day had tried to obtain relief by applying wooden screws to the afflicted parts and so drowning one torture in another. The King's heart, kidneys, lungs, arteries were affected, and dropsy swelled his already grotesquely distended frame till he could neither rest nor move.

In place of Leibniz's screws Frederick William must have noise. He took to doing carpentry in his bed; the hammering would penetrate far outside the palace as once the royal family altercations had used to do. His favourite generals had to come and sit with him and smoke and talk; above all they must talk, and keep on talking if the King managed to drop off to sleep—silence would wake him up at once. Hyperaesthesia developed so that other generals, not necessarily less meritorious than the favoured ones, were banished from the sickroom because their physiognomy grated on the patient: 'The sight of that man's face makes every pain more painful!'

The paintbrush came into its own again. From memory, albeit with the customary professional assistance, the King made himself a portrait gallery of his darling Longfellows. The Queen and the children took turns with the core of the Tabagie at entertaining the sufferer. He carried on with his business, digesting, dictating, signing papers for two hours each morning—but that still left twenty-two hours of the day to get through. Sometimes he wished for death, sometimes his whole being rebelled against such a fate, at not yet fifty-two. 'There stands my avenger!' changed to, 'Ruin my work, and I'll sit up in my grave and laugh at you!' Frederick tried to hold on to the thought that the illness, not his father, was his enemy; but it was hard to be berated in front of all and sundry as of old.

Early in 1740 the King's condition improved somewhat, and Frederick returned to Rheinsberg, not to stay hovering by the bedside with an assiduity that might be misinterpreted. He was working on a treatise which had grown from the unpublished *Considérations*, exploring the subject of political ethic along the lines of Montesquieu. In it the image of the exemplary ruler as presented by the *Henriade* was to be set against that of Machiavelli's *Prince* and refute the scientific amorality of the celebrated, premier handbook of autocracy. It incorporated the warning strictures of the inopportune anti-French pamphlet, though with not quite the same 'English' directness as before.* The work, which was to become known as the *Antimachiavel*, had reached the stage of revision and final polish, scheduled for summer publication at The Hague under Voltaire's supervision. Frederick was in a fever of budding authorship, which helped to take his mind off other things and preserve the equilibrium of his days at Rheinsberg.

The next time he went back to Berlin he learned on arrival that the King was so much better, he had had himself dressed and wheeled to the Red Room for a quorum session of the Tabagie. The Crown Prince hastened to attend his father there, and his entry, unannounced, surprised the company into rising to its feet, against the rule that in the Red Room one did not get up for anybody. The King who until that moment had been unusually blithe and talkative, flew into a towering rage and instantly left the room, to send word a few minutes later that the assembly was disbanded, for 'doing homage to the rising sun'. Messages of apology and appeal rebounded, unheard, unread. Only after Frederick had placed himself out of sight and mind again did the King take pity on his erring friends—not without voluptuous indulgence in the pleasure of unopposed recriminations.

* It is interesting to see the famous hypocrisy of the English having as yet no place in the mystique of international relations, although I find that Bossuet (1627–1704) is cited as the originator of the term 'perfidious Albion'.

The winter had been exceptionally hard and long. Towards the end of April the frost at last showed signs of abating, and the King decided to remove to Potsdam. Everyone believed here was a repetition of his 1734 deathbed: he would yet outlive them all. His parting apostrophe, 'Farewell, Berlin, I go to die at Potsdam!' was just the sort of thing he was always saying. But it was the winter weather which got a new lease of life; soon there could be no further doubt that the King's time was up.

'The King is very ill: you can use that as a lever—point out that anyone wishing to earn my gratitude had better look sharp about it,' Frederick, trying to negotiate a personal loan from Russia, wrote to his middleman, the Saxon Ambassador.

The King also faced the facts and took steps to prepare himself for the next world, in consultation with the Potsdam clergy. An ingenuous and moving dialogue has been handed down, between the dying monarch and Chief Preacher Roloff.

How would Roloff say that Frederick William was likely to make out before the throne of Divine Judgment? pretty well, no doubt, seeing that he had kept God's Commandments most conscientiously—uniquely so, for a king—? Chief Preacher Roloff temporized, observing that all men were sinners and only Jesus had been perfect. Frederick William would not let him off: certainly, he would not claim to be as perfect as that; but come, *for a king*, had he not proved himself very nearly perfect? He challenged Roloff to tell him of but one instance wherein he had not acted with perfect piety and justice. Roloff at this came back with several, recent examples—the case of a Königsberg official who had been hanged without trial; the King's oppression of the people of Berlin who were being forced to subsidize a great new building project; among others. Frederick William argued the point, but Roloff would not allow his justifications: there was nothing for it, Frederick William must repent if he wished to find favour with the Almighty.

Frederick William gave in. Very well, he repented. No, but his Majesty must show himself in earnest, and, as he hoped to be forgiven on high, forgive his enemies here on earth. Again the King prevaricated for a little: *his* enemies were such very particular scoundrels! Oh, very well, then, very well, he'd forgive them. 'After I am dead, Fiekchen, write and tell your detestable brother that I forgave him.' No, said Roloff, to do any good it must be done now; but in this Frederick William was not to be overborne: he would grant the Preacher skill in his trade, therefore let the Preacher concede the same to the King. '*After* I am dead, Fiekchen: it would not be safe, before.'

Finally he dismissed Roloff with the words, 'I must not keep you longer from the rest of your flock. You have not spared me, and that was right. You do your duty like an honest Christian.'

He asked to see his coffin, to make sure that his specifications had been carried out, then had it placed beside his bed, to be ready when needed. Every detail of his obsequies was settled. To keep expenses down, the King decided against mourning livery for the servants: crepe hat bands would do. The horses were a different matter; having ordered a rehearsal of the funeral procession which he watched from his window, the King noticed a groom in the act of fitting a yellow saddle cloth, and sent down one of his tobacco-puffing generals to give the fellow a sound thrashing on the spot.

On 26 May, Ascension Day, he sent a letter to Rheinsberg, his first ever to be headed, 'My beloved Son,' saying he hoped to live long enough to embrace Frederick at Whitsun. Frederick, warned by an express message from the chief physician that the end was near, was already on his way to Potsdam.

He arrived on the 28th, and found his father on the building site of the new royal stables, where, in his wheelchair and surrounded by a throng of onlookers, the King was watching the work in progress. The crowd parted for the Prince so that the King saw him from afar and opened his arms wide. Frederick sank to his knees by the chair and father and son wept in each other's arms. The excitement was too much for the dying man, who had to be taken home and put to bed.

By afternoon the King rallied again sufficiently to send for his heir, and, despite very severe shortness of breath, address him for an hour and a half on the subject of foreign affairs. After that his customary attendants were recalled and the King received them, saying, 'Has not God shown me great favour in giving me so good and worthy a son?'

The Crown Prince clutched his father's hand and covered it with tears and kisses; the father, sobbing loudly, threw his arms round the son's neck and so clung to him for some time.

Later, when at the King's request all joined in a hymn, which contained the lines, 'Naked I came into this world, naked I shall fare hence,' he interrupted: 'That isn't true, I shall have my uniform on.'

About one o'clock in the night from 30 to 31 May the King sent for his chaplain: 'My memory has gone, I can't remember a single prayer.' The chaplain prayed with him till four; after that the King demanded his wheelchair and went to see his youngest son who was just recovering from measles. Next he had himself wheeled to his wife's bedside and roused her: 'Get up, I am going to die.'

At five o'clock the Crown Prince and Prince Augustus William, Prince Leopold of Anhalt-Dessau, Generals Buddenbrock, Derschau, Hacke, and Bredow, the Ministers Podewils and Boden, and some confidential staff were summoned. In a voice too weak to rise above a whisper the King abdicated and formally laid the reins of State in the hands of his successor. He fainted and was carried back to bed; he regained consciousness and asked to be propped up with pillows that he might for the last time watch the Guard turn out; he fainted again, woke again. For hours he struggled thus in labour of his death. Suddenly he called for a mirror to see what his face looked like at this point: 'Hm, not so bad as I thought.'

He called for a surgeon to feel his pulse: 'Tell me how much longer I have got.'

'Alas, not long.'

'Don't say alas; but how do you know, anyway?'

'The pulse is gone.'

'Nonsense,' the King whispered, raising his arm. 'How could I move like this if the pulse were gone?'

Later on he said, 'Lord Jesus, in Thee I live, in Thee I die; Thou art my prize.' Those were his last words. At three o'clock in the afternoon he died.

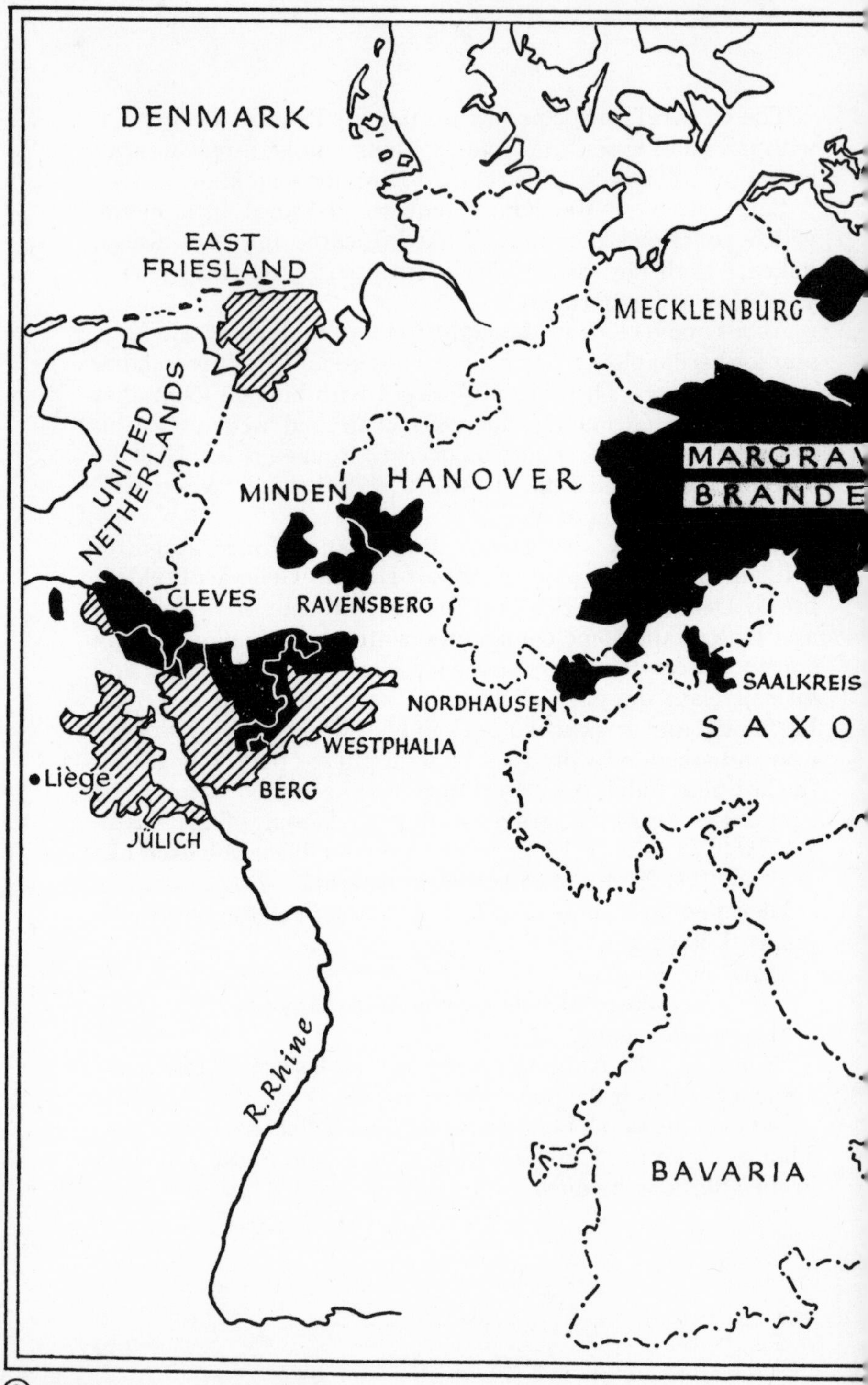
DENMARK
EAST FRIESLAND
MECKLENBURG
UNITED NETHERLANDS
HANOVER
MINDEN
MARGRAV
BRANDE
CLEVES
RAVENSBERG
SAALKREIS
NORDHAUSEN
SAXO
WESTPHALIA
Liège
BERG
JÜLICH
R. Rhine
BAVARIA

BRANDENBURG-PRUSSIA
AT FREDERICK'S ACCESSION, 1740

CHAPTER 16
THE SUNRISE

The longed-for dawn had come. The news that the old King was dead caused extreme joy among his people; strangers embraced in the streets and congratulated one another: Frederick William's bitterest anticipations were fulfilled. But the new sovereign, who for years had pined and dreamt and despaired of this hour, was beside himself with grief.

In floods of tears Frederick lingered over the poor, bloated, noisome corpse, was roused to answer some immediate call upon him, broke down afresh. Those first demands on him in his new guise afforded small distraction: he must have envisaged the opening of his reign so many times that the response was ready.

His mother came to do him ceremonial reverence, which he begged her to spare him: 'Always call me your son, Madame, a name more precious to me than Majesty.'

The old Prince Leopold of Anhalt-Dessau came, 'blubbering like a child, bawling aloud', to clasp the knees of the new master. For a spell the only two people to be so deeply affected wept together. But then the Old Dessauer in a breaking voice expressed his hope that there would be no changes as far as he was concerned: might he trust that he and his sons would continue in their posts and himself command undiminished authority? The King stopped weeping. 'Concerning your posts, I had not thought of making any changes. Concerning authority, I know of none in Prussia save the sovereign's.' The Old Dessauer retired in confusion; he might have been warned by the memory that a similar, over-hasty enquiry twenty-seven years since had been none too well received even by his fast friend Frederick William. Frederick went back to his grief.

The acclaim which greeted his arrival in Berlin that night was terrible to him. He went to bed at his old quarters and in the morning was awakened by a regiment taking the oath of allegiance under his window, followed by hurrahs. He leapt out of bed and rushed round the room, distraught, so that Baron Pöllnitz, coming just then to talk over the funeral arrangements, found the King 'half-dressed, with hair dishevelled, dissolved in tears, and as though out of his mind'. Pöllnitz offered the usual conventional consolation, speaking of a happy release. 'I know,' said Frederick. 'He suffered horribly; but he was with us. Now he is gone.' Presently Pöllnitz left, with instructions not to skimp the obsequies. Hardly had the door shut behind him when it opened again and the demented mourner of a moment before called after the Baron: 'Mind, no trickery now, no peculations!' Touché, Pöllnitz downstairs gave vent to his wounded feelings: 'I'd give a hundred Pistoles to have the Old Man back!'*

Elizabeth Christine, arriving post haste from Rheinsberg, was formally presented to the assembled royal family and court. Frederick led her by the hand, and saying, 'This is your Queen,' kissed her in sight of all. She also was astonished at the extent of Frederick's grief: again and again, she remarked, at any mention of his father, at the sight of any small object that had belonged to Frederick William, the son would utterly give way.

He received the generals of Prussia, he received the Ministers of his father's cabinet.

* Baron Karl Ludwig von Pöllnitz was a prototype of gossip writer. He had abandoned a military career for a post in Frederick William's household and took to supplementing a chronically mortgaged income by means of court-news letters which attained a fairly wide circulation. Wisely, Frederick as Crown Prince had treated Pöllnitz's proffered information service with great caution, but kept him on after Frederick William's death—chiefly for his amusing conversation. Frederick's concise verdict on Pöllnitz was, 'Entertaining at table; should be locked up between meals.'

'All of us have lost our lord and King, and together must try to take comfort. I hope you will help me in maintaining the splendid army which you helped my father to build up. . . . We know, you and I, that the oath of loyalty which you have come here to swear is really superfluous: without it, too, you would serve me as faithfully as you served my father. Between men of honour there is no need of oaths.'

For each group, however, there was a little rider: 'I am informed that there are charges against some of you, of undue harshness, avarice, and arrogance: see that you give no further grounds for these.' And further, 'Hitherto a distinction has been recognized as between the interests of the King and the interests of the realm. My father, though personally deprecating this distinction, had certain reasons for continuing to allow it. From now on, let it be understood that the interests of the realm are also those of the King. Should the two nevertheless conflict at any time, the interests of the country shall come first.'

The overall interests of his country were clear in Frederick's mind, but although during the last year or two he had gained some insight into the workings of his father's government, a great deal had remained closed to him. He knew himself a novice who could not start learning too soon, and did not wait for his tears to dry to immerse himself in state papers 'by the cartload'—so said the cabinet secretary who over the first week was kept busy day and night supplying and explaining material for the new King's scrutiny. Nor did the new King leave it at acquiring knowledge. There were things he knew about: general truths and precepts, requiring no further study to be put to practical application which had had ample time to be evolved.

Frederick William, who had not greatly loved his father, had therefore felt in pious duty bound to hold himself in check until his predecessor was under the ground. Frederick, in an ecstasy of filial sorrow, began to govern on the first day of his reign. The three weeks between 1 June and the date of Frederick William's funeral saw the introduction of the most revolutionary measures of the new epoch.

To start with, torture was abolished in Prussia as a means of judicial enquiry—uniquely in standard international practice.

Some subsidiary, related changes followed: no more public penance for unmarried mothers, meaning less incentive to infanticide; and, for convicted infanticides, death by beheading instead of drowning in leather sacks which the delinquents had been forced to sew with their own hands. Also severe penalties were decreed for ill-treatment and exploitation of newly enrolled members of the armed forces, as well as for recruiting outrages and excesses in disciplinary brutality.

Next, press censorship was lifted: 'The gazettes, if they are to be interesting, must not be muzzled.' (Frederick had long deplored a lack of respectable periodicals in Prussia and now instigated the foundation of two such in Berlin, one in French and one in German: for the former, the King offered his own services as a regular contributor.) Religious freedom was upheld absolutely: 'All religions alike are to be tolerated [so long as] none makes unjust encroachment on the others: for in this country everyone must go to heaven his own way,'—a terse autograph scribble whose substance sped round the world. An archaic corpus of marriage restrictions was abrogated, although the Crown thereby lost a regular income from the issue of dispensations. The extensive hunting privileges of Crown and nobility—bane of the agrarian population—were cut down to the minimum.

In the way of controversial acts, it was enough to go on with. There were other changes, more expected, less spectacular, though for Prussia equally marking a break with the old régime. Simultaneously with the announcements of his accession to the foreign courts, the new King sent out invitations to savants and scientists of note in other countries, to help him re-establish the Academy of Berlin. This had been founded under Frederick I by Leibniz, on the model of the English Royal Society, but under Frederick William had been starved to atrophy: out of a residual grant the Academy had had to defray the salaries of the royal court fools and the cost of occasional visiting acrobats, the while arts and sciences had gone into eclipse.

Christian Wolff was recalled to his old professorial chair, and the town of Halle accorded the philosopher a conqueror's triumphal entry. Yet this was an event which the old King had already set in motion some time before his death, having become converted to the blameless morality of the Wolffian doctrine. Likewise Frederick William had signed the order for the opening of the public granaries, which it was, however, left to his successor to ratify in happy inaugural munificence.

The winter of 1739/40 having been the coldest and most prolonged on record, there was great distress everywhere. Several times in the last months of his life Frederick William had been on the point of yielding to his Ministers and distributing the emergency stores; but to the end he had never quite brought himself to trust in reports which did not check with his own calculations and which he was unable to go out and verify. Frederick did add supplementary relief measures of his own: remission of dues, bulk importation of grain, the sale of game from the royal forests at nominal prices, and lastly, housing and employment schemes together with money grants to persons and communities in particularly grave straits, against what would be a late harvest and in all probability a poor one. Meantime merchants and manufacturers were asked to submit proposals for the expansion of Prussian trade and industries.

But there were two further departures all his own by which the new King of Prussia made a stir. One fell on the day of his father's funeral, 22 June, when the Giant Grenadier Guard, the dead King's 'only vice' (also known as 'the channel of grace'), paraded for the last time, being afterwards disbanded. The other did not occur till September, but, in the sense of the general impression that was created, might nevertheless be called complementary to the first. This was the publication of Frederick's *Antimachiavel*.

That profession of faith by one who had the power to practise what he preached, seemed to lend conclusive weight to the new reign's emphasis on liberalism and cultural renaissance, in conjunction with which the disbanding of the Longfellows had been taken as an earnest of drastic reductions in the Prussian army as a whole. It was widely believed, and confidently stated as on good authority, that Frederick was going to halve his standing forces; it was inferred—hardly less explicitly—that he was going to bear out all Frederick William's predictions and give his father's ghost something to laugh (or cry) at in his grave.

The *Antimachiavel* avowed a princely ethic based on the same standards of virtue and equity which were held binding in all other spheres of human life, and according to which duty outbalanced privilege and wisdom could only exist paired with truth. The ideas were not new, but their postulation by a crowned author was. From that point of view, it mattered little that the treatise dealt mostly with large abstractions (since the concrete attack on Fleury from which it had sprung had been toned down so that now it was barely discernible), or that it was flogging a horse already a long time dead. The Renaissance ideal of the amoral ruler had been one of the casualties of the Reformation; it was a literary curio, commanding no more actual following than the Gods of Olympus. But then, Frederick was not offering his work as a technical handbook, and his coeval readers did not take it as such. It was received, hailed or derided, for what it was: an ideological testament. There might be more brilliant and original propagandists of the Enlightenment, but a King of Prussia was an invaluable agent to the movement, which welcomed his debut as a philosopher with resounding enthusiasm. Frederick thus began his sovereign career with the support of the most articulate section of international society, whose influence was very much more potent than anything of the sort known in our day. As for the scoffers, they mainly resided in high places like Frederick himself and were not on the whole displeased to write him off as an impractical idealist and gilded dilettante, getting into his stride.

The fact that, at the same time as he disbanded the Longfellows, Frederick had created sixteen *new* infantry battalions* was somehow overlooked. The gesture appeared too strikingly symbolic to be accepted at its official face value, that is, as an incidental economy: the upkeep of the Giant Grenadiers had cost some 291,000 Thaler annually, compared with a maximum 72,000 Thaler for the ordinary infantry regiment. Likewise it was not especially noted that side by side with noble and proper sentiments denouncing ambition and conquest for their own sakes, the *Antimachiavel* contained a scattering of reflections

*Quite openly: he even wrote about it to Voltaire.

on the building, strengthening, and most efficacious employment in war of national armies. But only the eye of hindsight would pick these out, as the author, like Machiavelli himself, dwelt at least in passing on every aspect of a ruler's concerns. As with most first-fruits of literary talent, the author had given it everything he had got, keeping back none of his thoughts that had any bearing on the subject of his disquisition: proof of his complete sincerity, no less than of his vernal confidence that belief and expediency need not be mutually exclusive.

Frederick II was in his twenty-ninth year, to Frederick William's twenty-five at his accession; yet in the eyes of all, including posterity, it was as a youth that Frederick came to the throne. Perhaps it was because he was not yet himself a father,* perhaps because his career to date had been so very much that of a son; or because the phenomena of his advent gave it a flavour of Nativity.

'The prettiest, daintiest Majesty in the world,' the French envoy described him: with curled hair and big blue eyes, face rather tanned but hands very white and loaded with rings; height about 5 foot 7 inches, a little on the plump side ('hips too high and legs too thick' for the perfect manly figure); graceful, proud, swift if somewhat negligent in his movements; lively, pleasant 'though noble' of mien; smile indescribably winning, gaze radiant with attentive intelligence, calculated to loosen the most diffident tongue: in conversation his charm became irresistible.

The young Majesty was enjoying himself. 'Adieu!' concludes one letter to a friend. 'I must now write to the King of France, compose a solo for flute, make up a poem for Voltaire, alter some army regulations, and do a thousand other things!'

Voltaire proposed to call him 'Votre Humanité': 'Already you have fulfilled nearly all my predictions. Already you are beloved in your own dominions and in Europe . . . I am afraid you will work too hard . . . In the name of the human race, to whom you have become a necessity, take care of so precious a health!'

*It was not until 1744 that Frederick, designating his brother Augustus William as his heir, officially gave up hope of progeny.

The precious health was not, in fact, good; it was an added pleasure to work indefatigably against such advice and against doctor's orders. Another, kingly gratification, which Frederick had promised himself as long ago as 1730, was bestowing coals of fire. None of the expected dismissals took place. Frederick's former persecutor, Derschau, suffered no reduction; Grumbkow's son-in-law Podewils was confirmed in office as Grumbkow's successor. While the Old Dessauer complained that the new King disliked him 'on account of the past', an evident absence of affection was the worst he had to put up with. True, Seckendorf, like Grumbkow, was not there to put Frederick's forbearance to its most exacting test: the Imperial Ordnance Master in his turn was languishing in prison, far away at Graz in Styria, to atone for Austria's defeat in the war against Turkey. But again, of Seckendorf's brother's son, who had replaced him in Berlin, Frederick made a point of saying there was nothing wrong with the man except his name.

Now, too, the coals of fire became in part a burnt-offering to the dead. Apart from the momentous early edicts, tacitly indicting what they set aside, and apart from doing away with the old King's dearest toy, the Longfellows, as too dear—never was a father's memory honoured more reverently than by this son who, kicked, beaten, pilloried, had all but lost his life at the hands of the one he owed it to. 'We have passed over in silence the domestic chagrins of this great prince,' Frederick was to conclude his history of Frederick William's reign. 'The reader's indulgence is asked for the faults of the children, in consideration of the virtues of such a father.' The spirit of those words, though yet unwritten, informed the new King's every direct reference to the departed. Frederick had loved his father and loved him no less for the guilt which the living ever feel towards the dead, or for the deep necessity of salving bygone hurt by sublimation.

If the old King's abettors in oppression of the Crown Prince were not punished, it followed that the Crown Prince's fellow-victims must not be rewarded too conspicuously. Duhan was summoned in a warm personal note (3 June): 'Mon sort a changé, mon cher. Je vous attends avec impatience; ne me faites pas languir!' and provided for, in moderation. Katte's father was created a count and promoted field-marshal. A number of government posts and promotions went to the Münchow family—in no case exceeding professional capacity and merit. The elder Keith returned from England to take up an appointment as Master of Horse, in which he had little contact with the sovereign. Others received smaller compensation, some none at all. Nothing was done for Doris Ritter, now married to a small contractor and leading an obscure and hand-to-mouth existence.* Frederick's views on youth and its escapades changed when he stood in father's stead to his unmarried brothers and sisters, the eldest of whom was eighteen years old, the youngest a child of ten.

His views on friendship had not changed. Friendship of its nature was disinterested and its own reward. When the news of the old King's death had first reached Rheinsberg, some of Frederick's friends were playing cards, and, jumping up in their excitement, overturned the table so that the stakes rolled in all directions. As the rest scrambled to pick up the coins, Knobelsdorff cried, 'What, grovel for pennies now, when it is going to rain ducats?'

It did not rain ducats. It rained only poems.

> Tenderer than Philomel,
> Friendship in my breast shall dwell:
> More than monarch, let me be
> Brother, comrade, frank and free;
> Nursling upon Wisdom's breast,
> Just, humane my every quest;
> With this message from my soul:
> Peace on earth the noblest goal.†

Peace, tenderness, candour: but not ducats. If the King's friends wanted to come and see him, even by invitation, even from the ends of Europe, they had to pay their own fares. Any of them doing a job of work for him would get a fee: but no gratuities—except in verse. And if they were wise, Frederick's friends would not take him up too seriously on the point of comradeship, either: 'Monsieur, à présent je suis roi.'

*Voltaire who saw her once said she was then tall and haggard, with the look of a Sibyl but nothing to suggest a girl who had once been whipped for a prince.

† This, though a free translation, is not a notably unfair one.

Ruefully betraying the nature of their disappointed hopes, Frederick's friends in retrospect christened 1 June 1740 'la journée des dupes'.*

Others began to smart from the same cause. Trusting in the special favour of the former Crown Prince, the Ruppin district authorities applied for money to improve the road to Rheinsberg, and received the succinct refusal, 'I know that road, and the district chamber must take me for a great ass.' The Saxon envoy Manteuffel predicted that 'before long the father will be held up as a spendthrift and darling of the people, by comparison with the son'.

Exaggeration though this might be, certainly disenchantment was spreading among Frederick's subjects with the gradual realization that, after all, the new reign was not so very different from the old. In every detail, not only as regarded personnel, the Administration remained unchanged; the steep Prussian tariffs were not lowered, the niggardly civil service salaries were not raised. Unwilling to relinquish their King Charming so early in the day, men told each other that Frederick William on his death-bed had extorted a promise from his heir to leave things as they were for the first two years.

The reign was yet young; by and large rejoicing, pageantry, and royal bounty were still the order of the day. Frederick dispensed with a coronation. 'I leave for Prussia,' he wrote to Voltaire, 'to receive homage etc., without the holy ampulla and without the useless and frivolous ceremonies established by ignorance and superstition.' Frederick William had done the same, but for reasons of plain economy, unembellished by philosophical arguments or the voluntary services of the greatest publicist of the age. His son won far more credit for it, not least by one of the pithy sayings for which Frederick had so much more marked a talent than for poetry: 'A crown is just a hat that lets the rain in.'

Receiving the homage of the Provinces was, however, indispensable, although only in Königsberg, Berlin, and Cleve did Frederick put in a personal appearance; elsewhere he was

* A phrase coined in France upon a celebrated political démarche of the preceding century.

represented by deputies. Königsberg being officially the capital of the Kingdom, the question of homage had particular importance—the more as certain constitutional difficulties threatened to arise.

In Brandenburg the Electors had long ago suppressed any effective functioning on the part of the Estates, and the first two Hohenzollern Kings had gone some way towards achieving the same in Prussia proper. The Prussian Estates now demanded that the proclamation of the new King be preceded by a solemn guarantee of ancient privileges; but after some face-saving disputation yielded to an adroit technical compromise, in the negotiation of which Grumbkow's son-in-law Podewils gave proof of eminent ability. A commemorative medal boldly introduced the title, King *of* the Prussians, *Rex Borussorum*—the reverse bore the motto *veritati et iustitiae*. Replicas of it in gold and silver were scattered among the populace, also at Berlin, where the ceremony of homage was next repeated.

Here, after it was done and Frederick had stepped out on to the palace balcony to be acclaimed by the crowds below, he did what seems to have impressed everyone as an extraordinary thing. Certainly neither protocol nor tradition provided for it.

He remained on the balcony for a half-hour, silent, motionless, his gaze fixed on the multitude shouting and scrambling for the royal largesse.

CHAPTER 17
LA JOURNÉE DES DUPES

The New Solomon—a sobriquet popularized by Voltaire—had not taken up residence in the Palace of Berlin, fraught as it was with oppressive associations, but at his grandmother's nearby seat of Charlottenburg, which in those first months became something of a tourist centre. Natives and foreigners flocked to the little rustic town, where streets were unpaved mud tracks with improvised footbridges of raw timber, to catch a glimpse of the royal prodigy riding to and from Berlin. They could always pick him out with ease among his glittering entourage: for the King shone by *not* glittering.

Frederick, who had once risked his whole future for the love of fine clothes, now wore 'the shroud' day in, day out. But for the rings with which he covered his hands, he had begun to cultivate, not merely simplicity, but downright shabbiness in his person—set off by attendants sumptuously liveried as quasi-kings and thus rendering plainness of attire a kind of specific regalia. It was a leaf out of the books of Charles XII, Prince Eugene, and Frederick William, improved by artistic sensibilities which those three had not possessed, and thus being very far from decreeing a general, killjoy austerity.

It was not at all true to say that Frederick would soon outdo his father in parsimony. He was careful—as much careful of his dignity, in this, as of his resources—but he in fact initiated a new era of royal spending in Prussia. By his father's lifelong cheeseparing and administrative genius, he could afford it: Frederick I's wine cellars, at Frederick II's accession, were packed with barrels full of specie.

He at once saw to it that the cramping burden of a bizarre

frugality was lifted from the royal family, so that the Queen Mother and her children could live in fitting state and comfort. As for the Reigning Queen—to give her her due if euphemistic title—money was no object to settle her in a household of her own, apart from her husband, who thereafter would never stay for more than an hour or two, in company, under one roof with the Poor Soul.

Wilhelmine, whose financial position as Margravine of Bayreuth was still no better, might reasonably hope to benefit as well. Frederick on his way to the homaging in Westphalia arranged to make a wide detour to visit his favourite sister first. The whole journey, in fact, was planned to give him the sort of holiday he had always wanted and never got, combined now with an excursion in the Harun al Rashid manner.

He travelled, not at first incognito, with a party of only seven: Fredersdorf (lately raised to the position of chamberlain and, on the side, land owner)* and Prince Augustus William; the eldest son of the Old Dessauer and the youngest son of President Münchow; the Venetian Count Algarotti—one of the more recent luminary acquisitions of the Rheinsberg period; and two middle-aged colonels for sober ballast.

Wilhelmine had been looking forward to the first meeting with her brother since he had become King, with a passionate expectancy such as is nearly always disappointed. Perhaps she showed too much emotion—of the wrong, nostalgic kind—for his present comfort; perhaps she stirred up all his defensive perversity, appearing to rely on an impending rain of ducats. One can only attempt to read between the lines of her account of this most unsatisfactory reunion, once again overshadowed by a mysterious constraint on Frederick's part.

'I had so much to tell him: I told him nothing. . . . His caresses seemed forced. . . . His air of embarrassment put me off my stroke. . . . He paid far more attention to my visiting sister, the Margravine of Ansbach [between whom and Frederick there had not been any love lost previously] than he did to me. . . .'

* Fredersdorf incidentally had joined Frederick in entering the Brotherhood of Freemasons, an organization then considered dangerous and subversive by the ruling classes.

Only the erudite vivacity of Algarotti—author of a Guide to Newton 'for the Ladies'*—seems to have saved the company from complete petrefaction. Perhaps another meeting at Berlin would be happier: Wilhelmine promised to pay a return visit to her brother's court at the earliest date.

Frederick went on towards Frankfurt-on-Main, in high enough spirits, masquerading as a half-French gentleman, M. le Comte du Four, with his German friends Count von Schaffgotsch (Augustus William), Count von Pfuhl (Algarotti), and M. Fredersdorf—Prince Leopold the younger, Münchow, and the colonels were sent ahead to Wesel. The smaller the party, the better: the truant jaunt was supposed to be a deep secret, although some such possibility had been widely debated at home and abroad for weeks past. What more likely than that Frederick, ardent Francophile as he was, would take this opportunity to make a sortie into his cultural Mecca? It was an opportunity, too, to retrace and expunge the trail of the Crown Prince's journey under arrest, ten years ago.

Strasburg was the secret destination, which Frederick calculated they should reach in three days from Bayreuth.

> Mais le ciel, qui tout dispose,
> Régla différemment la chose.
> Avec de coursiers efflanqués,
> En ligne droites issus de Rosinante,
> Et des paysans en postillons masqués,
> Butors de race impertinente,
> Notre carosse en cent lieux accroché
> . . . . .
> Gravitant contre les rochers.
> Les airs émus par le bruyant tonnerre,
> Les torrents d'eau répandus sur la terre.
> . . . .
> Car des hôtes intéressés,
> De la faim nous voyant pressés,
> D'un façon plus que frugale,
> Dans une chaumière infernale,
> En nous empoisonnant, nous volaient nos écus.
> O siècle différent des temps de Lucullus!

* 'Much good it'll do the ladies,' sneered Christian Wolff.

Thus a fractional extract from Frederick's interminable jingling travel report to Voltaire in Brussels, where Frederick hoped to meet him face to face at last after he had done with Cleve. He spared neither his muse nor his reader, describing every episode of the adventure: how, making out their own passport at the last minute, they crossed the Rhine; how they amused themselves at Strasburg; how, to the consternation of the Governor, their true identities became revealed and the Prussian party found it necessary to split up and escape under cover of darkness from an excessive popular enthusiasm.

The whole lighthearted frolic is of interest only because it was Frederick's first and last essay in complete relaxation, and because, although being thus entirely without ulterior purpose, it of course had its more serious consequences in due time.

For one thing, as an unpolitical venture it was to say the least impolitic.

Ever since his accession the new King had been at great pains to preserve the enigma of Prussia's future alignment, which cogently occupied the major powers—notably England and France. Both these had their reasons for expecting Frederick's friendship, and it was his hope to make them bid for it against each other—principally in the old matter of Jülich-Berg—whilst keeping both equally in the dark. In this he was following his father's dying advice—given with quite remarkable clarity and acuteness for a man within twenty-four hours of dissolution.*

George II was waiting in Hanover to meet Frederick on the latter's way home from Cleve; Cardinal Fleury was waiting

* Concerning the other powers, Frederick William had directed his heir to render unto Caesar the things that were Caesar's, always remembering, however, that as head of the House of Austria Caesar was out to get rather more than his due, especially from Prussia. Further, Frederick should keep on good neighbourly terms with the northern German principalities, also with Denmark, but meet both Sweden and Russia with carefully sweetened reserve, watching out meanwhile for the occasional amicable stab in the back on the part of those old friends of Brandenburg, Holland and Hanover. Lastly, before resorting to arms, one should always reflect that, once started, a war could seldom be stopped again at will; however, if there were no other way out, one should see it through with inflexible determination.

to see the effect of the meeting with Voltaire on Voltaire's impressionable Prussian disciple. Tactically, Frederick's playful digression on to French soil had been an error, all the more if he wanted to avoid a personal conference with Uncle George just then, as he did.

At this very time, moreover, a matter of even more immediate political moment was rising to a climax, further concentrating attention on the equivocal beginner.

In 1732 the Prussian Kingdom had succeeded to the possession of Herstal, a small township in the neighbourhood of Liège which once had been the manor of Pepin, father of Charlemagne. Insignificant as this historic place was otherwise, its inhabitants did not wish to belong to Prussia and thus to be subject to the Prussian system of compulsory army recruitment. They had refused to swear fealty to Frederick William, who finally had extorted this by military pressure. The enforced oath was not observed. Backed by the Prince Bishop of Liège, with the solid support of the common people of the whole countryside, and under the leadership of an advocate of Liège named Defawes, the Herstal resistance had waxed so strong that it was no longer safe for Prussian officials to show their faces, or rather their detested uniforms, in that part of the world. Frederick William had seriously considered letting Herstal go—selling his rights, to be precise, for the sum of 125,000 Thaler; but the transaction had come to nothing.

Upon Frederick's accession Herstal declined to renew the oath of fealty, claiming allegiance to the Bishop of Liège, who had behind him both the Emperor and the King of France. The problem was one of the first on which the new sovereign had demanded a comprehensive Ministerial memorandum—and the first in which he gave an indication of what it was going to be like to work under him. Dismissing the expert opinion he had asked for, and which emphatically deprecated any action that might constitute a risk of war, he wrote in the margin of the report, 'So long as the Ministers talk politics, they are well enough; but when they start talking about war, it is like Iroquois discussing astronomy.' The story goes that Privy Councillor Thulemeier, acting head of the Department for

Foreign Affairs, had a stroke and died of the royal impertinence; though he survived the perusal for nearly two months.

In truth, the whole Privy Council was thrown into a state of panic tension. For after that one brusque communication, the King held tight and told them nothing, absolutely nothing more. Nobody knew what was going on, whether in respect of Herstal, London, or Versailles. Frederick kept all ensuing negotiations entirely to himself and his appropriate confidential envoys. The first his Ministers learned of a two-day ultimatum to Liège, was the Bishop's disdainful verbal message to the effect that this was no way to address a Prince of the Empire.

The next thing was that three battalions of Prussian Grenadier Guards and one squadron of Dragoons marched from Wesel into Liège territory, occupied the diocese, and levied an immediately payable war and provender tax, simultaneously distributing a printed manifesto which, sweetly reasonable, stated their King's case. The manifesto was dated to coincide with the action, Sunday, 11 September.

In other words, all this had been proceeding concurrently with the King's holiday. On the same day as Prussian military laid Liège under occupation, Frederick and Voltaire had their meeting, not in Brussels as previously arranged, but on Prussian soil, at a little place called Castle Moyland near Cleve.

Frederick was ill. In addition to certain rheumatic troubles, he suffered from malaria, which was very common in the marshy districts of Brandenburg, and at Cleve had been overtaken by an attack of the recurrent fever. Having had his sabbatical flight, he had refused to succumb until the serious business he had come for was completed; then, after a crowded and exhausting fortnight, he took to his bed.

'Confess that I am unlucky,' he had written to Voltaire from Wesel, 'for now when . . . nothing hinders me from seeing you, the fever intervenes. . . . Let us cheat the fever, my dear Voltaire, and let me at least have the pleasure of embracing you. . . . Everyone around me knows my intention was to come to you. . . . If the sight of you does not cure me, I will send for a confessor at once.'

Naturally Voltaire did as he was asked, although 'we had prepared a fine house for him. . . . At the door of the court [at

Moyland] I found, by way of guard, one soldier. Privy Councillor Rambonet [Frederick's messenger in the Herstal affair] was walking in the court, blowing into his fingers to keep warm. He wore big linen ruffles at his wrists, very dirty, a hat full of holes, an old official periwig one side of which hung down into his pocket, while the other scarcely touched his shoulder . . . I was led into his Majesty's apartment. Nothing but four bare walls there. By the light of a candle, I perceived, in a closet, a little truckle bed . . . on which lay a little man muffled up in a dressing-gown of coarse blue duffel: this was the King, sweating and shivering under a wretched blanket. . .' Thus Voltaire wrote twenty years later.

Now Frederick, writing a fortnight after the meeting: 'I have seen Voltaire whom I was so curious to know; but I saw him with the Quartan hanging on me, and my mind as unstrung as my body. With men of this kind one ought not to be sick; one ought even to be specially well, in better health than usual. . . .' However, 'He has the eloquence of Cicero, the mellowness of Pliny, the wisdom of Agrippa. . . . His intellect is at work incessantly; every drop of ink from his pen is a pearl of wit. . . . I could only admire and keep quiet. . . .'

And Voltaire again, on 18 October 1740—that is, before the beautiful friendship had soured but after the first sense of anticlimax of the actual meeting had faded—: 'I met one of the most charming men in the world, . . . who would be everywhere sought after if he were not King; a philosopher without austerity; full of sweetness and obliging ways; not remembering that he is King when he is with his friends; indeed so completely forgetting it that he made me too almost forget . . . that here I saw sitting at the foot of my bed a sovereign who had an army of 100,000 men. . . .'

In short, the moment and the setting were inauspicious; but at the time neither man was willing to admit to disappointment. Their correspondence lay dormant for only a week or so; then it continued with all its old ebullience.

Yet something had changed between them. It had always been Frederick who made the advances—never mind if the onus of advance lies upon princes; now Voltaire had been made to come to Frederick—never mind if it was only in the way of physical movement: no outward gesture but carries some inner effect. His fever had served Frederick opportunely (also giving him his pretext for not calling in at Hanover).

Another factor redressing the balance between master and pupil, was Voltaire's sudden appreciation of the little man as a lord of hosts, reflecting glory on his intellectual patrons. In the presence of 2,000 Prussian horse and foot—'2,000 good arguments,' said Voltaire, applauding—the Prince Bishop of Liège made haste to change his tune and the rebels of Herstal ceased singing. Six weeks after the bloodless invasion Herstal went to Liège, for an aggregate price of 240,000 Thaler, nearly double the sum originally proposed by Frederick William. The only help Liège had got from France or Austria was protest, censure, and invective.

The transfer was concluded on 20 October. Some hours before it was sealed Emperor Charles VI died.

* * *

Frederick was lying ill at Rheinsberg. Nobody dared go into the sickroom with a piece of news which in the King's present condition might prove too much for him. Fredersdorf finally was prevailed on to break it gently.

The patient took up his bed and walked. 'I am giving my fever the sack,' he wrote off at once—perhaps a little obtusely, since the addressee was Voltaire, for whom the said fever had not been thus dismissed, 'For I need my machine and must now work it to the utmost. A most unforeseen event prevents me from opening my heart to you as usual and from chattering as I would wish. The Emperor is dead. His death alters all my pacific ideas, and I think that next June it will be rather a matter of gunpowder, soldiers, and trenches, than of actresses, routs and theatricals [such as we were discussing]. My affair at Liège is quite finished, but the present affairs are of much greater importance to Europe. Now is the moment for a complete change in the old System of Europe: this is the rolling stone striking the idol made of four metals, which, in Nebuchadnezzar's dream, broke it in pieces. . . . Goodbye, my dear friend, do not forget me.'

* * *

'My rights to Silesia . . . I leave intact for my descendants to prosecute,' Frederick's grandfather, the first Prussian King, had set down in his memorandum of 1697. 'If God shall one day send the opportunity, those who come after me will know what they have to do.'*

In 1731 Colonel von Rochow had chanced upon a collection of papers in a cupboard, which turned out to contain a draft plan by the Great Elector himself for the recovery of Brandenburg's Silesian properties *in the event of failure of Habsburg succession in the male line.* ('This is worth more to me than 100,000 Ducats!' Frederick William had exclaimed on being presented with this oracular sanction of any such possible démarche.)

In 1740, directly the Emperor's death had become public, the aged Chancellor Ludewig of the University of Halle despatched to his young King a dossier, compiled in over forty years' research, and bristling with legal proof of the Prussian rights in Silesia.

No sooner had the court of Berlin gone into mourning for the Emperor than it was learned that Tzarina Anna Ivanovna of Russia had died eight days after him. She was succeeded by a nephew two months old, whose father was a kinsman of the King of Prussia. Another twenty days later, and the deceased Tzarina's anti-Prussian favourite (some said husband), Biron, had fallen from power. No untoward Russian interference in Prussian enterprises need now be apprehended. Frederick went into close retirement at Rheinsberg, where he was reported to be working furiously.

To what end, nobody but the two men knew who were closeted with him, one politician and one soldier: Podewils, rising star of the Foreign Department, and Frederick's old friend Schwerin. The rest of the world could only guess.

Not but what the rest of the world was getting busy too. The death of the Emperor without heirs male was an event long and avidly awaited. Whether or no the Pragmatic Sanction were going to be upheld, the heiress to the Austrian Crown Lands was debarred by her sex from any pretensions to

*See pp. 23–6.

Imperial candidature, a fact which greatly increased the possibilities of an imminent all-European reshuffle.

The first task of the Austrian Government was obtaining formal recognition of the Archduchess Maria Theresa's title as Queen of Hungary and Bohemia; the second was canvassing Electoral support for the candidature of her consort, Francis of Lorraine. Francis immediately wrote to Frederick, requesting an assurance of 'continued friendship' besides recognition, which he got, albeit with the oral qualification that it was up to Vienna to make friendship flower in Berlin. Francis, having met and liked Frederick in the past, and being of a sanguine temperament, believed what he wished: 'The King of Prussia is acting like a father* towards me and my wife,' he joyfully acknowledged Frederick's message, to the Prussian Ambassador Borcke, who had conveyed it. Maria Theresa herself, however, considered it advisable to put the worst construction on so guarded a pledge, and issued appropriate directions to her envoys.

Reports were coming in of very evident military preparations in Prussia. That sort of thing had happened before, and more than once, in Frederick William's day; 'The Prussians don't shoot as soon as all that,' was a fairly recent addition to the fund of German proverbs. Even if, spurred on by his success in Liège, Frederick were nursing serious aggressive intentions, his objective still remained in doubt. His most likely goal would be Jülich-Berg: in which case Austria had little to worry about, for France would never permit a Prussian coup so close to her own frontier. If, on the other hand, he had a mind to hold Maria Theresa to ransom for the Liegnitz bequest—the great province of Silesia was no little Herstal, and the mighty compound monarchy of Austria was not Liège. Meanwhile, the harvest everywhere in Europe proved extremely poor, as foreseen; and the military hibernating season commonly started about October. Even a tyro inflamed with delusions of grandeur by reading too many epics would defer an expedition till next year.

November came, without any flagging of mobilization in

*Archduke Francis was four years older than Frederick.

Prussia. Podewils and Schwerin were as close-mouthed as the King. The most wily and prepossessing foreign envoys could get no more out of the trio than could Frederick's other Ministers and his family—not even Voltaire, who also tried, under the promising auspices of mutual admiration. November passed.

At the beginning of December there was definite information that Prussian troops were concentrating near the Silesian frontier. On the 5th of the month Frederick himself hinted as much to the Austrian envoy, Marchese di Botta, in a passage of verbal sparring (Botta: 'Terrible roads, the Silesian ones at this season!' Frederick: 'The worst one will risk on them is a few splashes of mud.'). On the 6th, with a mixture of blustering and shamefacedness, he revealed his intention to the British Ambassador, Dickens; and finally gave out the official announcement that he had decided to 'advance a body of troops into Silesia'. On the 10th he sped the French Ambassador on his way home, with the words, 'Adieu, then. I believe I am going to play your game; if the aces fall to me, we will share!' On the 11th he disclosed to Botta the Prussian offer which Borcke had been instructed to submit in Vienna: Prussia would guarantee the Austrian possessions in Germany, join her in alliance with Russia, England, and Holland, subsidize Austrian rearmament, and vote for Francis in the Imperial Election—if Austria would cede to Prussia, not Liegnitz, not Brieg and Wohlau, but the entire province of Silesia.

On either that day or the next Frederick called together his generals and told them, 'Gentlemen, I am undertaking a war in which I have no allies but your valour and your goodwill. My cause is just—' Podewils was still working out the case for the just cause and making it better—'My resources are what we ourselves can do, and the issue lies in Fortune . . . Adieu!' he ended, after more in the same strain, 'until the rendezvous with glory which awaits us.'

On the 13th the Prussian army marched.

'The man is mad,' said Louis XV.

Within seven weeks the madman had got all Silesia.

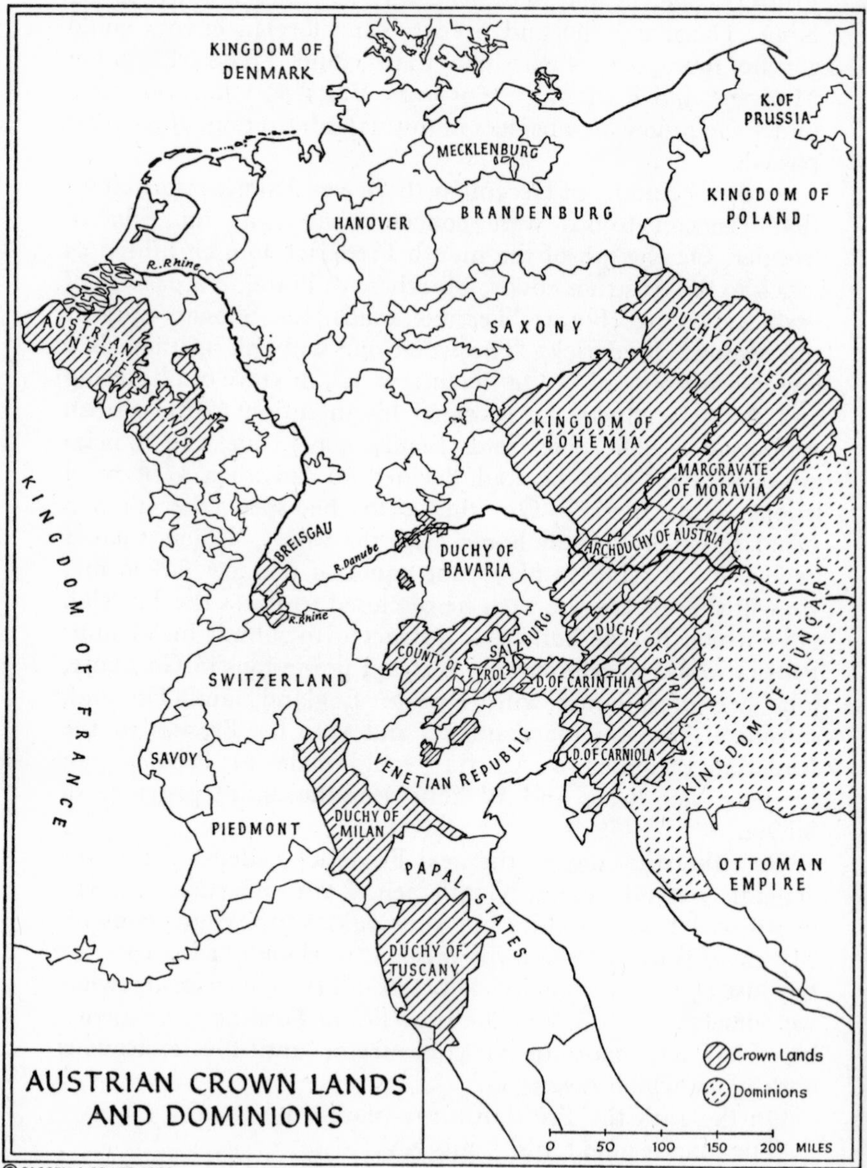
KINGDOM OF DENMARK
K. OF PRUSSIA
MECKLENBURG
KINGDOM OF POLAND
HANOVER
BRANDENBURG
R. Rhine
AUSTRIAN NETHERLANDS
SAXONY
DUCHY OF SILESIA
KINGDOM OF BOHEMIA
MARGRAVATE OF MORAVIA
KINGDOM OF FRANCE
BREISGAU
R. Danube
DUCHY OF BAVARIA
ARCHDUCHY OF AUSTRIA
R. Rhine
SALZBURG
DUCHY OF STYRIA
COUNTY OF TYROL
D. OF CARINTHIA
SWITZERLAND
KINGDOM OF HUNGARY
SAVOY
VENETIAN REPUBLIC
D. OF CARNIOLA
PIEDMONT
DUCHY OF MILAN
OTTOMAN EMPIRE
PAPAL STATES
DUCHY OF TUSCANY
Crown Lands
Dominions
AUSTRIAN CROWN LANDS AND DOMINIONS
0 50 100 150 200 MILES

CHAPTER 18
MARIA THERESA

'How different from the home life of our dear Queen!' the Viennese might justly have exclaimed with the apocryphal Victorian. In antecedents, character, and situation the contrast between Maria Theresa of Austria and Frederick II of Prussia could hardly have been greater.

The Kingdom of Prussia was not forty years old, the Holy Roman Empire getting on for a thousand. Frederick's father had been the second Prussian King, Maria Theresa's the fourteenth German Emperor of Habsburg race. In rank the latter was the highest temporal sovereign in Christendom, while the upstart title of the youngest monarchy was in some quarters still considered debatable and heretical. Where the Brandenburg Hohenzollerns were struggling to consolidate and enlarge their sparse territory, the Austrian Habsburgs were in centuries-old control of the largest landed possessions in Central Europe.

Vienna, though no more the actual capital of the Empire than Berlin was that of the Prussian Kingdom, in practice owned all the airs and fame of an Imperial residence. Berlin even yet was something of a joke as an aspiring major city, its artificial growth laboriously extended, inch by inch and year by year, in a continuous battle against sand and marsh. The court of Vienna, having no call to imitative ambition, was no pseudo-Versailles; but neither was the simplicity of the Imperial family life a strident profession of Spartan virtue like that decreed by Frederick William in Berlin. In France, thorough identification of the royal person with the mana of the State had brought ceremony into even the most private functions of royalty; in Prussia a conscious attempt had been made to remodel the whole nation (thereby incidentally castigating a whole degenerate world) upon the poor-but-honest pattern set by the sovereign household. In Austria, however, the Emperor's dual rôle as an extra-territorial dignitary and simultaneously head of a territorial power had casually brought about a separation of the office from the human being; more than anywhere else, indeed, the monarch was a man with a job, whose trappings he doffed outside office hours. In his home he behaved 'like anyone else', and unself-consciously so.

For all that from the hour of birth Maria Theresa formed the hub of Imperial policy, she was brought up so much a stranger to affairs and ceremonial that, the first time she saw the Emperor in his robes of state during a religious procession, she did not at once recognize her father. When she did, she jumped up excitedly and shrilly called down into the solemn throng, 'Come here, Papa, let's have a good look at you!' with that sunny spontaneity, and in that Viennese dialect, both of which were forever to endear her to her people while at times rendering her incomprehensible (both figuratively and in fact) to strangers. Always, too, the Emperor-figure as such would hold for her a touch of Santa Claus: glamorous disguise of a much-loved parent which she would give anything to see re-embodied in the males belonging to her, husband and son. Never would she lose the formative impressions of married bliss and family harmony—just as Frederick was marked for life by the reverse.

Happy the country that has no history: the childhood and adolescence of Maria Theresa are singularly poor in anecdote. Her training for office was nil, her education sketchy and informal. Music and theatre, outlawed at Frederick William's court, were the breath of life at the Vienna Hofburg. 'Resl' made her debut on the Imperial amateur stage at seven years old, in an opera performance for which the Emperor himself conducted the orchestra. She acquired proficiency in Latin (the official language of the Kingdom of Hungary) and French, a fair command of Italian, a smattering of Spanish. The study of history, to which Frederick William attached so much weight, was incumbent also on the Emperor's heiress—within limits; her primer appears to confuse the subject with speculative mythology, being full of such questions as, 'How many of the ten Patriarchs lived before the Flood, how many after?' 'By how many years did the life-span of Methuselah exceed that of Adam?' Modern history was more or less confined to the muster of Habsburg rulers from the thirteenth century onwards, culminating in a panegyric on Papa. Regarding literature, there was no ban on fiction, poetry, or drama; though the Emperor's preference was for Italian authors (as for Italian composers), he placed no embargo on the French. However, Maria Theresa was not naturally a great reader. The world as she knew it was circumscribed, black and white, intelligible, simple, elegant, and comfortable.

Married at nineteen to her kinsman Francis Stephen of Lorraine-Tuscany, whom she loved as a brother* and adored as a husband, she remained totally uninstructed in her future rôle which yet was the touchstone of European politics. She was happy. Her only unfulfilled desire, to bear a son, was shared by everyone around her. (Upon the birth of her second daughter, the Emperor had sought to encourage the disappointed populace by releasing one hundred doves, each bearing a necklet with a rhymed inscription to the effect, 'Third time, lucky.' The third child also was a daughter; but in 1740, the fifth year of her marriage, Maria Theresa was pregnant for the fourth time.) The death of her father was the first serious sorrow of her life: but even that was in the course of nature; the wound was clean and not the festering kind.

To her, then, accession came as a straightforward event, serious enough in all conscience, but without neurotic overtones.

Nor does this exhaust the points of contrast between her and Frederick. For Maria Theresa succeeded to a realm which as a co-ordinate whole had never been in worse case. Never had Habsburg suzerainty been less secure than it became at the

*Francis had lived with the Imperial family, a general favourite, from 1723 when he was fifteen and Maria Theresa six, to 1729.

moment it devolved upon her. If they had done nothing else, the decades of previous negotiation to ensure her safe tenure had served insistently to underline the weakness of her prospective position, in the eyes of her own people as well as in those of her neighbours. With Austria ceasing to be the seat of Empire, her military strength dwindled to the borderline of weakness, as the States of Germany were no longer bound to supply their contingents of troops on demand. In Spain, in Italy, Bavaria and Saxony claims on the Habsburg heritage were ready. Despite Maria Theresa's personal popularity with her subjects—tempered as it was in any case by mild contempt, sometimes shading over into distrust, of her husband*—there was every doubt as to a woman's capacity to keep the realm together at such a time. The leading candidate for the Imperial throne and leading pretender to the Austrian Crown Lands, Elector Charles Albert of Bavaria, had as good a connexion as Francis, if not a better, with the Habsburg dynasty—in right of descent from a sixteenth-century Archduchess of Austria and by marriage with a daughter of Emperor Leopold. He in addition had behind him the support of France—France, otherwise the arch enemy of Austria and the Empire.

Defeatism rather than intransigence was bred of the quandary, and, assisted by secret agents of France and Bavaria, the feeling spread through Austria that it might be as well to switch allegiance to Charles Albert before it was too late—before, that is, Maria Theresa had her coronations in Hungary and Bohemia and received irrevocable homage.

Over and above a true and simple piety, Maria Theresa therefore had every reason to wish for a speedy coronation with the full sacramental trimmings, lacking which her title could not carry real power—just as formal recognition of that title by the other countries was an indispensable prerequisite for its realization. Whilst being deeply convinced of the divine origin of her royal portion, and devoid of personal ambition,

*Francis held no possessions within the Empire. The Duchy of Tuscany which he had got in compensation for renouncing Lorraine, was little more than a titular amenity—not quite as empty, if not quite so high-sounding, either, as his decorative style of King of Jerusalem.

she was thus under the paradoxical necessity of winning what was lawfully hers.

Her equipment for this onerous task was, again, quite other than Frederick's. Where Frederick found a fiscal surplus, a smoothly running administrative machine, and a huge and exemplary fighting force, Maria Theresa inherited a deficit, administrative confusion, and an army discredited as well as depleted by its ineffectual performance against the Turks—an army which, moreover, numerically comprised never more than a percentage of its statutory strength on paper, whose leaders were mostly in prison for defeat, and in which drill had been reduced to the minimum so as not to tire the soldier, trained with the aid of dummy rifles only, to conserve munitions. The fading laurels of Prince Eugene* and a Privy Council composed entirely of men in their seventies and eighties were dubious assets.

But her heaviest liabilities—her ignorance and her sex—became her greatest advantage. The one reinforced her native courage and optimism, the other gained her universal sympathy, even among those who looked to profit by that great primary drawback.

'I may be only a poor Queen, but I have the heart of a king.' 'Had I not been with child all the time. . . .' Such phrases as these, which are her own,† point straight at the responsive feelings she excited. Those were statements of fact, not pleas of self-pity. Marie Theresa had the heart of a lion, and she was hampered throughout the most critical years of her reign by pregnancies and accouchements. But when all is said a kingly heart inside a King is not as much a matter for amazement; indomitable defiance becomes the more magnificent when emanating from a creature in the throes of creature-business. Even Frederick, who evinced no such susceptibility to any other opponent, always admitted to a somewhat guilty conscience regarding the Queen of Hungary.

They never met to test upon each other their different brands of a personal appeal which according to the general testimony both exercised to so marked a degree. Maria

* Died 1736.

† It is unlikely that she had ever heard of Elizabeth I's Tilbury speech.

Theresa's greatest charm was the uncalculating, confident spontaneity of one who never in her life had met with unkindness—until 1740, when her character was formed—and which might allow her to feel diffident, but never shy. Her intelligence, characteristically, was of the type defined as *mother*-wit. It might be sometimes narrow in its vision, sometimes distorted by tenderness; but it would not be blinded.

She loved her husband and to take the sting out of his position lavished on him as much of apparent authority as she had to bestow; that did not mean endowing him with faculties which he obviously lacked.

Francis had been conducting the talks with the Prussian Ambassador, and he it was who received and spurned Frederick's proposals which Borcke submitted on 17 December—four days after Frederick and his armies had entered Silesia. Sooner than let Prussia have that province, cried the Archduke, he would wish the Turks at the gates of Vienna, sooner see the Netherlands go to France. The wretched Borcke—hating his commission, since knowing as well as Frederick did himself that it was asking the impossible—did what he could to calm Francis down, and presently succeeded so well that Francis began to talk of possibilities of compromise. At this Maria Theresa, having evidently taken the precaution of listening behind the door, burst in and, asking innocently: had anybody seen her husband? stopped the interview.

What compromise could there be, in honour? 'So long as there be even one single Prussian soldier on Silesian soil, we shall have not one word to say to your master.'

Maria Theresa was not unaware that France, and Spain, and Sardinia, and Bavaria, and Saxony all had designs on her inheritance, of one sort and another; and that roughly speaking the rest of Europe was standing by to see on what side it should become most worth while to come down. This filled her with anxiety but not with such a passion of disgust and loathing as Frederick had inspired in her. True, he had already acted, before anybody else was ready; but in any case she took Frederick's perfidy personally as she would not that of any other sovereign.

To her it was incomprehensible that a man who owed his

THE FOURTEENTH HABSBURG EMPEROR
Charles VI of Austria

THE HEIRESS
Maria Theresa of Austria as a child

WILHELMINE
Margravine of Bayreuth

KING IN THE REPUBLIC OF LETTERS
Voltaire

life to the Emperor (as witness his 1730 letter of thanks) could so go against common gratitude as to rob that Emperor's daughter. Legal quibbles were as foreign to her mind as historical general knowledge. She could not get over it that Frederick's father, grandfather, and great-grandfather had all renounced the Silesian claim, never mind if they had each done so under duress, never mind that the claim had rested on legal contract and not on aggression and conquest: a promise was a promise. Furthermore, her revulsion from the perjuror was strengthened by profound religious antipathy, and she could not sleep for thinking of the Protestant wolf rampant in the Catholic Silesian sheepfold.

CHAPTER 19

THE ANNEXATION OF SILESIA

The international outcry seconding Maria Theresa had an unmistakable note of resentment. The same sources which had previously poured scorn on the *Antimachiavel* now unctuously contrasted its virtuous message with the author's procedures against the Bishop of Liège and the Queen of Hungary. The aggressor's perfidy was the more perfidious for the deception practised upon his colleagues by their own obstinate, wishful picture of him, and also for the object lesson how easy it would have been to act as he had done, if only one could have been as quick.

By 22 December the Prussian advance through deluges of rain and lakes of knee-deep mud had appropriated a broad swath of Lower Silesia from Krossen to Glogau; on 1 January it arrived at Breslau, capital of the province. Not a shot had been fired, the only casualty so far a soldier's wife drowned at a torrential river crossing. But then, Prussia was not at war with Austria. Frederick had come, not as an enemy, but as a friend, bringing his army along to help the Queen of Hungary defend her own against the scheming rapacity of Bavaria, Saxony, and France. Silesia, richest of her provinces, was merely to be taken into a species of protective custody, for the present.

Such was the gist of another aspect of his just cause as preferred in Frederick's *Proclamation to the Silesians*, distributed in thousands of copies in the opening stages of what was called the Silesian Undertaking. The Old Dessauer called it 'political infamy'.

The grapes were sour. As early as November the Old Dessauer had started importuning Frederick to tell him what was going forward, till Frederick acidly put a stop to it: 'Your Serenity will learn in due course what my orders are, without disquieting yourself about them, as nothing has been forgotten or shelved.—F.' When the secret was out, it transpired that the Prince of Anhalt-Dessau had no part in the project. Deeply hurt, the father of the Prussian army dashed off another agitated note: how could Frederick do this to him? how would it look, for him to be passed over in this way as if he were good only for the scrap heap, the while his pupils were allowed to gather laurels?

The reference to pupils was perhaps ill-advised. Frederick took full advantage of the opening:

> You may be sure I honour your merits and capabilities as a young officer ought to honour an old one, who has given the world so many proofs of his ability; nor will I neglect your Serenity on any occasion when you can help me by your good counsel and co-operation. . . . But as to this present expedition, I reserve it for myself alone, that the world may not think the King of Prussia marches to war under a tutor.

There was a barb in every clause, and every one found its mark. Not even a vaguely soothing interpolation—that this Undertaking after all was the merest bagatelle, and that the King was reserving the Prince of Anhalt-Dessau against the event of possible complications developing from the direction of Saxony as the immediate neighbour of both Prussia and Silesia—could appease the fuming old warrior. Physical combat had never been his only mode of warfare. With a will the old warrior applied himself to spreading alarm and despondency, not only as to the moral turpitude of Frederick's action, but forecasting its end in disaster. And when it came to the point, most of the elder generals obeyed their marching orders with considerable misgivings. By the civil population—aside from the King's young brothers, who clamoured prettily to be allowed to come too—the Undertaking was viewed with apathy at best.

But all that was changed before the end of the year. The generals felt a lot better, and the people of Berlin waxed quite bellicose.

Yet the secret of Frederick's success was at least as much of a political as of a military nature, for all the indisputable strategic value of speed, surprise, force of numbers, and high degree of organization.

* * *

Everywhere the Prussians passed, the *Proclamation to the Silesians* was posted on church doors and handed round.

More important than the introductory précis of Frederick's motives was the promise that the King of Prussia would respect 'and indeed secure, by His royal protection and puissant guardianship, to all inhabitants, whatever their religion, estate or calling, of their every, ancient Law and Justice, Liberties and Privileges *in publicis et privatis, in ecclesiasticis et politicis*, so safely as ever they could wish or demand; further He intends to keep such Discipline and Order among His troops as shall ensure that no one is molested and annoyed, still less disturbed in the peaceful possession of his goods'.

More important than the promise was the fact that it was kept.

* * *

The province of Silesia, divided into two halves by the River Oder, was rich in arable land, green pastures, timber forests, richest of all in its vast subterranean funds of coal, iron, and other minerals, worked by a hardy and industrious people. However, as a political entity the country laboured under a number of disadvantages, inherent in its footing as an adjunct of the Bohemian Crown.

The obligations of the Silesian Estates stood in no relation to their civil emoluments. They could boast a specious independence which charged them with full administrative responsibility, but yet left them fully accountable, and in practice wholly subservient, to the central authority. They had, as it were, power to argue with the central authority provided they then bowed to its decisions.

Exchanging one distant overlord for another could not in itself cause any suffering. On the contrary—the Silesian burgess who watched the Prussian eagle replacing the (double-headed) Austrian one over a public building, and said hopefully, 'That bird has only one head and one crop: maybe it won't eat so much as the other one,' voiced the feeling of many.

No very tangible benefits accrued to the Silesian from his place within the Habsburg monarchy, apart from the questionable one of military protection. The country's whole economy had been subordinated to the weal of the mother State, and, worse, drained for the support of outlying sister provinces. Frederick, though promising to maintain the status quo ante, in fact could not but improve on it, by detaching the province from the interests of others with which she had nothing but a bond in common.

Like the rest of the Austrian Crown Lands, Silesia was experiencing the relayed symptoms of a disordered central exchequer. The cruel winter of 1739/40, followed by failure of crops, had wrought havoc on the staple means of subsistence; and by a combination of forced loans and tax increases, with a forbidding tangle of inter-commonwealth customs barriers, crafts (which were very manifold) and commerce had all but come to a standstill. There was a dearth of foodstuffs and of ready money; there was a glut of manufactured products; there was distress.

The invading army brought its own provisions and an abundant supply of hard cash; it brought life to a stagnant market. And the Prussian soldier did in truth belie the proverbial brutality and licentiousness of his calling, to which the regular transit of Austrian garrison troops had accustomed the population. A very few infringements of discipline were punished with the utmost severity, and did not recur. Collaboration with the enemy was painless.

As for the religious freedom which the King of Prussia had promised to preserve—that yet remained for him to institute in the first place. One of the earliest and most vigorous centres of Protestantism, the province of Silesia had been forcibly restored to the Catholic order in and after the Thirty Years War. There existed a large minority of Lutherans, barred from civic office, deprived of clergy, compelled to observe the Catholic feasts and marriage regulations, exposed to constant pressure for conversion, and in constant fear of pogroms. To this section of the population the Protestant invader appeared as a saviour, of whom it was even related that a Voice in the night had commanded him to the rescue of the oppressed.

The one claim Frederick never put forward for the justice of his cause was Divine instigation. But he was true to his principles and constant in his beliefs, which remained forever insulated from his steadily maturing, occupational cynicism. He made it his particular business to see that the hopes of the Protestants were realized and the Catholics' corresponding dread of reprisals was allayed, in every district that came under Prussian occupation: that the disabilities resting upon the one denomination were lifted without being shifted to the other.

No fundamental change occurred in the position of the Jews, a minority of minorities, very small, scattered, powerless, and unloved. The dynastic tradition of religious toleration in which Frederick had been born and raised had never gone a very long way with regard to the Jews who, in Brandenburg as much as in almost every other country in the world, laboured under crippling social restrictions and special financial burdens. Frederick, though opposed to all persecution as such, and though holding that, 'All religions are equally good . . . so long as those professing them be honest folk . . . Ay, and if Mohammedans were to come offering themselves as colonists, we'd build them mosques!'—made an implicit exception of Judaism. Though he would avail himself of the services of individual Jews, he entirely shared the confirmed anti-semitic prejudices of his kind. Maria Theresa, however, surpassed the average, with a positive hatred of the killers of Christ, and under her rule the anti-Jewish laws were enforced with notable harshness, Jewish privileges whittled down; so that the Jews looked forward to the Prussian advent with something of the same feeling as the Protestants. (Indeed Frederick did soon after repeal the expulsion of the Jewish community from Breslau, enacted by Charles VI in 1738.)

* * *

Thus the deeper founts of resistance were sapped in Silesia.

Military resistance was slow to materialize. Against Frederick's expeditionary force of 40,000, the garrisons of all Silesia between them could muster no more than 3,000; and for want of money to repair them the province's few major fortresses were falling to pieces. Rounding up relief from other parts of the Austrian dominions—themselves short of troops and destitute of funds—was no easy matter.

There was flurry in Vienna, but no attempt at reorganization. There were attempts at stopping up one gap by creating another, but none at any serious investigation into the causes of deficiencies; there was a plethora of cross-purposes. The danger was not yet so near that it could galvanize accustomed inertia; virtually the only person with an appropriate sense of urgency was the Queen herself.

Even so, Maria Theresa appointed as Chief of Defence her husband, whom she would not like to feel slighted, and who was after all descended from some noted warriors, although he had given small proof of such heredity in the Turkish War. Francis, from equally commendable but irrelevant loyalty, appointed as his chief executive his former military tutor, General Count Wilhelm Reinhald Neippberg. Neippberg was one of the generals in disgrace for losing the Turkish War—in fact had narrowly escaped beheading on his return—and had to be released from prison to take up his new command. (Seckendorf was let out at the same time. But he had had enough and as soon as possible left Austria to offer his services to the contender for the Habsburg succession, Charles Albert of Bavaria.)

In the meantime, pending general replenishment of the army, one might as well look on the bright side. Bartenstein, the Secretary of the Privy Council, who by his loud voice and dogmatic manner carried much weight*, gave out that Austria was better off with Frederick as an enemy than as a friend: in the Rhine campaign the Prussian contingent had been more hindrance than help.

Everyone felt duly reassured, the more as Glogau, the first town to defy the Prussian call to surrender, remained in Austrian hands. Frederick, having no siege artillery on the spot and not wishing to wait for it to come as it was important to continue the spectacle of his lightning progress, bypassed Glogau though leaving it masked by a reserve of 10,000 troops, under the Old Dessauer's eldest son.

*He was given to shouting the Queen down so that his vehemence was audible several rooms away.

The rest of the army went on—with hardly any maps, in weather which had extinguished all civilian traffic, the roads of which Botta had justly given warning now utterly vanished. 'Do not ask for poetry from a man who is at present following the occupation of a carter,' Frederick wrote airily to Voltaire, 'and of a carter sometimes stuck in the mud.' (Voltaire did not ask Frederick for poetry; he sent him some. Mme de Rocoulles was sending him knitted comforts.)

The march was in two columns, the one commanded by Schwerin making for Liegnitz; the King wanted to take Breslau himself.

Breslau was the capital of Silesia, yet did not belong to the Habsburg compound, being one of the free cities of the Empire which owed allegiance only to the Emperor. There was no Emperor at that moment, and at all times the city guarded its independent status with jealous vigilance. Thus although Breslau was the seat of the Provincial Government with its Austrian affiliation, the town kept a standing embargo on Austrian troops, who were not permitted even to pass through save in infinitesimal trickles escorted by the municipal guard and with the transit route sealed off by strong chains. However, inflexible in little things, in big the Town Council tended to grant the Government's requests.

With the King of Prussia at the gates, the Town Council was willing to admit Austrian troops for the defence of the city; but guilds and burgher companies opposed what they suspected of being the thin end of the Habsburg wedge. Their own militia would rise to the emergency, they argued—not with a great deal of enthusiam. The weather had changed, the moat was frozen solid, provisions were scant, and the Prussians were going to win anyway: so why burn the suburbs and undergo the perils and privations of a siege? A large proportion of the inhabitants were Lutherans; while in the suburbs which it had been proposed to raze the Catholic Church was the foremost property owner.*

* Prominent in knitting together the younger and more refractory elements of both Faiths was a self-appointed pro-Prussian agitator named Döblin, a cobbler by trade—the trade that, oddly, furnished many a popular demagogue before the days of mass production.

However, as the argument continued the militia drilled, arms were issued to the population, the town gates were closed and sentries reinforced.

The sentries, naturally, were the first to show the Prussians what manner of reception would be theirs in Breslau: 'Welcome, dear sirs!' some of them cried and all presented arms when the enemy vanguard appeared on Sunday, 1 January 1741.

The militia manned the walls, jostled by civilians, all together craning to watch the splendid sight of the Prussian army, in magnificent order, taking over the suburbs. The suburbs breathed again, safe now from officious arson. Negotiations went swiftly.

On 3 January Breslau opened her gates to Frederick, with unmistakable delight. The descriptions of his entry irresistibly remind the modern reader of a film star mobbed by his fans. Frederick himself was a little puzzled. He had done nothing more wonderful than guaranteeing Breslau's neutrality, in return for permission to set up a Prussian depot in one of the suburbs: and here were these semi-republicans rendering him voluntary homage. Silesia was evidently at his feet.

CHAPTER 20

SECOND PHASE: BATTLE

'My dear M. Jordan, my sweet M. Jordan, my tranquil M. Jordan, my good, my benign, my pacific, my humanest M. Jordan—I announce to Thy Beatitude the conquest of Silesia.' So Frederick wrote on 14 January—from Ottmachau, where the Austrian defence had made its first stand and accounted for the first round dozen Prussian dead.

The Prussians were in control of the entire province. With the exception of Glogau and Brieg, sealed off for future attention at leisure, there was not one strongpoint inland, hardly a supply depot, which had not fallen to them intact; Schwerin's force held the Jablunka pass across the Beskid mountains bordering the extreme south tip, which gave access to Hungary beyond. Only at the edge of the long mountain chain which divided Silesia from Bohemia and Moravia there remained a potential base for Austrian counter-attack: Neisse, the country's largest and strongest citadel.

On 17 January Frederick wrote again to Jordan: 'I have the honour to inform Your Humanity that we are in good Christian fashion preparing to bombard Neisse . . . if the paltry place will not surrender gracefully, we shall be under the necessity of pulverizing it. . . . In ten days it will all be over. . . . The whole conquest has cost us only twenty men and two officers.'

But the pulverizing action of the Prussian siege artillery was not as prompt as had been hoped. At Neisse the defenders ruthlessly destroyed their handsome suburbs; the moat was daily de-iced and the ramparts were daily watered so that they presented an unscalable glassy surface. The Prussian supplies were running very low; their lines of communication were stretched to near breaking point. The population of southern Silesia was solidly Catholic and hostile. The great landed magnates showed that they were not minded to become like the Prussian nobility, powerless. The great merchant houses had begun to feel the pinch of blockade upon their international commerce and also developed methods of resistance. And the Prussian army, which had been on its feet for six weeks, was tired. The assault on Neisse was broken off on 23 January.

Frederick left the army to recuperate and repaired to Berlin for three weeks of intensive office work. People remarked that he looked in better health than ever before. He was using the recess in playing for position outside Silesia. 'Troops and Thaler,' as the Imperial Chancellor Sinzendorf had once said apropos Frederick William, 'are worth nothing, without allies.' It had been the canker of Frederick William's life that alliances meant only a choice of dependency and that service was expected to precede reward. His son was hoping to reverse both these premisses, right from the start of his reign, on the basis of Prussia's overnight increase.

While complex and delicate negotiations went on in every direction, the diplomatic fencing between Prussia and Austria continued without either break or progress. Frederick now took the line that the road lay open before him to Vienna, but that he still had no wish to make war on Austria: he did not want more than was rightly his—or not much more. Maria Theresa reiterated that, in honour and conscience bound to stand by the Pragmatic Sanction, she would never renounce a particle of Silesia: though provided Frederick instantly withdrew his troops to the last man, she would let him off without war indemnities.* She knew that God was on her side and that English subsidies were in the offing.

* * *

For England was at war with Spain, Spain was supported by France, France was using Bavaria as a stalking horse against

* Francis wrote to Frederick to the same purport but in a different key, closing his letter with kind regards and the hope of undiminished mutual esteem.

Austria and therefore working towards an alliance with Prussia, Prussia had been wooed impetuously but in vain—in the short term between Frederick's accession and the invasion of Silesia—by England who anticipated French attack in Hanover and who was accordingly in sympathy with Austria, against Prussia who was about to make a deal with France, who was the partner of Spain.

* * *

Frederick returned to Silesia towards the end of February and embarked on a criss-cross tour all over the country to inspect the Prussian positions. To enliven the dreary hours of incessant travel, he provided himself with civilian good company: Jordan, Algarotti, and the French mathematician, astronomer, and President-designate of the Berlin Academy, Pierre Louis Moreau de Maupertuis, who was one of the most famous men of science of the day.

The Prussian positions were in excellent order; but during the past month numbers of mounted Austro-Hungarian irregulars had got in, and, harrying the countryside, were proving a serious annoyance. Sketchy though military intelligence was, it became clear that an Austrian offensive was on the way. An army of 15,000 was assembling in Bohemia on the other side of the Sudeten mountains. This side, Prince Leopold the younger had meanwhile taken Glogau, 'whereat his Majesty fairly jumped for joy.' His Majesty hastened to send effusive congratulations to Father Leopold upon the military achievement of his son; the Old Dessauer was on home guard duty—manœuvres, ostensibly—with a large force concentrated near the Saxon border.

Four days later, 13 March, Maria Theresa scored a resounding success in her own sphere. She gave birth to her fifth child, and it was a son at last: 'I wish I were already six months pregnant again!' the happy mother exclaimed when she held the babe in her arms. Vienna went delirious with joy; it even conceded the father's share in the event. Among countless banners and transparencies with which the town was decorated, one depicted Archduke Francis as a woodcarver, turning out boy infants; the caption prophesied more of the same article from that shop. Many others testified to a sudden rise in his popularity. The rest ranged from elaborate allegories and pictorial puns to sturdy declarations like, 'The royal confinement with pleasure has filled/The whole worshipful Tailors' Guild.'*

The birth was taken as an indubitable sign of heavenly blessing, and, coupled with the exploits of the Hungarian horsemen in Silesia, caused a great upsurge of confidence in the Austrian camp. Now it would not be long till the King of Prussia was 'chased back to Apollo and the Muses'.

There was no lack of over-confidence in the Prussian camp, either. The weather had turned colder again, with renewed, heavy snowfall. So long as the snow lay, the land was without a blade of grass to aid raiding cavalry and the mountains must be impassable. Thus it appeared to the invaders from the plains who, having encountered, at the very most, only passive resistance among the people of Silesia, could not conceive of popular loyalist movements in other parts of the Austrian Crown Lands, such as were in fact growing. Having themselves broken all the rules of season, climate, and terrain, last autumn, the Prussians implicitly counted on it that the Austrians, notoriously comfort-loving and convention-bound, would for their part abide by these.

But there was an ardent and unreasonable woman at the head of affairs in Vienna, who did not, would not know the rules. Also, Austria was on the verge of concluding an agreement with England and needed to show that there was life in the old Habsburg compound yet—that England's assistance would not be thrown away on a supine, disintegrating nation. Lastly, the Prussians were preparing to re-occupy the trenches before Neisse and must at all cost be forestalled. With Neisse gone, any hope of recovering Silesia would become remote indeed.

Neippberg, it seemed, was better than his reputation. He had managed to double the forces hitherto available for Silesia and grouped them round a core of tough veterans of the Turkish War. A large proportion of the fresh Bohemian levies were highlanders who would be in their element during the

* 'Über die königliche Niederkunft/Freut sich die ganze Schneiderzunft.'

forthcoming operation. The Croatian, Serbian, and Hungarian volunteer corps swarming to succour their Lady brought with them the élan of adventure and freely offered service; and the local mountain folk pressed forward to act as scouts and guides.

In the second half of March, ice and blizzards notwithstanding, Austrian posts established themselves all over the Sudeten barrier. On 1 April Neippberg began the descent into Silesia, surmounting difficulties of transport so immense that the initial Prussian feat, the great march through the mud, paled by comparison.

The fourth April had been the date set for the resumption of the siege of Neisse. The plan was to concentrate all the Prussian army in that area, for the dual purpose of assault and preventing relief. The bulk of the younger Prince Leopold's force could now be withdrawn from the Glogau region, and Schwerin was ordered to evacuate the Beskid approaches, since nothing stirred in that quarter. Frederick with the remainder went to meet Schwerin between Troppau and Jägerndorf, to ensure a sufficiently dense coverage of what both thought Neippberg's only feasible route into Silesia.

Neippberg was taking the infeasible, the non-existent road. On Easter Sunday, 2 April, the Prussian high command received the first intimation of this, quite by chance, through a deserter, whose information necessarily was neither comprehensive nor exact.

While the Prussians, amid a confusion of argument, recriminations, and ambiguous orders, were yet manœuvring to complete their deflective pattern, the Austrians—dragging everything they had, baggage, fodder, cannon, pontoon timbers; thick, driving snow in their faces all the way—reached the plains. On 4 April their whole army was safely on Silesian soil, and the Prussians, so far from proceeding to the bombardment of Neisse, were separated into three sections that could no longer communicate, although they had yet to discover this. At mid-day on the 5th Neippberg entered Neisse from the south, to the cheers of the inhabitants.

Still neither army knew precisely where the other was. Their scouts saw nothing, heard nothing, even though at times enemy columns marched or bivouacked almost within hailing distance. The snow kept on falling, obscuring vision, deadening sound, erasing tracks, and obviating dust, that standard clue of military detection.

With Neisse giving him an undisputed base of operations, Neippberg turned towards Brieg and Ohlau, to break the blockade of the former and recapture the latter with its large Prussian munitions depot. The town and fortress of Neisse lay on the eastern bank of a river also called Neisse which, taking a roughly rectangular turn north before joining the Oder below Brieg, thus formed two sides of a moat-like square with Brieg at the opposite extremity, a distance of twenty-eight miles from Fort Neisse. Twice Frederick and Schwerin found themselves frustrated in effecting a crossing of this river. The tables had been turned: the threat to Brieg and Ohlau involved the whole of Lower Silesia.

At length the King, forced farther up the river, managed to get across. Once more the enemies vanished from each other's ken, once more trying to beat each other to the goal, blind. A pitched battle was what both desired now. Frederick on 8 April wrote a tender letter of farewell and testamentary dispositions to his brother and heir. Neippberg stopped in his advance on Brieg to grope hither and thither for the opponent.

On 9 April the wildest snowstorm of that spring immobilized both parties. The Austrians were encamped by a group of hamlets named Mollwitz, Grünigen, and Hünern, the Prussians, not two hours' march away, at the twin villages of Pogarell and Alzenau—with a stretch of woodland fortuitously interposed between each other's patrols.

In the morning of 10 April the snow lay two feet high but abruptly ceased to fall. The sky cleared, calm and blue, the sun shone brightly, and two villagers of Mollwitz made their way into the Prussian camp to tell about the Austrian. The whole district was uniformly Protestant, and the Austrians themselves received no warning—not until the Prussians, forming up in battle order diagonally south of Mollwitz, were sighted from the look-out turrets of Brieg.

As Frederick later analysed the situation, he failed to exploit, and thus forfeited, the advantage of surprise. It was not only his first battle to direct, but the first he had ever seen. The world was watching; all his gains were in the balance; here was the chance of turning annexation into conquest.

Carefully, conscientiously, the four Prussian columns were put through the accustomed manœuvres, deploying in two lines—the first commanded by Schwerin, the second by the younger Prince Leopold—300 paces apart, artillery at their head, cavalry in flanking positions at once covered and somewhat compressed by a spinney on the right and a small stream to the leftward. Thus they began to advance in flawless unison, with fife and drum and flying colours, having given the enemy time to form up too behind a screen of cavalry activity. At the rate of '90 shots to a Paternoster', the Prussian artillery began to rake this vanguard; the white ground was ploughed black and covered with fallen bodies. The Austrian guns were not yet ready.

Numerically the opponents were about equal in strength. However, in the Prussian army infantry predominated, and its cavalry was far outweighed by the Austrian. Both Frederick William and the Old Dessauer had carried home a traumatic contempt for cavalry from an incident at Malplaquet, the effects of which were about to become manifest.

Maddened under the Prussian fire, the main body of the Austrian cavalry broke formation and stampeded in roaring descent upon the Prussian lines. The Prussian cavalry disintegrated at the first impact and was driven back piecemeal into the ranks of its own infantry, between, before, behind the two extended lines, pursuers and pursued inextricably mixed.The King, on the right wing, was sucked away into the mêlée and in furious despair tried to stem the rush, crying, 'Brothers! Children! Lads! Your country's honour! Your King's life!'

He succeeded in collecting a few squadrons, only to have them swept asunder again, and thereupon forged on alone until he reached Schwerin, on the extreme left. The Prussian infantry still stood unshaken but had lost its bearings, firing in all directions and hitting friend as well as foe. It seemed a miracle that Frederick had not been touched by either; all round the casualties were mounting thick and fast. His generals desired nothing so much as to get him out of the way; Frederick

REMUSBERG
The Chateau of Rheinsberg

THE BRIDE
Elizabeth Christine of Bevern-Brunswick

FREDERICK'S FACTOTUM
Michael Gabriel Fredersdorf

FREDERICK'S FOREIGN MINISTER
Henry von Podewils

himself believed the battle lost, and believed that the others thought so too.*

He was persuaded—with how much or how little difficulty it is hard to ascertain—to leave the field. With a small escort, he was advised to ride to Oppeln, a safe Prussian post with a bridge across the Oder, thirty-five miles away.

The Prussians were not to know that the enemy charge had irretrievably spent itself, the Austrian cavalry now scattered, exhausted, partially bogged down in marshy ground beyond the brook on the left Prussian flank, out of reach of orders; while, having seen their horsemen disappear, the Austrian infantry could scarcely be brought to move. Yet the rooted, inflexible Prussian discipline and adherence to method now paid off.

Disembarrassed of concern for the King's safety, the senior generals bent their whole attention on the infantry. With an eye to the abiding antagonism of foot and horse, Schwerin addressed the unbroken front: no battle had ever been won or lost by cavalry alone; everything depended on the infantry now; their King was unharmed. Under the spell of the eleventh hour and with what seemed like telepathic co-operation on the part of all commanders, the regiments that had stood like a wall moved forward, like a wall now walking, across the corpse-strewn field—a credit to the Old Dessauer, a vindication of the much-mocked 'Drill Sergeant' Frederick William, a terror to their target.

'I never in my life saw anything more beautiful,' an Austrian officer who lived to vent his aesthetic appreciation, wrote after the battle. 'They marched with the utmost composure, arrow-straight, their front like a plumb-line, absolutely level, as if they had been on parade, their side arms glittering with the most superb effect in the declining sun, their volleys sounding without pause like a continuous growl of thunder.'

The Austrian infantry, with its large bolstering of raw recruits, wavered, fell apart, hid one behind the other, expended its ammunition out of range, formed 'sheep-like huddles,'

* 'The crisis was so severe,' he wrote in his memoirs, 'that old, experienced officers saw no solution. . . . Let this be a lesson to young warriors, not to despair too soon.'

Neippberg raged, 'between which one could have set up whole cavalry regiments,' standards crowding together in very bundles; broke up; began to run. Just after sunset, about eight o'clock, the rout was complete. The Austrians poured back into the quarters they had left at noon with instructions to have their soup kept hot, but only to evacuate them now at speed. In the darkness the retreat continued as far as Grottkau and the Neisse River—nearly the same distance from Mollwitz as Oppeln. The pursuit was not pressed; Schwerin, twice-wounded, was in favour of doing so but yielded to Prince Leopold's dissuasion. The losses on both sides were almost equal: 4,613 Prussians killed, wounded, and missing, 4,410 Austrians; also four Austrian battle standards and nine cannon.*

Only an hour after Frederick's departure Schwerin had sent a messenger after the King, to say that with God's help he now had hope of winning the battle. But Frederick rode too fast and was not found for ten hours. Most of his attendants having gradually dropped behind, it was night when he reached Oppeln. But Oppeln in the meantime had been taken over by Austrian raiders. The sentries, to their everlasting chagrin afterwards, gave fire, and the King galloped off again into the night.

After more than forty-eight hours without either sleep or food, Frederick's spirit now gave way; he muttered to himself despondently while doubling back across the River Neisse to a place called Löwen, where on the way out he had left part of his escort. Remembering what had happened at Oppeln, he wished first to make sure Löwen was still in Prussian hands; he could not believe it when an adjutant came out to meet him with the news of victory at Mollwitz.

At daybreak, 'in the shop at the corner of the market place' of Löwen, one Widow Panzern made the King a cup of coffee and served with it a roast fowl. He ate and drank and then rode back to the field of victory from which he had fled.

* Among those taken prisoner was Frederick's distinguished travelling companion, Maupertuis. He had been treed and captured by a party of Austrian hussars, who robbed him of wig, watch, and nearly everything else he had on him. Transported to Vienna and released on parole, he complained to Archduke Francis, who immediately pulled out his own watch and gave it to Maupertuis.

'Mollwitz,' he wrote later, 'was my school,' and would list in minute detail his mistakes, the lessons to be drawn from them, and the feats of heroism and skill of those 'who won the day for me'. About the ride to Oppeln, he never wrote nor said a word. Garrulous as he was about his faults, his follies, and the more discreditable of his motives, those ten hours joined the year of 1730 in that limbo which possibly accommodated also a certain surgical misadventure about 1728.

BRANDENBURG
to Berlin
Wittenberg
Dessau
Halle
Leipzig
SAXONY
LUSATIA
KOTTBUS
Krossen
Görlitz
Meissen
Dresden
Kesselsdorf
Katholis
Hennersd
R. Elbe
Prague
Chotusitz
R. Elb
BOHEM
R. Sazaw
R. Moldau
Sahay
R. Danube
BAVARIA
UPPER
AUSTR
Linz
to Munich

TERRITORY OF THE
1ST & 2ND SILESIAN WARS
gau
W E R
L
E
S
I
A
Liegnitz
Breslau
POLAND
icht
Striegau
Ohlau
Brieg
henfriedberg
Mollwitz
Löwen
Oppeln
Grottkau
U P P E R
autenau
Soor
Eypel
R. Neisse
Neisse
Glatz
Ottmachau
C. OF GLATZ
R. Oder
Jägerndorf
Troppau
A
Olmütz
M O R A V I A
Brünn
HUNGARY
O W E R
A
Vienna
MILES
0
25
50
75
100

CHAPTER 21
THE WAR OF THE AUSTRIAN SUCCESSION

By common maxim, the object of a battle was to drive the enemy off the field. This the Prussians had overwhelmingly achieved at Mollwitz. Although the contestant armies had been equal in strength, the contestant nations were not; in the eyes of the world, mighty Austria had played Goliath to little Prussia's David. Neippberg was reviled in Austria and despised everywhere else, while Frederick was inundated with congratulations and foreign overtures. Frederick could not have received more applause had he been personally responsible for the victory and had the Austrian army been annihilated instead of remaining in possession of Neisse and with that in control of Upper Silesia, which previously the Prussians had already held.

He wrote the good news to Wilhelmine, he wrote it to Voltaire, and the dammed founts of poesy sprang again, richly.

'To write verses, and good verses, after a victory,' Voltaire returned in the same incense-offering spirit as was universally abroad—though with his characteristic technique of keeping flattery in bounds by laying it on with the trowel and a little grit of irony, 'is unique and thus reserved to your Majesty. You have beaten Neippberg and Voltaire. Your Majesty should put laurel leaves in your letters, like the ancient Roman generals. You deserve at once the triumph of a general and of a poet, and you need at least two laurel leaves. . . . Among what dangers and labours you pass your wonderful life!'

But Frederick, who with his earlier, easy success had in private shown all the insufferable symptoms of conceit, did not let adulation go to his head this time. His demeanour was uniformly modest; and, apart from giving out the text, 'Let the woman learn in silence with all subjection. But I suffer not a woman to teach, nor to usurp authority over the man, but to be in silence,'* for the Victory Thanksgiving service, he possessed himself with diplomatic reserve and circumspection. He still held back from finally concluding the agreement with France.

Since the middle of March—after an abrupt revision of foreign policy in St Petersburg—an agreement most dangerous to him had been in process of negotiation, designed to put a stop to the Prussian 'Undertaking' before it should turn into 'War', a war, that is, involving everybody else willy-nilly and beyond selective planning. The intending signatories were England, Holland, Saxony, and now Russia, in concert with Austria; signature had been delayed by the difficulty of adjusting the projected partition of Prussia to the demands of all five allies. Nonetheless troops were already gathering in Hanover, Saxony, and Russian Livonia. Frederick had been hesitating to accept the French offer precisely because his patent need of such an alliance placed him in an inferior position to France and so affected the terms.

Mollwitz caused an immediate change in the situation. Saxony and Holland drew back, Sweden prepared to disengage Russia's attention from Silesia, England and Austria were left alone together. France sketched out a provisional repeal of the Pragmatic Sanction, by which Upper Austria, Bohemia, and Breisgau were to go to Bavaria, the Austrian Milanese to Spain, Moravia and Upper Silesia to Saxony; Prussia to retain Lower Silesia, leaving the Queen of Hungary with her titular Kingdom and Lower Austria, Styria, Carinthia and Carniola —less than two-thirds of her guaranteed inheritance. A French emissary was despatched to Germany in the hope of promoting general secession from the Pragmatic Sanction on the basis of that sketch. He was Marshal Count Charles Louis Auguste Fouquet Belle-Isle, a brilliant and versatile man, at fifty-three

* Timothy I, chapter 2, verses 11–12.

leader of the 'young' war party at Versailles, and whose mission in itself, therefore, was a set-back to the pacific conservatism of Fleury. The official purpose of the mission was to help Germany decide on her next Emperor.

England was threatened with a still greater increase in weight to the Bourbon combination than what she had been striving to prevent.

The news of Mollwitz did not get to London for a fortnight —by which time the victor's headquarters already resembled the venue of an international congress. Now England entered the fray in the rôle of arbitrator, in an attempt to save the Pragmatic Sanction by a compromise between Austria and Prussia. Lord Hyndford at Prussian headquarters, Sir Thomas Robinson in Vienna—the British ambassadors laboured tirelessly and thanklessly, as Maria Theresa would not agree to yielding an inch of Silesian soil and Frederick laughed at the suggestion that he should give up his conquest for two million Thaler and a renewal of the vexed Jülich-Berg guarantee.

However, Frederick kept Hyndford dangling the while he was yet finessing with Belle-Isle, whom he had regaled with a ringside seat at the smart and efficient siege of Brieg. 'When there is a chance of profiting by honourable procedure, let's be men of honour,' Frederick gaily wrote to Podewils, 'and when duplicity is called for, we'll be knaves.'

Of all Frederick's correspondence, it was of course this letter which fell into Austrian hands and was publicized far and wide with appropriately damaging effect to the author's reputation. Not published was the paragraph leading up to the impudent avowal: 'To persist in acting as a man of honour among knaves is an immensely dangerous thing, and to deal honourably with a pack of swindlers is a desperate enterprise with extremely dubious prospects.'

Brieg capitulated after a week, on 4 May; its Austrian garrison marched away to Neisse on parole not to take arms against Prussia for two years. To all intents and purposes the armies of Frederick and Neippberg stayed where they were, doing little more than bare their teeth at one another. Frederick used the interim to overhaul, restock, and exercise his cavalry. 'Our infantry are heroes to a man,' he had written after Mollwitz.

'As for our cavalry—the devil wouldn't take it as a gift.' Perhaps he was not altogether sorry that his father and the Old Dessauer had left something for him to add to the war machine he had inherited ready-made.

On the Prussian side Podewils was acting as Fleury's counterpart, doing his level best to dissuade Frederick from a pact with France which at that juncture must inevitably lead to war in Europe. But there was no holding the two prime negotiators, to whom such a war presented itself as a justified gamble. Belle-Isle was carrying all before him at the courts of the Empire, and Frederick saw a good chance of an eventual settlement in which he would obtain more than his factual acquisitions to date, instead of less as variously proposed hitherto.

On 4 June France and Prussia signed a pact of mutual defence, binding for fifteen years, but not as yet to be revealed; while in sanguine mood Maria Theresa was preparing for her coronation in Hungary.

On 19 June she started down the Danube on her state voyage to Pressburg, the capital of Hungary, where a crowd of thousands welcomed her with heart-warming ovations. However, for all their human responsiveness to so young and charming a Queen, the Hungarian Estates had not lost sight of their opportunity to win back sundry ancient privileges and extra rights which had gradually passed into desuetude under her predecessors. It took five days to arrive at an acceptable formula, and Maria Theresa drove to her coronation looking noticeably paler and less radiant than at her coming. Francis had accompanied her, but as a husband only: without any official standing whatsoever in Hungary, he had to find a place among the spectators. Alone, Maria Theresa was invested with the mantle, sword and crown of St Stephen, the first Christian King of Hungary* and was acclaimed with the nicely devised flourish, 'Vivat domina et rex noster!' Then, mounted on a black charger, she accomplished the most exacting part of the rite and galloped up the 'Hill of Coronation', on the summit of which she swung St Stephen's holy sword towards the four quarters of the globe, in token of the ancient Magyar chieftains'

* A.D. 977–1038. The Hungarian Crown passed to the House of Habsburg, by female inheritance, in 1526.

proud style of Rulers of the World. That done, she recovered the glow of health and happiness, enchanting everyone at the festivities which followed.

A few days later came the news of the Franco-Prussian pact. Her Ministers, reported Robinson, 'sank back into their chairs, pale as corpses'; only one heart remained steadfast, he said—that of the Queen.* She needed all she had in her of fortitude to steel herself and sustain everyone around her against a tide of bad news of which this was only the start.

The harassed efforts of the Austrian Government to make the German States guarantee their old guarantees of the Pragmatic Sanction, foundered against the eloquence, the nervous stamina, the bribes, and not least the vicarious display of the French Crown's wealth and power, of Marshal Belle-Isle—who, travelling with a dazzling retinue of 130 and voluminous baggage, transformed his every resting-place into a temporary fairyland of authoritative splendour. One after the other, the guarantees—as Prince Eugene had predicted—proved worth less than the parchment they were written on. Frederick's argument—that Prussia had given her guarantee on the understanding that the Emperor guaranteed her succession to Jülich-Berg, whereupon the Emperor had promptly signed away Jülich-Berg to the Palatinate—was by far the least flimsy. One by one the Electoral votes swung into place behind Belle-Isle's leadership. For a time only did the French-sponsored candidature hang in the balance as between Augustus III of Saxony and Charles Albert of Bavaria; then it settled definitely on the latter. Although the fact that he could claim never to have supported the Pragmatic Sanction at all, was not what had decided the issue in his favour, at least it lent him some aesthetic countenance.

The official announcement of Charles Albert's candidature was hardly out when French troops wearing cockades of the Bavarian colours, blue and white, crossed the Rhine and moved into German territory. By the middle of August the Bavarian

*Maria Theresa disliked the British Ambassador for what she deemed his patronizing manner and brutally practical advice: yet Robinson worked indefatigably in her interests; Frederick spoke of him as besotted with adoration.

army, thus swelled by 40,000, was on the march in the direction of the Upper Austrian frontier.

Maria Theresa, having all this time withstood, in solitary defiance, a concert of pessimism, gave in at last. She signed the cabinet order authorizing the offer of Lower Silesia to Prussia, with the words, 'Placet, because no other way out, but with greatest sorrow. Maria Theresa.'

It was too late. The offer which not many weeks before would have found ready acceptance, was rejected. The Queen's advisers in their turn had no alternative but to concur with her last hope, which was to call the whole Crown Lands to arms, starting with Hungary.

Two centuries of Habsburg maladministration now bore fruit. Torn between vindictive obduracy and the temptations of blackmail, the Hungarian Diet was united in resistance to the Crown's appeal. In the course of stormy discussions a flood of venom became launched against the Queen herself. Maria Theresa was deeply hurt by an onslaught of hatred and scurrilities which in view of the recent demonstrations of loyal enthusiasm appeared to her as the blackest treachery. She wept bitter tears, but still her resolution did not falter. She could not understand and so would not believe that men might really be so insensible to their moral obligations. She would speak to them herself.

Her Ministers raised fresh objections, foreseeing a Hungarian rebellion directly Austrian arms supplied the necessary means. Against all warnings, the Queen asked a group of the most influential magnates to a private talk and threw herself upon their loyalty and courage—with that gift of extempore oratory which, going straight to the heart, was so effective an expression of her personality. The response was instantaneous; the Hungarian magnates there and then swore to support her to the death. It may be that the gloomy prophecies of her Ministers, which had become known, unexpectedly aided the Queen: for when the scene was repeated at a plenary assembly of the Diet, there were shouts of *death to any who would come between the Queen and her Hungarians!* Vowing life and blood to her cause, the Hungarian Estates in a rapture of love and pity granted everything she wished. Hungary would furnish an army

100,000 strong and grant Archduke Francis the title, if not the powers, of co-regent.

This celebrated session took place at Pressburg on 11 September 1741. On 15 September the Elector of Bavaria entered Linz, the chief city of Upper Austria, which opened its ill-defended gates without a struggle to his combined forces. Neippberg's army was tied down in Silesia; the promised Hungarian army did not yet exist; other potential relief, such as it might be, was far away. Moreover, a Saxon army was gathering close by to assist in the dismembering of the Habsburg lands. The whole of Upper Austria paid homage to Charles Albert. Vienna, divided in its sympathies, deserted by most of the Government and fast emptying of all who could flee, was as good as lost.

'Only in Rome can the Romans be beaten,' the King of Prussia urged his new allies. But Charles Albert's heart was set on seeing himself crowned King of Bohemia, the dominion where Maria Theresa had not yet had time to be invested with anoïnted sovereignty; and he would not be cheated of his victory celebrations meanwhile. Every day that passed with festivities and debate at Linz, favoured the organizing of resistance at Vienna.

Maria Theresa had got an ally, and that, in a sense, where she most needed one, at home: Field-Marshal Count Ludwig Andreas Khevenhüller, of long and distinguished service in the Austrian army, recommended by Prince Eugene as the best general he had, unblemished in the Turkish War, and now President of the War Council. Just as, almost alone, Khevenhüller had stood with the Queen in taking a more balanced view of Neippberg's defeat at Mollwitz, he backed her militancy at this hour of greatest peril. Charged with the defence of Vienna, he confounded the reputed Austrian pace and did wonders, both in last-minute repairs of the fortifications and collecting and shaping manpower. The drooping spirit of the remaining civil population rose; the University hung out its war flag, and everywhere the able-bodied drilled.

About the middle of October the Bavarian advance along the southern bank of the Danube suddenly halted. The allied armies turned sharply about, crossed the river, and made straight for Bohemia. Vienna, and with it all Lower Austria, was saved.

Indeed the prospect had been darkest before the dawn, though by how much it had brightened for Austria was known only to a very small group of people.

On 9 October a mysterious meeting had been held at a certain secluded castle, named Klein-Schnellendorf. It was situated in the Brieg-Neisse region, midway between the Prussian and Austrian headquarters in Silesia. The owner was from home. On 8 October all his servants and retainers were scooped up under wholesale arrest by Austrian military and taken away for twenty-four hours 'on suspicion of treason' (and afterwards released without further explanation).

The meeting was convened by the British Ambassador, Lord Hyndford, and those circuitously coming to attend it with him were Field-Marshal Neippberg and one of his generals, Lentulus, and the King of Prussia with his adjutant Goltz. They came without guards, without grooms, without secretaries: entirely unattended. Hyndford himself wrote out three copies of a summary of the proceedings, the upshot of which was nothing less than a secret armistice.

His Majesty of Prussia, and Field-Marshal Neippberg on behalf of her Hungarian Majesty, pledged their word of honour, the one to allow the Austrian army in Silesia to retire to Moravia, the other to hand over Neisse to the Prussians after a pretended siege of fourteen days. The whole transaction was to be surrounded by continuous sham—but only sham—hostilities. Frederick was to be left in possession of Lower Silesia and Neisse, and to winter in Upper Silesia, undertaking to cause no serious damage and to pay his way. All being well, a formal treaty should be signed before the end of the year; meanwhile both parties bound themselves not to join in any attacks on England, whatsoever and wheresoever. Frederick reserved the right to disavow the contract if the condition of absolute secrecy were violated.

For Frederick was, of course, breaking faith with his allies. The manner in which the Franco-Bavarian invasion had been conducted, together with the ambiguities of the surrounding inter-allied negotiations, had convinced him that it was the old story, all over again: that he had been cast for the rôle of cat's paw and, eventually, vassal at best, in the same relationship to the King of France as Frederick William's to the Emperor. He wished to arm himself with some provisional safeguard, and at the same time create a cheap diversion in Moravia-Bohemia: it was not at all in Prussia's interest to see Austria wholly crushed and France, unchecked by any counterweight, with a free hand in Western Europe. Under the present, secret, gentleman's agreement, Neippberg's army would be freed for the defence of Bohemia, allowing Frederick's army to rest and re-equip in peace. Should the situation change, Frederick would be able to break an unsigned compact just as well as a formal treaty.

On 1 November, Neisse surrendered as agreed; on 7 November Frederick received the homage of Lower Silesia, in Breslau, amid the usual pomp and jubilation; on 11 November he arrived in Berlin. On the night of 25 November his allies captured Prague and enabled the Bavarian Elector to style himself King of Bohemia. Unfortunately for Neippberg's rescue operation, Archduke Francis had been placed in supreme command over the armies released from Silesia and with cumbrous to and fro had wasted the precious time which had been gained by the enemy's previous hesitation at Linz.

About the same time, before word of this came through to Prussia, Frederick, meeting Hyndford by chance, had stopped to tell the British Ambassador in passing that the secret of Klein-Schnellendorf was out: 'The Court of Vienna told the Empress Dowager Amelia,* who told the Court of Munich; the Austrian Minister in Paris has told Fleury; the Austrian Minister to Russia has told it at St Petersburg; Robinson through the British Minister in Saxony has told it at Dresden; and members of your Government have talked of it publicly in London.' Without further comment other than a shrug, Hyndford reported, the King had then gone on his way.

In other words, while it was not yet known how matters were going to turn out at Prague, Frederick had shown himself provided with cause to repudiate the Klein-Schnellendorf agreement, should events recommend this as the better part.

* Emperor Joseph's widow, aunt to Maria Theresa and mother-in-law to the Bavarian Elector.

The fall of Prague to his allies did so recommend it.

The news reached Frederick on 29 November, and he publicly drank the health of the new King of Bohemia.

He no longer had his reputation as a man of honour to worry about: that ballast was already lost. His father had worried himself to death about *his* integrity; and what had this profited Frederick William, or Prussia?

CHAPTER 22

END OF THE FIRST SILESIAN WAR

'In no other war,' wrote Clausewitz, discussing what became known as the First Silesian War, 'has strategy been so saturated with politics.'

In a general appreciation of the wars of Frederick, Clausewitz therefore gives very little space to it, and significantly places the beginning at 1741, not 1740. He might have gone further: for if, by Clausewitz's famous dictum, war be nothing more than the continuation of politics by other means, then the Silesian Undertaking never rightly became a war at all. The 'other means' only entered into it in sample form, exhibiting potentials, underlining seriousness of intention, and, to be sure, as a deterrent.*

The War of the Austrian Succession, which Frederick's (as it were) pseudo-war precipitated, was real war, in that at every stage the issue rested on armed combat. Yet finally the outcome was determined by the *political* factor of Frederick's *military* participation in it.

Upon the capture of Prague by a Franco-Bavarian army under the noses of Neippberg and Archduke Francis, Frederick recommenced hostilities in December. The greater part of the Prussian forces made a successful push south and before the year was out were established on the Moravian plateau.

For the moment there was nothing to be gained by Prussia from holding aloof and so losing any influence on the course of

* Frederick became one of the first advocates of a universal arms race as the medium of universal Peace.

the war, incidentally forfeiting a share in the spoils. Also, both the resources and the goodwill of Lower Silesia, which had had Prussian armies quartered on it for well over a year, were becoming exhausted. It would be well to open up new pastures, at the same time getting hold of a piece of territory that would come in useful for purposes of bargaining, in relation alike to Frederick's allies and his adversary.

Although Frederick had broken the agreement of Klein-Schnellendorf with an alacrity verging on the grotesque, the motives from which he had entered into it stood fast. Austria must not be destroyed, or it would be the worse for Prussia.

In much the same way Frederick's allies—France, Bavaria, and now also Saxony—passed over the 'secret' betrayal, transient as it had proved. France was not championing Bavaria in order to make Bavaria great in the place of a reduced Austria. Bavaria had no wish to see her Saxon confederate and rival doing too well out of the joint enterprise. Saxony hoped that Prussia in the end result would pull the Moravian chestnut out of the fire for her. With Prussia active in the coalition, the rest could play her off against each other and simultaneously keep her under some restraint.

Austria was making an unexpected recovery.

The mobilization of Hungary being in full swing, Maria Theresa had returned to Vienna, also in December. As before labouring against a consensus of pessimism, against her own qualms, and, not least, against the handicap of another pregnancy, she forced through her own defence plan, of attack. In the third week of January her mainstay Khevenhüller led his army out of Vienna—leaving the town all but defenceless, but yet with a euphoric send-off at the hands of its inhabitants–and marched on Linz, the principal Bavarian garrison in Upper Austria.

The irresolution for which the luckless Neippberg was universally blamed appeared at an end. The waste of time was all on the other side, as the leaders of the French, Saxons, and Prussians wrangled for supreme command or at least a mutually acceptable modus operandi. Khevenhüller raced them to Linz and thus not only recaptured that important stronghold, but also eliminated—under parole for one year—10,000 French troops.

In a matter of days almost the whole of Upper Austria was regained. From there Khevenhüller followed the Danube into Bavaria, thus drawing off the Bavarian complements of the French second army on the River Moldau. What had been planned as a diversion developed into conquest. Within a week or two Khevenhüller had the mastery of all southern Bavaria—albeit nominally under Archduke Francis. Francis had been recalled from the northern theatre of war in time to partake of the first major success of Austrian arms since the heyday of Prince Eugene. His northern post was filled by his brother, Prince Charles of Lorraine, whose first act of reorganization was to get rid of Neippberg.

Charles Albert of Bavaria took no part in his own especial war. He was detained at Frankfurt-on-Main, the hallowed city of high Imperial functions, seething now with princes, diplomats, and sightseers for the Election. The principle of status once again proved its overriding power: nothing at that moment could have persuaded the winning candidate to leave for home. On 24 January he was elected Holy Roman Emperor of the German Nation, by unanimous vote; the vote of Bohemia having been declared void in virtue of the sex of Maria Theresa, with whom technically it still rested.

While an Austrian army swept across his hereditary lands, the Emperor-elect stayed on at Frankfurt, engrossed in the preparations for his coronation—with a fixed avidity that might strike one as incomprehensible, had not Maria Theresa shown herself similarly affected. To her, too, the enemy's symbolic-social triumph appeared for the moment to outweigh his actual reverses.

On 12 February the Elector of Bavaria was duly crowned Emperor Charles VII—though disappointed of recognition as Archduke of Austria and King of Bohemia, titles which Khevenhüller's huge recoupments had cancelled. On that same 12 February Khevenhüller for his part crowned his campaign with the occupation of Munich, capital of Bavaria. 'Et Caesar, et nihil,' mocked the Viennese wits. Caesar's ally, the King of Prussia, was moved to remark that the Bavarian Field-Marshal Count Törring resembled a drum: one only heard of him when he was being beaten.

Frederick never could find it in him to forgo either a good quip or a bad pun, regardless at whose expense, regardless of damage to himself. He called the indefatigable Hyndford 'Lord Hundsfott' or Blackguard; he rewarded Podewils' loyal political contortions on the King's behalf by addressing him as, 'My dear Mountebank'. He early ensured the antagonism of the new Tzarina Elizabeth—which he could ill afford—by his irresponsible shafts; and he did not now spare the Saxon King-Elector or his commanders (Counts Maurice de Saxe and Rutowsky, two of Augustus the Strong's glamorous bastards, with a third in reserve, called Chevalier de Saxe), and the French Field-Marshal de Broglie offered an irresistible target.

Unfortunately from Frederick's point of view, Belle-Isle, that man after his own heart, as able in the council chamber as in the field, had been laid low by rheumatic fever soon after the Imperial Election which he, as good as single-handed, had steered to the desired goal. Belle-Isle's Moravian command had gone to Broglie, another veteran of the Spanish Succession Wars, but one who had not worn so well as some (for instance, Belle-Isle himself, Khevenhüller, the Old Dessauer, Buddenbrock, Schwerin and various others in both camps—one might think the conflict of 1701–1714 had been especially health-building for generals). At one stage of his career Broglie had won considerable negative fame by narrowly escaping capture —minus his trousers. At another stage, more recently, he had been commandant of Strasburg: he it was whom Frederick's incognito visit there had caught embarrassingly off balance. Frederick lost few opportunities of alluding to those two incidents and drawing analogies to Broglie's generalship in the present war. Broglie, a stickler for etiquette and rank, in any case regarded the King *in* Prussia as an upstart, and accordingly wounded Frederick's dignity in return. French and Saxons compared notes on their arrogant and uncomfortable partner and sent home reports intended to set their respective governments against him, not without effect. Since in this as in all military alliances co-operation was perpetually subject to considerations of national and personal pride (to say nothing of proportionate future rewards), every drop of bad blood poisoning relations between the allied leaders had its logistic consequences.

If the military operations were fraught with politics, policy was influenced by personalities to an exceptional degree. Just as Maria Theresa had felt the blow of Charles VII's election more keenly than the balm of victory, so, from scarcely less emotional causes, was she more occupied with the loss of Silesia than with any inroad into her other provinces. Conversely, her personal feelings towards the Emperor were nothing like as bitter as those which Frederick elicited. Both Charles VII and Augustus of Saxony were as much members of the family as her own 'dear Old Man' Francis, since their wives were the daughters of a Habsburg Emperor, her uncle Joseph I—never mind if their attacks on the Austrian Crown Lands were based on that fact. Blood was thicker than water, and she did not hate them. Nor did the quibbling falseness of Cardinal Fleury incense her to the same extent as the brazen cynicism of Frederick, the little Margrave of Brandenburg, merest vassal to her father and as such holder of the subaltern feudal office of 'Imperial Basin-bearer', the heretic, the ingrate, the destroyer from within. Frederick to her was the worst, the real enemy; and she was quite right.

Whatever the motives, now frivolous,* now patriotic, which Frederick at various times attributed to himself—the mainspring of his aggression had undoubtedly been the longing to achieve, at the very outset of his career, what ancestor after ancestor of Frederick William's despised son had toiled for in vain: the ultimate cohesion, and commensurate power, of their State. Although regression now would not necessarily mean ruin, it would send him right back to where the Great Elector had had to stop, forced to write off everything he had staked on the attempt. In this sense, then, the issue for Prussia, as for Austria, was one of life or death; none of the others had as much to lose, for all that they stood to gain as much or more.

Yet, by the perverse algebra of human transactions, a separate peace between the two deadly foes was in the interests of both. Once Prussia resigned from the contest, Austria was

* 'I was young, had plenty of money, a big army, and wanted to see my name in the newspapers.'

certain to come out on top, now that English subsidies, fiery Hungarian levies in their thousands, and the Austrian successes in the south had brought new vigour to her war effort. Frederick, on the other hand, would be wise to strike a bargain while yet his bargaining position appeared sound.

Factually his position was not good. His war fund had sunk from 10 million to 3 million Thaler and was still sinking fast, provisions were more and more hard to come by, communications still harder to maintain, his troops worn down by incessant skirmishes and guerilla resistance, his allies less and less amenable to the ostensible, common purpose.

Thus it was that secret peace talks between Austria and Prussia were carried on almost uninterruptedly, having been resumed as speedily after Frederick's repudiation of Klein-Schnellendorf as this had followed on the agreement itself. To Maria Theresa it seemed she was alone in drawing the obvious inference from that affair: namely, simply, that Frederick was not to be trusted. But had she known it, Frederick in his private reflections expressed the wonder, which cannot but touch the posthumous onlooker too, that anybody ever bothered with treaties at all.

Whilst unwillingly giving her consent to these parleys—English pressure was cogent, and to talk Frederick round, man to man if possible, had become a pet scheme with Francis—Maria Theresa backed her belief that the only way to eliminate Prussia from the war was to do so in physical fact. After profound heart-searching, she decided to halt Khevenhüller's progress in the south, ordered him to send 12,000 men—more than half his fighting strength—to the support of the Prince of Lorraine in Moravia, and authorized the main offensive there.

The Emperor was reported on his way to Prague, to have himself crowned King of Bohemia after all. Prussian hussars were raiding the approaches to Vienna, penetrating almost to the gates; Glatz, in its strategic eminence on the borders at once of Silesia, Bohemia and Moravia, was about to fall to the Prussians. However, owing to the Saxons' refusal to honour their military commitments, the allies had had to abandon the siege of Brünn—the strongest fortress of Moravia, which was to this province as Neisse to Silesia.

Dissension among the enemy, it was well-known in Vienna, had reached a pitch where the Saxons were about to drop out and the French met every Prussian-recommended plan with bland equivocation. What with the fresh Hungarian levies infiltrating the Beskid heights, to descend into Upper Silesia from the east and cut across it laterally, this was the moment for the Prince of Lorraine to move midway between the two defining points of Prague, the Emperor's destination, and Frederick's Moravian headquarters at Olmütz, thus to foil the one and threaten the other's line of retreat to Silesia.

It was now April. Frederick had already decided on retreat early in March, but held out until the last possible moment, for the sake of the peace negotiations which, however, failed to prosper in time. As he put it in an 'easy little military lesson' to Jordan: Moravia, a poor country, could not be held for lack of victual, having been reduced to such a state of want and desperation that no enemy could subsist on it.

That concise sketch of an appalling picture applied equally to the conditions surrounding the Prussian withdrawal—arduous, hungry, harassed, and very bloody.

Nevertheless Frederick's situation, taken by and large, was not as bad as might appear in close-up detail. Though in his rear Olmütz, which he had much desired to keep hold of, had had to be evacuated, on the same day (25 April) Glatz, far more important, came into Prussian hands. Though Moravia had returned, entire, under Austrian dominion, Prussia's tenure of Silesia remained secure, particularly as the Old Dessauer, called in at last with his reserves, punctually entered Upper Silesia and cleared the Beskid mountainside of the Hungarian outposts. The Prussian magazines had so far everywhere been saved, and food supplies—meagre and tardy enough—were coming through again; also, by Hyndford's offices the negotiations with Vienna were continuing.

Characteristically for the whole tangle of events, it was through those negotiations that Frederick conceived a sudden violent desire to end them, whatever the risk. Tenor and substance of the Anglo-Austrian proposals had changed in accordance with Frederick's deteriorated position. It was to have been expected, but it was intolerable. Hints had moreover reached him that a French agent was at Vienna, where presumably possibilities were being sounded as to a separate peace with France instead of Prussia.

Like Maria Theresa, Frederick now reacted first of all emotionally, though serviceable rationalization was never difficult to marshal. The French had been playing him along throughout; but Austria and England, by showing how weakened they deemed him, were openly insulting him.

He fumed at 'being held in contempt like my father, though much more powerful', and talked of nothing but *revenge*—so the secretary Eichel* informed Podewils, who also had to bear his share of Frederick's irritation. (Podewils had always been against the French alliance, and Frederick in his rage wildly accused him of taking English bribes.) Eichel, who from long association with Frederick's father knew all about such moods, wrote appropriately in the tone of an old nurse: 'When we are good, we can be quite wonderful; but when we are in a passion—oh dear me!'

So Frederick wrote straight off to Cardinal Fleury, announcing his resolve to give battle at the earliest opportunity, with a gratuitous exposition of the indissoluble unity of interests of France and Prussia, and—only gleam of his old humour—requesting a mass for Prussian victory. This was on 11 May.

Prince Charles was of the same mind as the King of Prussia. Their two armies were advancing at right angles to each other, the Austrian south to north and the Prussian east to west. On 13 May, Whit Sunday, the distance between them was not above fifteen miles. So long as neither was prepared to swerve, their paths must cross between the Elbe and Sazawa rivers. By 16 May it was clear that the collision must occur in the neighbourhood of Czaslau on the road to Prague. In fact Prince Charles had taken over Czaslau, his main army encamped at Ronnow, and Frederick was at Kuttenberg, with Prince Leopold the younger approaching from the heights of

* As with the whole Administration, Frederick had taken over his father's secretaries. There were three: Eichel, Lautensack, and Schuhmacher—or Acorn, Lute-bag, and Shoemaker. The Berlin establishment ran to fortuitously whimsical names; Frederick's chief musicians were called Graun and Hasse, or Horror and Hate.

Podhorzan, a little to the north-east. As the crow flies, the opponents were not more than six miles apart. But armies did not yet possess the art of flying, and between them there lay every vagary of undulating wooded terrain.

However, this time there were no snowstorms, and the screening knolls afforded also look-out posts. Before nightfall each contestant knew roughly where the other was. 'This time' —both were very conscious that this would be the return match after Mollwitz. Prince Charles was determined that there should be no Neippberg-like hesitancy on his side, and that the Austrian foot soldier should recoup his reputation in pitched battle against the same opponent to whom he had lost it. Frederick likewise was anxious that his cavalry should make good its shame, and himself improve on his unhappy performance, the last time.

'This time' the Austrians were going to get in first. To promote the right spirit the commander-in-chief broadcast a warranted promise that in future promotion would be more dependent on merit, which hitherto had played little or no part in this. Then, at nightfall, the Austrian troops marched out of Ronnow, without lights or signals of any kind, leaving heavy artillery and baggage behind for silence and speed. The object was to fall upon the road-weary Prussians before dawn, before breakfast, before they had time so much as to form up.

The Prussians had no inkling of the nocturnal manœuvre, but they were guarding against a surprise move of some sort. Also, they were not spread over several villages as Prince Charles supposed, but assembled in one single camp at Chotusitz, a small market town forming the apex of a triangle whose base would be described by Kuttenberg and Czaslau, with a church spire serving as a focal point of the already settled battle order.* Further, the exigencies of a secretive approach prolonged the process. The attack was not ready to be mounted until nearly 7 a.m. The Prussian bread wagons

*Frederick's directive to Prince Leopold, 2 a.m., 17 May: 'Take Chotusitz for your centre, see that you lean your left wing on something near the Dobrowa [stream] . . . then range your right wing westwards till you lean again on something there. Two lines; leave room for me and my forces on the corner nearest the right extremity.' The actual disposition adhered closely to this outline.

had not yet arrived, but there was time for an issue of gruel.

Before eight o'clock, when the sun was already hot, the armies faced one another in full array, in the traditional two lines of infantry with cavalry on both wings. The Austrians had thirty-eight battalions and ninety-two squadrons, the Prussians thirty and seventy; their respective strength is estimated at 30,000 to 28,000 or thereabouts, with a slight Austrian advantage as to infantry but a considerably larger one in point of cavalry.

It was the Prussian cavalry that opened the engagement. General Buddenbrock—the 'venerable ancient' of 1730, when he had bared his breast at Frederick William to save Frederick—at three score and ten again proved the salubrious properties of Marlborough's wars, heading a cuirassier charge that overset both lines of cavalry on the Austrian left 'like a house of cards'.

At Mollwitz there had been deep snow, atomized to vanishing in the area of battle. At Chotusitz the weather was warm and dry and the ground sandy as anywhere in Brandenburg, in spite of certain rills and quagmires, hedges and gardens figuring significantly in the tactical procedure. The clouds of dust whirled up by the Prussian charge and ensuing mêlée completely obscured what was happening, confused the Prussian infantry command which should have followed up the first thrust, and robbed the attackers themselves of orientation as they were taken in the flank by Austrian infantry, with Austrian hussar reserves plunging into their rear.

Meanwhile on the Prussian left the cavalry had been forestalled by simultaneous Austrian attacks from all directions—whether owing to an oversight of Prince Leopold's, as Frederick maintained, or as Prince Leopold maintained by the fault of one of his sub-commanders, or as seems the most likely by a combination of the two plus the patently inconvenient lie of the land in that quarter. Soon the waiting Prussian lines became involved and began to be forced back; the Austrians broke through them and right into Chotusitz proper which was their centre, set fire to the houses to assist in mopping up, and tried on either side to get between the Prussian double file.

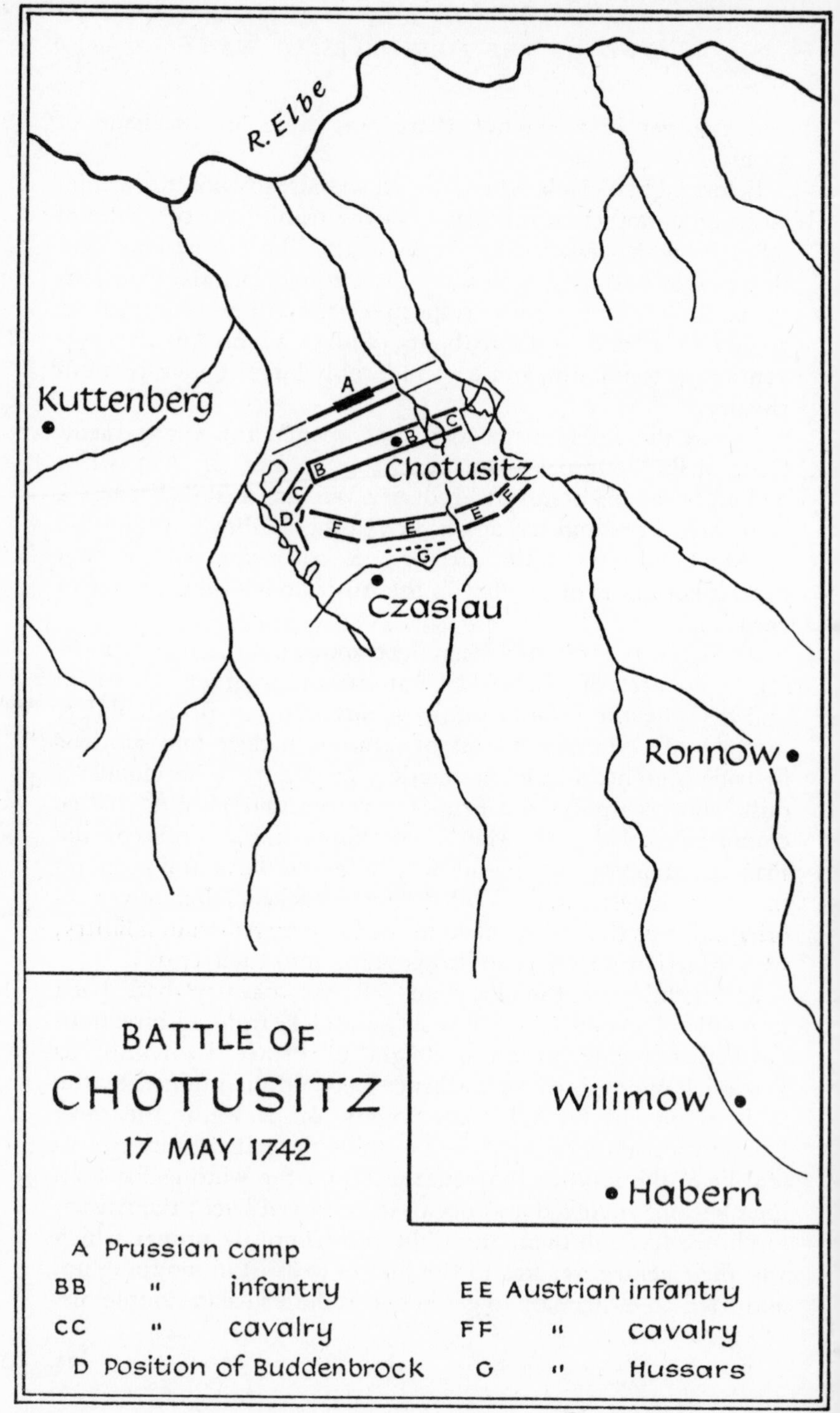
R. Elbe
A
B
C
Kuttenberg
B
Chotusitz
C
F
D
E
E
F
G
Czaslau
Ronnow
Wilimow
Habern
BATTLE OF
CHOTUSITZ
17 MAY 1742
A Prussian camp
BB " infantry
CC " cavalry
D Position of Buddenbrock
EE Austrian infantry
FF " cavalry
G " Hussars

Prince Charles's adviser General Königsegg said he had never seen as murderous hand-to-hand fighting; Frederick records the sight of very swaths of men, cut down rank on rank with their muskets beside them as though in consummate obedience to some freakish order.

Now two things happened. First, their impetus carried some Austrian squadrons beyond Chotusitz into the Prussian camp, where they succumbed to the temptation of plunder. Second, the great heat generated by the thatched timbers of the burning village turned it into a furnace which laid an impenetrable no-man's-land between attackers and defenders.

For a space the Austrian pressure slackened.

In the respite several units of the dispersed Prussian cavalry of the left rallied and returned. The Prussian infantry lines began to reform, in constantly changing, smoothly interlocking order which roused something like horror in their opponents as time and again it seemed the beaten and the dead were coming on for ever renewed. For the nonce the Austrians were halted, but without as yet yielding an inch of ground. Prince Charles had already thrown in almost everything he had got on his right; he now decided to bring up artillery support from the left.

Slightly to the south and west of Chotusitz there was a small hump, and thither the Austrians now hauled a battery. But suddenly, concealed until the last by an elevation in the ground, a broad wave of Prussians appeared 'as though growing out of the earth', preceded by incessant barrage from a row of light mobile field pieces in front and many more grouped nimbly at the sides. This was the Prussian right wing, having held back until the fog and baffling tumult in that sector had died away with the dissipation of cavalry activity. These troops were still fresh, their powers taxed by nothing but the strain of waiting, their ammunition intact; comprising twenty-one battalions with a total of seventy-six of those agile light field guns with which Frederick had replaced a customary, heavier type during last year's lull. What was virtually a clear field stretched before them, right across from the straggle of ponds which marked the western boundary of the pitch, to the thickened Austrian concentration hammering away at the disputed embers of Chotusitz. The King was in command; it was his move.

Within minutes this fresh force was practically upon the Austrian rear and deployed to encircle the enemy. The Austrian left wing crumbled, fell back upon the centre, and all threatened to pile up pell-mell on top of the right, where the Czaslawa brook made a ditch to entrap them for certain slaughter.

The sun stood high, noon was not far off, the Austrian regiments battering away at Chotusitz had been hard at it for nearly four hours; those making merry in the Prussian camp would soon be lost beyond hope of contact. Prince Charles saw no other way to avoid annihilation but to withdraw as best he could, as soon as might be, and as rapidly.

The Prussians pursued the Austrians off the field, only as far as Czaslau; but the Austrians did not rest till they gained Wilimow and Habern, fifteen miles away, their combatant strength reduced to 15,000. The victor let it be known that he had refrained from demolishing them in order to spare the poor Queen of Hungary the last humiliation. His chivalry looks somewhat dubious in the light of the Prussian losses, which were enormous: 4,074 dead and wounded—the greater part of them cavalry—including one general and three colonels, against the Austrians' 3,000 dead and wounded (with 3,300 missing, however, as compared to but 700 Prussians taken prisoner). Of more than one Prussian regiment less than a third survived, and the Austrians bore away eleven regimental colours and one standard, against seventeen cannon captured by the Prussians.

The return match ended in what was an even less genuine and for all that even more impressive victory for Prussia than that of Mollwitz; over and above which the King had now shown himself a man of valour and independent judgment. His action had decided the day; and even if without further tests chance could not be ruled out, the intangible faculty of luck was itself an accepted part of gifted generalship.

'There!' Frederick wrote exultantly to Jordan. 'For the second time in thirteen months behold your friend victorious! Who would have thought a few years ago that the disciple of Jordanesque philosophy, Ciceronic rhetoric, and Baylean dialectic was destined for the rôle of warrior? Who would have thought that Providence would choose a poet to overturn the

European System and upset all the calculations of Kings?' Jordan replied that he was not in the least surprised.

To Broglie Frederick wrote, also hot from the field, that it would be to France's eternal dishonour not to follow up and emulate her ally's triumph. Broglie replied that the spirit of the French required more brake than spur, and on 25 May fought and won the battle of Sahay, of which Frederick ungenerously said that the couriers sent out with the glad news had far and away outnumbered the casualties inflicted on the enemy.

Nine acres of Chotusitz land were purchased by the King of Prussia for the burial of the fallen. Carlyle not quite a hundred years later tried in vain to locate these acres, as the whole battle plain was indiscriminately covered with rye, barley, miscellaneous pulse, and potatoes—'mostly insignificant crops'.

CHAPTER 23

INTERLUDE

Prussia and Austria made peace. Its real architect, the much-maligned 'Lord Hundsfott', by way of reward asked permission to add the Prussian eagle to his coat of arms, which was 'most civilly' granted. Under the Treaty of Breslau, ratified 28 July 1742, Prussia received the whole of Silesia except the principality of Teschen with Troppau and Jägerndorf, which laid a slanting wedge between Upper Silesia and the county of Glatz, and an adjoining strip of Moravia—it required twenty days of strenuous work on the part of a bi-governmental commission to define the boundaries. Frederick took over a loan contracted on behalf of Silesia by the late Emperor Charles VI, payable to England and Holland; and solemnly pledged himself to respect the Catholic religion in his new province.

Within a few weeks Saxony also withdrew from the Succession War in which unofficially she had ceased to take part some months before—Augustus III was so vague about these to him uncongenial matters that after Chotusitz he had enquired whether his troops had done well in that battle.

Upon the French Court Prussia's separate peace fell like a thunderbolt. Cardinal Fleury, in his ninetieth year, burst into tears and then wrote to Vienna, fairly begging for a parley and disowning any responsibility for the Franco-Prussian alliance. Vienna declined his request and gloatingly published the letter, which was reprinted in every European gazette. Fleury nevertheless renewed his attempts at negotiation and over the head of Belle-Isle, who by this time had recovered from his illness, appointed Broglie as his deputy.

'To be sure,' Belle-Isle wrote scathingly, 'at Vienna they like M. de Broglie a good deal better than me—seeing that he has brought the French army into disrepute and by his own unaided efforts succeeded in alienating from us the one Prince whose friendship was a necessity for us.' His was about the only voice of note raised in defence of Frederick's action, an open, signed and sealed betrayal this time.

'The Saxons,' Frederick defended himself, 'had acted like traitors, the French like fools.' The missing wedge of the Teschen district was, indeed, a direct result of the failure of allied military support both before and after Chotusitz. 'Can I help it that Marshal Broglie is no Turenne? I could not make a night-owl into an eagle. Shall I be arraigned because I did not fight twenty battles for France? It would have been a Penelope's task, M. de Broglie having the peculiar mission of breaking down what others build up. . . . Is it so great a crime that I withdrew from an alliance which by his own admission the head of the French Government deplored from the first?'

But even Frederick's best friends, the constituents of the Republic of Letters, declared that he had gone too far. He had gone against France. France, when all was said, was the spiritual centre of the philosophes, whatever their opinion of current French policy; whereas to the champions of enlightenment the whole 'System' of the Holy Roman Empire represented Western Europe's Old Man from the Sea, by whose antiquated stranglehold Progress was retarded: while the administration of the good and charming Queen of Hungary was among the most reactionary of the day. By letting France down in this way Frederick had put his whole case in a different light. Even Voltaire—who had supported Frederick's high-handed proceeding against the Bishop of Liège and the people of Herstal, with a manifesto from his own mighty pen—reproached him now.

Frederick replied:

> It is easy for you to inveigh against those who support their rights . . . by force of arms; but I remember a time when, had you possessed an army, it would have marched at once against

> Desfontaines, Rousseau, van Duren, etc., etc. . . . We made an alliance as people make a marriage contract; I promised to make war as a husband promises to satisfy the concupiscence of his new wife. But, just as in marriage the woman's desires often exhaust the husband's strength, so in war the weakness of one ally may increase the demands upon the other past capacity. And to conclude the comparison, when a husband thinks he has sufficient proof of his wife's infidelity, nothing can prevent him from obtaining a divorce.

With the relief from strain, Frederick had recovered some of the sensitivity to criticism which he had deemed well lost. His case looked too unprepossessing; still, given the circumstances as they were—given the initial aggression which so many of his present critics had condoned—he did not see what else he could have done. He relieved his feelings in an ode rebutting the 'Judgment of the Public upon those who follow the Unhappy Calling of Politics', and next penned a pamphlet attacking the accusers of the King of Prussia, which Podewils had difficulty in preventing him from publishing 'anonymously'.

But just as Frederick's first discarded polemic had led to a larger and less ephemeral work, the *Antimachiavel*, so this second one gave rise to a worthier sublimation of the impulse which had inspired it. Instead of excusing himself, he would explain; instead of arguing, he would relate. Forthwith he began to plan what became the first volume of his *Histoire de mon temps*, covering the political events of his lifetime up to the end of his recent war.

For Frederick and his especial literary mentors, the highest reaches of the art of letters lay in the sphere of historiography, but lately reborn as a novel synthesis of event and diversely causal background, which only the disciplined creative imagination could properly condense and illuminate. At one and the same time he might now ascend to that level, assuage his need for truth—that intense urge for which he never thought to claim credit, and for which therefore credit has seldom been allowed him—work off and thereby dissipate his discomfiture, and indulge his passion for writing to his heart's content.

As a writer Frederick had a conscience. As a historian, he

THE QUEEN WITH THE HEART OF A KING
Maria Theresa as Pallas Athene

MARIA THERESA'S CONSORT
Archduke Francis Stephen of Lorraine-Tuscany

HOME LIFE OF THE IMPERIAL FAMILY

Maria Theresa and Francis with some of their children on St Nicholas's Day (6 December). The custom was for children to put out their shoes overnight, which the saint filled with sweetmeats and toys for the deserving or a birch for wrote well: lucidly, intelligently, without humbug or special pleading, and with the reticencies only of a design which by the ruling laws of Taste and technique had no room for any but the most generalized human emotions. Although of course his interpretation was conditioned by the Prussian interest, he made no attempt to overbear posterity with a flattering self-portrait—rather the reverse. From the professional point of view it needs to be said that the monarch happy in being his own historian did nothing to misuse this advantage. He wrote from true conviction, which needed no bush: let but the history of his time be understood, and he would need no self-advertisement. He would compel recognition on his own terms; it was no good to him otherwise. In the same context, and thus characteristically, he absolutely discountenanced eulogistic representations of himself, whether in paint or sculpture, whether in form of allegory or monument; in fact, he never again so much as sat for his portrait.

'Regarding the security of our new possessions,' Frederick summed up his immediate programme to Podewils, 'as I see it this will be founded on a good and numerous army, a full treasury, forbidding fortresses, and prestige alliances to impress the world if they do nothing else. The thing is now to accustom the European powers to seeing us in the position which the war has given us, and I believe this may be brought about by showing a great deal of moderation and tolerance towards our neighbours. A happy quiescence must be the guiding principle of our policy for the next few years; we need peace to consolidate the State.'

Indeed they did. The depleted exchequer stood at 150,000 Thaler, the army was badly in need of refurbishing, and the full and permanent integration of Silesia was to be neither lightly nor cheaply encompassed. The latter process in fact took several decades to complete, and even with the best will in the world could not be carried on without hardship to many; so it is an extraordinary thing that in Silesia, in the raped and conquered province of all places, there should have grown unto Frederick a potent antidote for the sickness of his reputation—a plant proliferating with such vigour that in time it swamped what it had helped to cure. In Silesia, so early in the day, the Frederick-legend had its birth.

The legendary Frederick was no outright travesty of the real. The image, as is the way of two-dimensional images, merely was one-sided, and presented his best side, from the popular, functional, romantic point of view. His accessibility, contrasting with the generations-old remoteness of the Habsburg rulers, probably had something to do with it; coupled with the further contrasts of success with simplicity of manner and attire, and of power with a punctilious personal concern which was constantly in evidence and did not stop short of practical proof. With the aid of true anecdotes no less colourful than their spawn of apocrypha, the instinct of worship created the father-figure of a lovable eccentric full of humane method in his crusty madness, a hero in ragged clothing, Justice and Wisdom speaking with the voice of slang. It was an image so attractive and in its category so rare, that it could not help spreading beyond the confines of its birthplace.

In any case, as Frederick might have known, reproach seldom sticks to conquerors. The storm of moral indignation blew over in the natural course of world events, to which 'for the next few years' Frederick intended to be but a watchful spectator.

While the War of the Austrian Succession went on without him, slowly but surely favouring Maria Theresa, the King of Prussia sat back to be wooed and enjoy his peaceable pursuits. He took the waters for his rheumatism, saw the inauguration of the reborn Academy of Sciences and the opening of Berlin's new Opera House: 'Buildings are my dolls,' he confessed, forgetful that a passion for building ranked among his grandfather's reprehended vices. The palace of Charlottenburg received a new wing, and he had begun to toy with plans for a summer residence near Potsdam. Fitly to deck his dolls, competent friends were sent to Italy with authority to buy up fine paintings: 'But no scoundrelly saints undergoing martyrdom, if you please: make it scenes from classical mythology or historical pieces!'

He made music, played and composed. He wrote—letters, essays, dissertations, poems of all shapes and sizes on every subject under the sun, satires, dramatic pieces—such as a farce for the occasion of Keyserlingk's wedding and libretti for the Opera's repertoire—in addition to the everyday transactions of government and the serious work on his History. The latter no one was as yet allowed to see, excepting Podewils who was helping on the research side, and Voltaire, to whom selected passages were submitted with all the self-conscious reservations typical of authors in an interesting condition.

For Voltaire came on another visit. The British Ambassador reported sourly that the King and his star guest were inseparable; the whole court talked of nothing but Voltaire, who read from his tragedies to the Queens and Princesses till they were bathed in tears: nobody without the works of Voltaire either in his head or in his pocket counted as an educated person. Voltaire concurred:

> I am in France here. French is the only language; German is only used with soldiers and horses. I meet people, brought up in Königsberg, who know my poems by heart and are not forever trying to trip me up!

The real purpose of the visit was diplomatic. So far had France, like Austria before her, forgiven Frederick's defection, that she now wished to coax him into a fresh alliance. George II wished the same for England. Ever since the fall of Walpole early in 1742, the King of England had been gravitating towards more active intervention on Maria Theresa's side, to which end it was hoped to bring in Prussia too. Hence the British Ambassador's disquiet on seeing Voltaire sweep the Prussian court off its feet—and hence also a passing chill in Frederick's relations with his idol who, it seemed, flattered himself that his personal influence might further political ends.

There was no such thing as personal pull with Frederick. Friendship and business were things apart; from the first he guarded his autocratic independence, jealously. His remark to Keyserlingk, soon after 'la journée des dupes', typified a general attitude: 'My dear Caesarion, you're a dear fellow, you are well-read, you have a pleasing wit and a nice singing voice: but your advice is that of an imbecile.' Yet as a person there was no one of whom he was fonder; Keyserlingk's early death prostrated Frederick and he never forgot him. In the same way, Frederick's devotion to his mother, now again very marked, was utterly devoid of political connotations—a fact which the Britannic court was very slow to face. Even yet it was hoped in

London that through Sophie Dorothee Frederick might be brought round; and for some time the wishful rumour persisted that Frederick would divorce the unloved wife who had been forced upon him and redeem his protestations to Queen Caroline of ten or twelve years ago and more. Nothing was further from Frederick's mind. So long as he did not have to see Elizabeth Christine, he was perfectly content with his marriage, which saved him from invidious proposals.

That did not mean he was ready to immolate his nearest and dearest on the altar of expediency, as yet.

Tzarina Elizabeth of all the Russias was making enquiries about a suitable bride for her nephew and heir, who like most of the males of her stock was showing signs of mental instability. Relations between Berlin and St Petersburg were good at the time: what better opportunity thus to strengthen the connexion? But Frederick shrank from consigning a sister to a life among raving savages, which would be her portion at the court of Muscovy. The Tzarina herself had come to the throne by a palace revolution, typical of the rapid turn-over of sovereigns in her country, and such as were usually accompanied by frightful atrocities from which the principals were not exempted. He excused his sisters and after deliberating with Podewils suggested the latter's choice, the young Princess Sophie Friederike of Anhalt-Zerbst.

Frederick and Podewils did not know it then: but this fourteen-year-old, country-bred female was in many ways his counterpart—so much so that later it was sometimes averred, entirely without foundation, that he had fathered her. Her actual father was one of the least of minor German princes, an upright man subsisting on his Prussian army pay and his salary as Governor of Stettin. Her mother, née Princess of Holstein-Gottorp and close kinswoman to the Tzarewitch, was, one feels, a sort of forerunner of Mrs Bennet. Their household was straitened and provincial. And the product of these was the future Catherine the Great.*

* So far the only way in which she had publicly distinguished herself was by oblique impertinence on her first visit to Berlin as a tiny child years before. Obviously the little girl had overheard her elders on the staple topic of Frederick William's ridiculous meanness; when told to kiss the old King's coat, she objected that she could not reach it because it was so very short—causing much suppressed amusement all round.

The Tzarina was delighted with her, and to return the compliment of matchmaking now proposed the marriage of one of Frederick's sisters with the heir to the throne of Sweden, a much-coveted parti: both George II and Augustus III had already submitted portraits of their daughters at Stockholm. So, although Frederick himself would have preferred to send his younger sister Amelia, whom he judged to be physically more robust and better equipped temperamentally, he yielded gracefully to the Swedish insistence on the elder (as being necessarily of higher rank than her junior), and Ulrike became the envied bride.

Or so the story goes; the ins and outs of it are obfuscated by another story, itself ultimately inscrutable, concerning Amelia's debated love affair with a young officer on Frederick's staff, Baron Friedrich von der Trenck, afterwards famous for the barbaric persecution he suffered at the King's hands. At all events, Amelia was withdrawn from the marriage market at about this time and made Abbess of Quedlinburg, a Protestant foundation for noble spinsters.* Whatever the possible inaccuracies and exaggerations of Trenck's autobiography, there can be no doubt that he was treated with a primitive vindictiveness unique in Frederick's dealings. (The details chronologically belong elsewhere. However, Trenck spent—and, incredibly, survived in good health—ten years captive in a damp and lightless dungeon of Magdeburg, where he was chained to the wall by neck, waist, wrists, and ankles; his several attempted escapes more than rival that of Casanova from the Leads.)

Some deep-lying nerve of archaic sexual mores must have been struck in Frederick. For his general attitude to carnal transgression, even aberration, was humane to a point where, in the view of many, leniency became scandalous. The mildest

* Amelia's life was cast in a pattern of blighted hopes from the outset: born 9 November 1723, she was named after the Princess Amelia of England, at a time when the marriage of Frederick and Amelia appeared a happy certainty. However, by way of light relief, the birth as such had its piquant features—terminating as it did one of those pregnancies which are misdiagnosed from start to finish. Amelia of Prussia was the twelfth child born to Queen Sophie Dorothee, yet she arrived quite unexpectedly after a bout of presumed colic, with no better-qualified midwife at hand than King Frederick William, who himself effected the delivery.

instance is the protection he habitually extended to any young ladies of the court, caught out in the natural consequences of amorous indiscretion; the most flagrant his marginal note, laconically commuting the death sentence passed on a soldier for sodomy with his mare, to one of, 'Transfer to the infantry!'—punishment enough.

In civil Law, all the penalties hitherto obtaining for fornication and unwedded motherhood were abolished—one of numerous interim edicts of this peaceful period, during which the project of comprehensive judicial reform was taken a stage further.

In recognition of the defects in the existing Law, and pending entire revision of the code, a decree was promulgated empowering each and every subject of the King to come direct to him with petitions or appeals. The practice continued even after the reformed Code had come into being. Until the end of Frederick's life, every day that he was not away at war, humble litigants came to interview him and were heard; now and again foreign house guests of the King were alarmed to see stray plebeians wandering about the royal terrace, peering in at windows, looking for him.

National security, as outlined by Frederick, was to rest on 'a good and numerous army, a full treasury, and awe-inspiring fortresses', in the main. In fulfilling these conditions the new province, bringing Prussia between one and two million extra inhabitants and a revenue of 4½ million Thaler, was of great assistance. But money and men were not everything; the army must not be left resting on its first-crop of laurels. One must try to keep ahead of imitators and attend to the deficiencies which the Silesian campaigns had disclosed. Here Frederick started at the top, with an intensive attempt to raise the level of education of the officer corps. Frederick William might have introduced compulsory schooling, but this did not embrace much more than the three Rs. Frederick had found that the transmission of orders, and indeed of overall tactical directives, was often hampered by the cheerfully unlettered ignorance of his doughty Brandenburgian nobles nor could they be asked to study the great classic campaigns of the past without first extending their very vocabulary, to say nothing of their intellectual horizon.

There was much general overhauling; numbers of regiments were reconstituted and received highly circumstantial new regulations. The special efforts to develop the cavalry continued: prizes were given for equestrian tricks and resourcefulness, during exercises which in some respects recall the rodeo. Troop reviews and manœuvres changed from mere tests of mechanical accuracy to mock-battles under war conditions, on natural terrain. Another change was that Frederick, who between 1741 and 1742 had expressly invited foreign observers to attend the cavalry displays demonstrating the improvement in this arm, now strictly excluded outsiders from all such events, placing even the most insignificant amendments of military organization under seal of secrecy.

He had very soon found that his expressed hope of 'happy quiescence' was untenable. So long as there was war in Germany, Prussian neutrality could not but prove a mirage.

CHAPTER 24

TO THE EMPEROR'S RESCUE

Less than a year after Prussia's withdrawal from the War of the Austrian Succession, the prospect had altered so radically as to be almost in reverse. The Austrians had recaptured Prague, Maria Theresa was crowned Queen of Bohemia, the armies of France were in full retreat, right back to the Rhine, the forces of Bavaria split up into ineffectual particles while their country was overrun once more and about to be annexed by Austria; in Italy Sardinia now espoused the cause of Austria, against Naples and Spain; and on the Lower Rhine George II, with an ever-anxious eye on both real and imaginary threats to Hanover, assembled a 'Pragmatic' Army—16,000 English, 16,000 Hanoverians in English pay, a corps of hired Hessians, and some Austrian regiments bringing the total up to 40,000—ready to march upon the Main. So even at Frankfurt France's puppet Emperor, bereft of puppeteer, was safe no longer.

On 27 June 1743 George II, in his sixties, won the great personal satisfaction of inflicting a heavy, surprise defeat on the French at Dettingen, which resulted in their complete evacuation of German territory. Emperor Charles VII—'the Imperial Vagabond', as he called himself, afflicted 'with all the ills of Job' including gout, stone, and penury—lost the last semblance of authority, even in the transactions of the German Diet.*

* The Diet was a congress of representatives of the Empire, comprising its princes, ecclesiastics, and Free Cities—founded under the Carolingians, and in permanent session since 1663. The business of the Diet had largely degenerated into, one might say, heraldic disputations: it was, however, the only official working sphere of the Emperor.

There was talk, notably by English spokesmen, of setting up a 'Roman *King*' in opposition to the disendowed Imperial figurehead. England thus was patently abandoning the scheme of Prusso-Austrian parity which she had been sponsoring, and wishing to restore Austria to domination within the Empire, instead. The outlook for Prussia in Silesia became less bright—distinctly unsettled.

'Listen, Milord,' Frederick barked at Hyndford, 'I don't care what you do to the French anywhere outside Germany—in France itself, in Flanders or Lorraine: but I will not have you stirring up trouble inside the Empire; I will not let you despoil or dethrone the Emperor.' He added a frank threat: would Hyndford be so good as to remind King George that Hanover was within very easy reach of Prussia? Podewils had hard work of persuading the British envoy that Frederick had not meant what he said. Frederick had meant every word.

Prussia having helped to instal the Emperor, her dignity and her security declined with his. With the collapse of Charles VII, the whole idea of a German Emperor whose hereditary lands and prime interests lay inside, not outside Germany, would fall to the ground again. Further, not three months after Dettingen, a coalition was formed at Worms of Austria, England, Holland, Sardinia, and Saxony. The secret terms of the Treaty, which Frederick got wind of, reaffirmed the Pragmatic Sanction (i.e. indivisibility of the Austrian Crown Lands as existing at the time of the previous Emperor's death), and laid down future territorial provisions for the other four allies in which the guaranteed cession of Silesia to Prussia was entirely ignored. The inference, that in due course that cession was to be rendered void, was substantiated by a letter in which, apropos Silesia, George II significantly reassured the Queen of Hungary, 'Madame, ce qui est bon à prendre, est bon à rendre.' A copy of this letter had also come into Frederick's hands. If more proof had been needed, Saxony's change of front was another. Frederick must work quickly or pay the price of isolation.

A breathing space occurred with the seasonable lull, as the warring armies went into winter quarters on both sides of the Rhine while in Italy the conflict stood at sanguinary stalemate.

In the spring of 1744 Frederick, like his father in 1730, embarked on a thinly disguised tour of soliciting support for the Emperor in the Empire ('to restore Germany's liberty, the Emperor's dignity, and Europe's peace'), with indifferent success. Frederick's prophetic notion of an all-German Imperial Army under Prussian leadership came to nothing, as the Emperor had no money and France would not grant the necessary subsidies; also, France had never been more unpopular with the German princes, the Emperor's dignity afforded small inspiration, and Frederick's unselfishness seemed rather too good to be true. So besides the King of Prussia and the Emperor, only two others (the Landgrave of Hesse-Cassel and the Elector Palatine, both with relatively insignificant capacity) entered into the 'Union of Frankfurt', 22 May 1744, based on Frederick's undertaking to rescue Bavaria and reconquer Bohemia for Charles VII. The price of this service was to be the missing wedge in Silesia and a part of Bohemia which would extend the Prussian dominions right up to the Elbe. France was an as yet unofficial party to this arrangement.

For some months past Frederick had been negotiating secretly with France. Podewils, who after Frederick's impolitic violence towards Hyndford had exclaimed, he wished the King would either leave foreign affairs to him or take them over altogether, had had to eat his words, as the King ceased entirely to let him know what he was doing. Apart from the Prussian agent extraordinary to the court of France, Count Rothenburg, nobody knew. For the only other person in the confidence of the King did not count as a separate entity.

'My secrets,' Frederick boasted, 'are safely locked inside my breast. I have only one secretary, whom I know I can trust absolutely; so anybody wishing to find out my intentions would have to bribe me, myself.'

This secretary, as unbribable as his master, was August Friedrich Eichel. By ten years' work under the old King schooled in Frederick William's opinion of the Crown Prince, Eichel had started serving under 'the young gentleman' with misgivings, turning into chronic anxiety, turning into acute despair ('If it were possible to have one's wish, I'd wish myself dead—at least for a year or two—that I need not be a witness to these disastrous courses!')—which presently turned into steady hero-worship.

'Monsieur Hecle', as the foreign envoys garbled a name they had no occasion to see in writing, was variously described by them as a mystery man cum slave: 'Unseen by mortal eye, he dwells in complete seclusion and yet knows everything; closely guarded like a prisoner of State, he is on duty all the year round with not so much as a half hour's vacation; wherever the King goes, he goes too; his bureau is the true seat of government; every effort to get speech with him is vain.'

Substantially true, this was yet slightly misleading. Eichel was in constant contact with Podewils, with whose frustrated policy of safety first he had every sympathy; and his aloofness from the King's other Ministers and the generals of the army was self-imposed. He was approached often enough with flattering requests to use his special influence: it was said of Eichel that he could easily have risen to cabinet rank but preferred to see men of position crawl to him, the lowly, deferential underling. If so, that was his only perquisite. Nor, for all his solidarity with Podewils, did Eichel breathe a word of the King's clandestine negotiations to the King's Foreign Minister.

The Treaty of Paris, uniting France and Prussia in a pact of mutual aid, was concluded on 5 June. Podewils was not told of it till 5 July—and that was sooner than Frederick had intended. The tempo of events had forced his hand.

France after three years of fighting strictly under the Bavarian colours had declared war on Austria. The plan was to follow this up with a renewed, double invasion, simultaneously across the Upper and the Lower Rhine. Once the campaign was well under way, Prussia should attack in Bohemia; and by way of additional diversion, the King of France prepared to resuscitate the Stuart cause to harry and distract the King of England.

The French offensive in Flanders started with éclat, having the benefit of one of the most brilliant generals of the age, Maurice de Saxe, and the presence of Louis XV himself. Maria Theresa's answer was a bold move to invade France on the Upper Rhine. Khevenhüller had died in January; in his place another Austrian commander of renown, Field-Marshal Count Otto Ferdinand von Traun, was recalled from the Milanese to act as Chief Military Adviser to Prince Charles of Lorraine. Thus excellently well advised, Prince Charles effected the Rhine crossing of 70,000 Austrian troops in a record time of four days (30 June—3 July) and triumphantly carried the war into French territory, Alsace and Lorraine. The Prussian diversion in Bohemia must be launched without delay, before a protective triple alliance, which Frederick had been negotiating with Russia and Sweden, could be concluded.

On 12 July Frederick informed Louis XV that the Prussian army would start for Bohemia a month hence and should reach Prague before the end of August. He hoped to capture Prague, hold on to it, and thereafter maintain a purely defensive stance, which ought to suffice to draw off a part of the Austrian forces from the Rhine. It was not that he disagreed with Podewils' analysis, by which Prussia faced ruin if anything went wrong: but Frederick argued that he risked the same if he took no action till, as might well be, it was too late, while if his action succeeded, he was likely to gain more than the continued security of his possessions.

Frederick could deal with Podewils' anguished objections easily enough. To force his views upon his allies was more difficult. Count Schmettau, Frederick's new second-in-command,* hastened to French headquarters at Metz to press home his master's proposal, which was that the Austrians should be kept busy on the Rhine till the Prussians had established themselves in Bohemia, that they should then be pursued as far as Passau, and that in the meantime a Franco-Bavarian expedition should threaten Hanover from the direction of Westphalia.

King Louis arrived at Metz on 4 August, but almost immediately fell ill. He was thought to be dying; the French high command was as though paralysed. Virtually unhindered, the Austrians recrossed the Rhine at their own convenience, and by 24 August were in full advance towards Bohemia. For

* Frederick had quarrelled with Schwerin over the evacuation of Olmütz, which the King obstinately held could have been avoided.

Frederick had given notice to Vienna of his imminent intervention on the 7th of that month, and the Prussian army had begun its march on the 15th—preceded once more by a Manifesto* in which the invading sovereign declared he had no quarrel with the sovereign of the invaded country.

'The Monster!' cried Frederick's former friendly correspondent, Archduke Francis, and hotly demanded that he instead of his brother, Prince Charles, be placed in supreme command against Frederick. His wife had the utmost trouble in averting this unexpected danger arising in her own camp.

Her first resort, to laugh her 'Old Man' out of his ambition, was singularly unsuccessful. 'I then took refuge in the wonted tactics of our sex and tried caresses and tears,' Maria Theresa wrote to her only sister, newly married to Prince Charles. 'But what use are these with a husband of nine years' standing! Even with this best of husbands they did not get me anywhere. So then I got up my anger, and this served me so well that both he and I ended up sick.' Prince Charles, with Traun at his side, remained in charge, to Frederick's great cost.

* * *

'Throughout this campaign,' Frederick wrote in introducing his analysis of it, 'the advantage was with Austria. M. de Traun played the part of Sertorius, the King [of Prussia] that of Pompey. No general committed more mistakes than did the King.' He ended, 'The conduct of M. de Traun is a model of perfection, which every soldier who loves his business ought to study and try to imitate if he have the talent. The King confesses that he must regard this campaign as his school in the art of war and M. de Traun as his teacher. Good fortune often is far more injurious to princes than ill, in that the former will intoxicate them with presumption, whereas the latter teaches circumspection and modesty.'

The King confessed, between the lines of that last sentence, that he had overreached himself.

What Traun performed in such virtuoso fashion was the classic strategy of avoiding battle, yet thereby outmanœuvring

* Entitled, 'Advertisement of the Causes which have induced His Prussian Majesty to send His Roman Imperial Majesty Some Auxiliary Troops.'

the enemy till the latter wholly ceased to be master of his own movements. What Frederick did in his admitted presumption was to give him the initial opportunity. What Frederick had desired above all was to prevent a war for and in Silesia; and what resulted was precisely that.

* * *

The enterprise opened well enough. Equipped with an Imperial 'Requisitorial' demanding free passage through Saxony 'for Our August Ally, in transit on Imperial business', two-thirds of a Prussian expeditionary force of 80,000 took that route,* the remainder advancing via Silesia. The three columns, commanded respectively by the King, Prince Leopold the younger, and Schwerin, met before Prague only a little behind schedule, and after seven days of its third siege in three years the Bohemian capital surrendered (16 September).

But thereupon Frederick departed from his original plan and pushed on further south, the more surely to trap the Austrians coming from the Rhine between two fires and at the same time menace their home frontier. His communications were thus strained to breaking point; but he was banking on a short and sharp campaign. Even when to his incredulous amazement he learned that there was, alas, no question of two fires—that neither French nor Bavarians had moved so much as in feigned pursuit of Prince Charles and Traun—Frederick would not remodify his operations.

'You and your French friends,' he wrote to his old foe Seckendorf, now in command of the Bavarian-Imperial contingent, 'are a lot of wet hens cowering in the rain. Since I have no word from either of you, I'll manage by myself.'

Prince Charles, reassured and equally astonished that he really had not been followed, wrote to Vienna in pious gratitude, 'I verily believe that God has turned his wits, for his moves are those of a lunatic.' While Frederick announced to Podewils that he would shortly cross the Moldau, engage and beat Prince Charles, and secure Bohemia for the winter, Prince

* King Augustus was away in Poland and his Ministers did little more than go through the motions of protest, in face of 'a frightful quantity of big guns'.

Charles outlined his intention to cut the Prussians off from Prague and from the Elbe, and to starve them out.

Bohemia's natural resources were poor at the best of times. Transport difficulties were extreme. The population was Catholic and hostile to the Prussians, and willingly obeyed the Austrian Government's order to bury all stores and hide out in the forests. News as well as nutriment was at a premium, as ubiquitous Hungarian light cavalry completed the havoc wrought upon the invader by starvation and disease, intercepting almost every Prussian patrol and completely isolating fortified encampments.*

By the middle of October Frederick had lost the initiative, scurrying hither and thither to save his threatened magazines. Before the end of the month he was in retreat. In the first week of November he was forced to go back across the Elbe, in the fourth week every last Prussian garrison, including that of Prague, had been eliminated from Bohemia. The majority of the Prussian army was in a lamentable state, large numbers of sick and wounded jolting along in overcrowded, stinking carts. Deserters absconded in shoals, at a rate seldom paralleled: the recorded figure soon exceeded 17,000. On 4 December the campaign was over.

'We no longer have an army,' the Chief of the Silesian Administration, a son of Frederick's 'benefactor' President von Münchow of Küstrin, wrote as the tattered remains arrived to take up winter quarters in the province. 'All we have is a rabble barely held together by habit and the authority of their officers; and the officers themselves are disaffected. . . . At the slightest further reverse, or for that matter a continuation of the war at this season, we may expect wholesale revolt, such as one would have thought impossible under Prussian discipline.'

The King himself set no very edifying example, with frequent, peremptory unfairness towards his immediate subordinates assisting the vicious circle of strain, privations, discouragement, and more and more virulent bickering and backbiting. His

* So effective was Austrian activity, that Frederick sometimes was without news from Silesia for weeks together, once for as long as a whole month. Sometimes an entire regiment would have to be sent out to ensure that his orders to some other section of the army reached their destination.

subsequent estimate of his own mistakes was no less just than his admiration of the enemy. But he was now helpless in the grip of circumstances which he had called into being. Where during the First Silesian War he had been most careful to include all kinds of non-military factors in his calculations, the desperate gamble on a tour de force in Bohemia had led him to sacrifice sense and sensibility alike to an essay in shock tactics—seeming to present a short cut which turned into a long and painful detour.

He returned to Berlin to make his preparations for next year. The rank and file of the army in Silesia were in not quite such hopeless condition as the younger President Münchow estimated. Of those retaining the use of their feet, only the staunch, after all, had stayed with the colours. A great many of the deserters came from other German countries, hired or pressed into the Prussian service; the core of native Brandenburgers had a certain natural cohesion and besides could feel they had some stake in their King's enterprise. As in the twenty-six months of peace Frederick had increased his total force to 140,000, there were still good reserves to draw on. All the experts were agreed that the Silesian fortresses had been made impregnable, and the Treasury was not yet empty. Finally, Prussia had her allies.

One mistake which Frederick of all men might have known better than to commit, was trusting in the promises of allies. The most his allies were willing to do at that juncture was severely to reproach one another for not helping Frederick. The French having taken Freiburg from the Austrians had returned their concentrated attention to the Austrian Netherlands. Seckendorf and his weary Imperial Master ('I don't want to die in a hole like Frankfurt!') had made good their bid to regain at least a part of Bavaria and were not going to leave Munich again voluntarily.

Frederick's hope of keeping the enemy out of Silesia for the duration of the winter also proved mistaken. The Austrian pursuit would not be halted at the Elbe; and no sooner had the King left for home than Upper Silesia and the county of Glatz became flooded with Austrian troops, so that everywhere the Prussians were confined to the shelter of their permanent

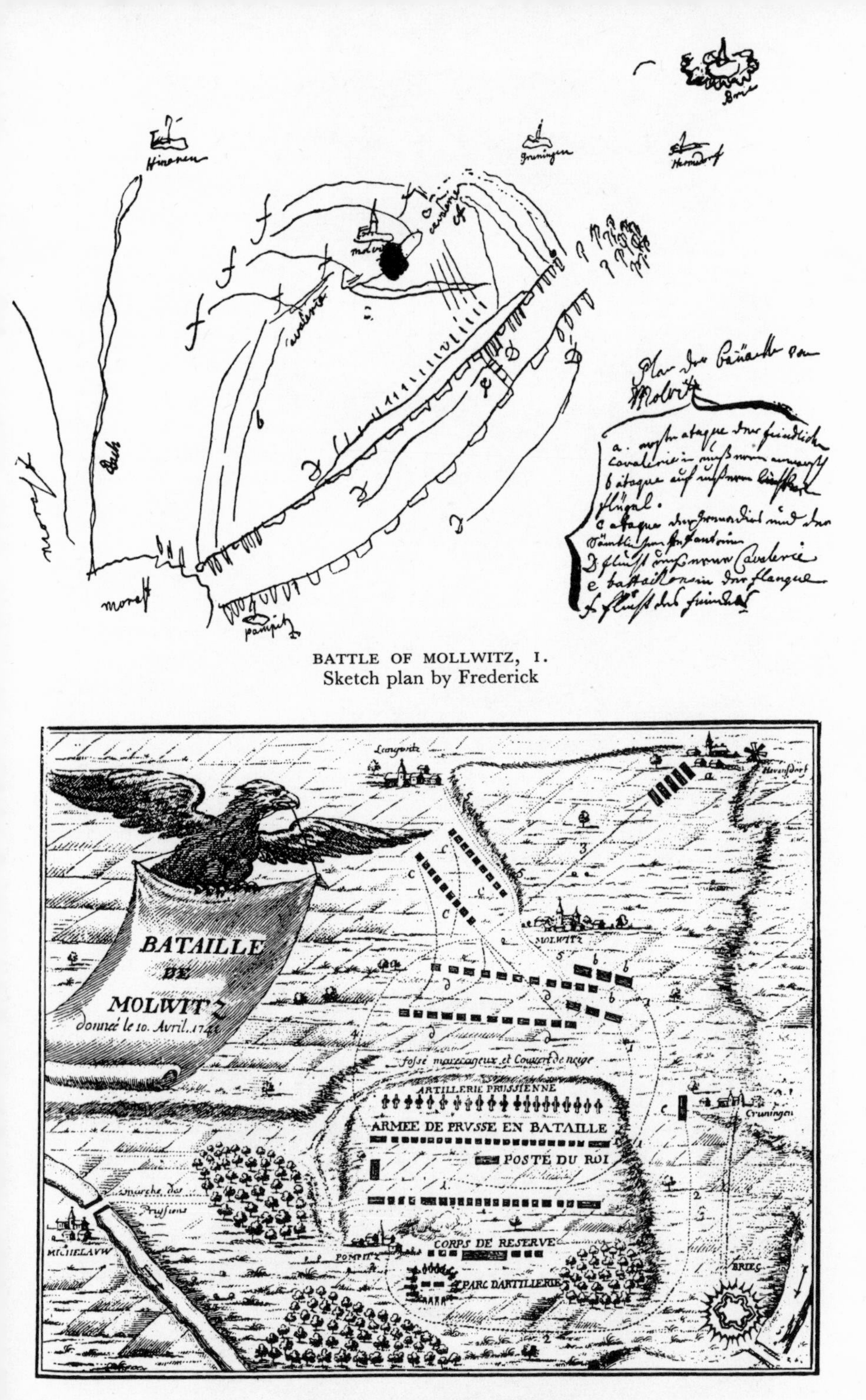

BATTLE OF MOLLWITZ, I.
Sketch plan by Frederick

BATTLE OF MOLLWITZ, 2.
The official engraving (main part)

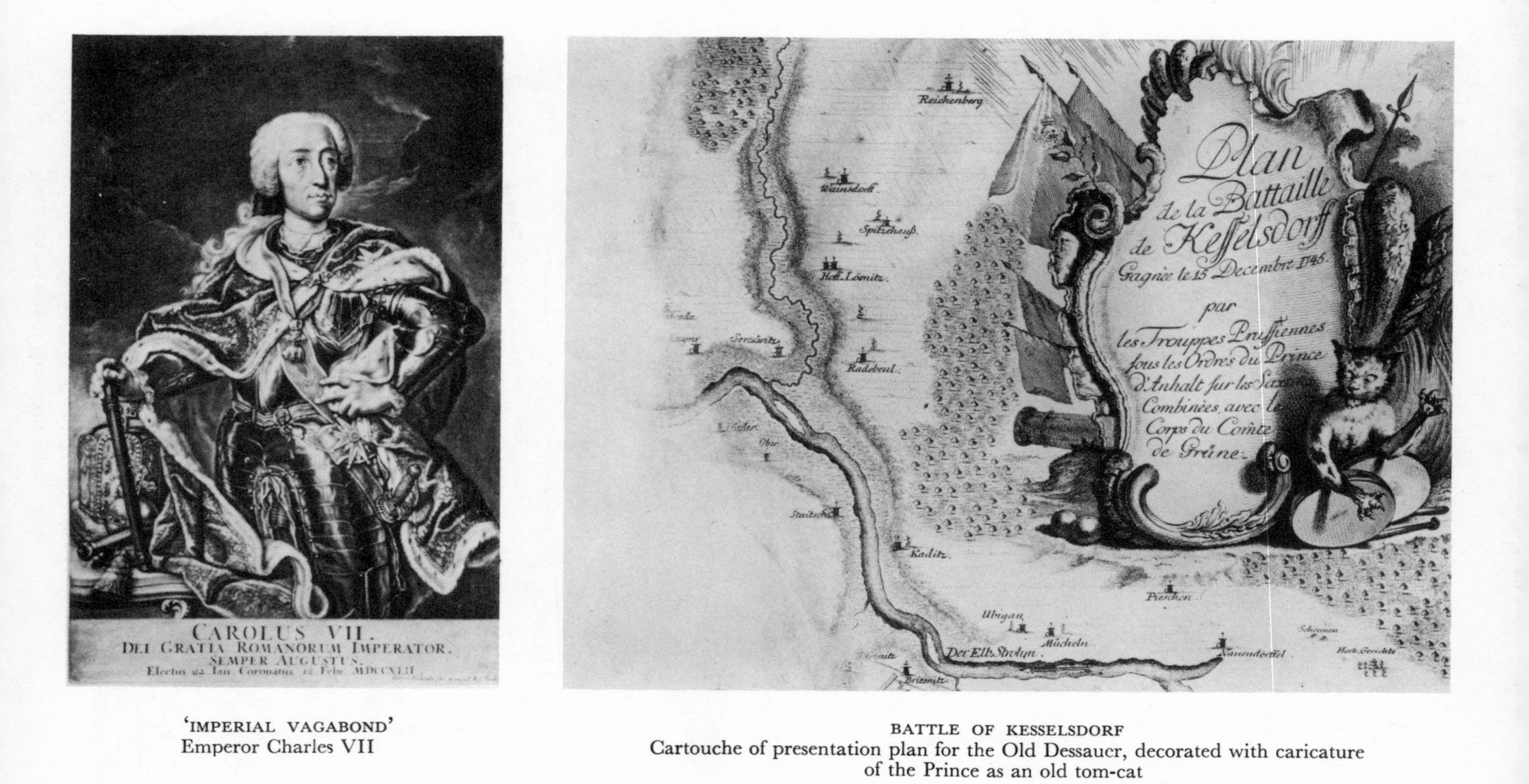

'IMPERIAL VAGABOND'
Emperor Charles VII

BATTLE OF KESSELSDORF
Cartouche of presentation plan for the Old Dessauer, decorated with caricature of the Prince as an old tom-cat

fortifications. A paper war of manifestos ensued: Maria Theresa absolving her Silesian subjects from their oath to Frederick and reminding them of the good old days of 'bliss' under Habsburg rule, Frederick reminding *his* Silesian subjects of all the ills from which he had brought them release.

This duel was as short as it was inconclusive. The Prussian reserves came into play, and with them the Old Dessauer, to whom the King had delegated the Silesian command—no unmixed satisfaction to the old man, as he was far from well and in addition to the burden of so formidable a task had to bear a continuous barrage of royal criticism from Berlin. He had to take the field in a cart, rattling irately ahead of his crack regiments across snow and ice, his fever-stricken son and second-in-command scarcely able to keep in the saddle beside him. The dramatic augury of such leadership was not belied: in an unbelievably short time—three weeks—the two decrepit heroes drove the Austrians out again. The liberation Te Deum was sung in Berlin on 21 February 1745.

A litany of more prolonged resonance had sounded earlier in the new year. On 20 January Emperor Charles VII had died at Munich, in his forty-eighth year. With him died Frederick's formal casus belli—yet thereby only rendering Frederick's war the more vital. The Imperial throne was vacant again; Archduke Francis had another chance; and Maria Theresa's most immediate object was to get Silesia back.

How good her chances appeared in Vienna was shown by the fact that Charles VII's son, the young Elector Maximilian Joseph of Bavaria, was offered peace and restitution of his lost patrimony, against the promise of his vote for Francis at the next Election.* The reconquest of Silesia seeming assured, Austria no longer needed compensation in Bavaria. Francis's only other likely rival, Augustus of Saxony-Poland, had already pledged his Electoral vote to the Archduke. Although Augustus had not grown insensible to the attractions of the Imperial title, he had formed certain commitments, less than a

* Seckendorf used the negotiations to make his own separate peace with Austria and now deserted the son of Charles VII as he had previously deserted the daughter of Charles VI.

fortnight before the Emperor's death, from which he could no longer extricate himself.

He was in receipt of English subsidies binding him to furnish military aid to the Queen of Hungary 'whenever invaded in her own dominions'. This was part of a new secret agreement (Union of Warsaw, 8 January) between England, Austria, Holland and Saxony, which aimed straight at the recovery of Silesia and the disintegration of the Kingdom of Prussia.*

Little as Frederick was able to discover of what was brewing against him, he could guess. Even if his guess fell short, he could not be in doubt as to his desperate situation. His military preparations for the spring had left him with a deficit of 4½ million Thaler. He was unable to raise a loan abroad and had no better luck with the Prussian financiers. The Estates of Brandenburg were more helpful but could not scrape together much more than one million. Secretly, at dead of night, Fredersdorf shipped all the solid silver furniture of the Berlin palace (including tables, chandeliers, great mirror frames, chimney gear, and the whole of Frederick William's celebrated silver 'trumpeters' gallery') down the River Spree to the mint. The King, back in Silesia since the middle of March, worked night and day at making bricks without straw and trying to find a crack in the massive wall of opposition closing round him. Eichel wrote to say his heart was bleeding

* George II went so far as to moot the following: Austria in addition to regaining Silesia and Glatz might share with Saxony and Hanover in dividing the Prussian Duchy of Magdeburg; Cleve should be lopped off too, together with the recent windfall to Prussia of East Friesland. Russia with any luck would be brought to join in with the bait of East Prussia. The residue of Brandenburg should be sequestrated to reimburse England and Holland for their outlay in general subsidies. What George left out of account was the religious factor—the very one which had so lately brought the House of Hanover to the English throne. His Government refused to contemplate a scheme by which the painfully built-up Protestant bloc would be instantly destroyed; and the proposal went no further. In this connexion, it is well to bear in mind that England as Austria's ally was at war with France but not with Prussia; England's and Austria's ally, Saxony, was not at war with either France or Prussia; England's and Austria's and Saxony's ally, Sardinia, was at war with France's ally, Spain, but not with France; England's, Austria's, Saxony's and Sardinia's ally, Holland, was not at war with anybody.

for the poor King; Podewils believed the end of Brandenburg was at hand. To neither was it any comfort that they had the right to say, 'I told you so.'

'I shall win,' said Frederick. '. . . What ship's captain, having failed in every bid for safety, would not have the courage to blow up his powder magazine? A woman, the Queen of Hungary, refused to despair when the enemy was at the gates of Vienna and her best provinces were gone: should we possess less fortitude? As yet we have never lost a battle; some fortunate issue may yet raise us up higher than we have ever stood. . . . *It is my pride that I have done more than any of my forbears** for the greatness of my House, that I have played a distinguished part among the crowned heads of Europe; to maintain myself therein is, as it were, a personal duty which I shall fulfil, even at the cost of happiness and life. I have no choice now: either I will uphold my power, or . . . have Prussia's name buried with me. . . . If I must perish, let it be with glory, sword in hand.'

He had the courage of his egotism, and the one was equal to the other in heroic proportion. The quality of heroism has the peculiar power of eclipsing by its pure dazzle the dross of any baser matter from which it may have sprung. Invariably it will gild the cause it serves. With Frederick there was no exception. In fact, the final motif of his life and legend was now clearly stated for the first time: the spectacle of man rising to the heights of his human powers in adversity—never mind the origins of that adversity. Reproach and laughter in the world were stilled. And the cry of, 'I shall win, or none of us shall see Berlin again,' so far from repelling those whom it promised to immolate, diffused inspiration.

Frederick when he wrote those words had thought he knew the worst. He had been wrong. About the middle of April he learned that a Saxon army was setting out from the north-western corner of Bohemia to join the Austrians in the south-east. Not only did this bring the troops at Prince Charles's disposal up to well over 110,000, but with Saxony's entry into the struggle for Silesia Brandenburg and Berlin itself were very seriously threatened. Podewils, his 'hair standing on end', as

* My italics.

he wrote to Eichel, received the King's directives for the civilian evacuation and military defence of Berlin.

Three things helped to raise Frederick's spirits which, 'Thanks be to Heaven!' he had recently stabilized on an even keel of stoicism. Traun was no longer with the Austrian army in Bohemia, having been transferred to the Frankfurt region to render the Imperial city safe for the forthcoming Election. Then, the King had found the refurbished Prussian armies in Silesia in far better fettle than he had dared hope. And now the French in Flanders repaid the English for Dettingen, at Fontenoy on 11 May. Though Frederick wrote caustically to the King of France that a victory on the banks of the Skamander or the capture of Peking would be about as useful to the Prussians in Silesia as that distant coup, his heart beat higher and he began to think Fontenoy might mark the turn of the tide.

In any event, the head-on collision which he had vainly courted all last year was coming now. 'Anything is better than this waiting and uncertainty. . . . The great emetic will either kill or cure, within but a few hours.'

CHAPTER 25
THE GREAT EMETIC: THREE DOSES

Frederick likened his design—which he said he would submit with confidence to the shades of Condé or Turenne—to a mouse-trap. The entrance to it were certain passes across the southern mountain barrier of Silesia; the bait was the Prussian army, the greater part of which had been drawn together about the selected area at the opening of the plain. It remained to ensure that the mouse—80,000 strong, against the bait's 65,000—chose the desired approach and that the bait would prove fatal.

Slowly effecting their concentration in the course of May, the Prussians had got to know the district inside out; and the local peasantry was friendly to them. It had been a mistake on the Austrian side to compose the liberating forces sent into Silesia mainly of levies from other provinces who did not speak the language and behaved like conquerors. Not only were there no leakages as to Frederick's manœuvres, but he succeeded in insinuating false reports into Austrian headquarters by which Prince Charles was led to believe the Prussian army in an advanced state of demoralization and about to retreat towards Breslau. Finally a series of carefully executed feints made the Prussians' imminent expulsion from Silesia to appear so certain, that all the Saxon heavy artillery was diverted north to Wittenberg, in readiness for the attack on Brandenburg which was to follow immediately on the expected allied victory.

On 3 June the combined Austrian and Saxon armies began to debouch from the hills and spread over the plain, affording the hidden watchers a panoramic picture of their strength and dispositions. In return the Austrian leaders on their observation post, the gallows' hill of the village of Hohenfriedberg, were treated to the calculated spectacle of a winding Prussian column making for Striegau, another village some five or six miles to the north-east. Here the decoy troops duly encamped for the night—and duly turned their camp into a dummy, silently moving out again as soon as darkness fell, with the fires left burning. At the same time the Prussian main army deployed and from two sides advanced upon the Saxon contingent, which had settled north of Hohenfriedberg at a place called Häslicht. The night was clear and starlit, potholes in the roads had been quietly filled in beforehand, drums and hooves were muffled, and everything proceeded precisely to plan.

At 2 a.m. on 4 June the King held a final conference with his generals. At 4 a.m. the first Prussian cannon-balls produced their murderous surprise among the Saxon outposts; by seven o'clock the entire Saxon wing had been destroyed, thickly tangled mounds of dead testifying to a valiant resistance.

No message had got through to Prince Charles, who tranquilly deduced that the echoes of a cannonade which 'seemed to set the mountains trembling' signified that the Saxons were capturing Striegau, and stayed in bed. Not so the inhabitants of Breslau, who also heard the thunder. Protestants and Jews flocked out into the streets and held public prayers for a Prussian victory; Catholics barred their doors and prayed at home.

When Prince Charles received the news of the accomplished disaster, the Prussians were already wheeling to outflank and engage the Austrians next. There was just time to receive them in battle order, and the fight was severe; but by 9 a.m. this second part of the battle also was done.*

At first the Prussians could not credit having captured seventy-six colours in all; there was a recount. Sixty-six cannon had been taken; the number of prisoners ran to 6,000, of whom 200 were officers, including four generals. The Saxon

* One Prussian regiment, the Bayreuth Dragoons under General Gessler, alone put twenty Austrian battalions to flight; Frederick himself led three battalions in a successful charge upon an Austrian gun emplacement, which only 360 men survived with him.

losses were about 2,950, the Austrian nearly 4,700, to 900 Prussian dead and 3,800 wounded.

Frederick, with the quiet radiance of the delivered, referred all praises to the hand of God. Only in a hasty note to his mother—signed also by his brothers Augustus William and Henry, to prove to her that they were alive and well—did the remark escape him that there had been nothing like it since Blenheim. Henceforth the only other person to whom he would occasionally betray a hint of candid self-satisfaction was his factotum Fredersdorf—and that in much the same way as to his mother: to share a morsel of agreeable personal news with one whom he could give no greater pleasure. The urge of boastfulness had passed with the need. Gilding the lily of his reputation now could only have dimmed its lustre.

Also, there was smaller occasion for rejoicing than Frederick had had reason to expect. The victory of Hohenfriedberg, which in the literature of war ranks as a set-piece of its kind and as one of the principal proofs of Frederick's military genius, failed to bring him 'advantageous peace, and a long rest', such as he had looked forward to. The great emetic had not worked this time.

Three years before, when it had done so, the circumstances had been very different. Then the French still stood in Bohemia, with Bavaria and Saxony behind them. Now the Bavarian army had ceased to exist, Saxony was Austria's ally, with English and Dutch also fighting on Maria Theresa's side. Only in the north were French armies disputing her possessions: and the Austrian Netherlands were as nothing to her in comparison with Silesia.

Further, Frederick by failing to pursue the enemy into the mountains gave him time to bind his wounds and recover from the moral shock of defeat. Although Frederick later accused himself of remissness in this respect, it is hard to see how at the time he could have acted otherwise. His forces were badly fatigued, and owing to lack of money food transportation was almost wholly dependent on requisitioned farm carts with scant and poor stocks of draught animals, while the mountain communities had been razed bare after two successive occupations by the allies. And he could not risk depleting the standing defence of Silesia, or for that matter of Brandenburg, which remained liable to attack from Saxony or Hanover.

The latter danger, at least, began to recede. About the middle of July Prince Charles Edward Stuart sailed from Nantes for Scotland and landed in the Hebrides early the following month; on 19 August the standard of the Jacobite Rebellion was raised high in Britain. The heart of Pharaoh, as Frederick said with reference to his Uncle George, was softened. Very much against his personal inclinations, King George yielded to the pressure of his Ministers and agreed to the Convention of Hanover (26 August), which re-affirmed Anglo-Prussian friendship and renewed the English guarantee of Silesia as a Prussian possession. With this went an undertaking to bring in England's allies, Saxony and Austria, into the compact as soon as might be.

But that proved an over-optimistic view. In fact, the danger emanating from Saxony increased.

Shortly before the Convention of Hanover came into being, Frederick had directed a threatening manifesto, tantamount to a declaration of war, at Saxony for her part in the invasion of Silesia. He had left it at that only because on the conclusion of the new agreement it was felt that Saxony would hardly hesitate to follow the English lead. However, Saxony meanwhile had secured a Russian pledge of military aid in the event that the allied attempt at reconquering Silesia resulted in a Prussian attack on Saxony—a pledge too good to waste. Saxony stood as firm as Austria herself in resisting England's persuasion.

That was as far as it went for the moment. For nearly four months Prussians and Austrians conducted their small war about the Bohemian Elbe country, 'contending for hay and laurels'—that is, warily wrestling for position whilst trying to take the food out of each other's mouths. The two commanders took up semi-permanent headquarters on opposite sides of the river, Prince Charles at Königingrätz, Frederick at Chlumetz, where he was able to relax sufficiently to catch up on his reading, play the flute, and dote upon his dogs.

His fancy, the graceful whippet breed, had become as necessary to him as flute and books and ink and snuff; the favourites of his kennel went everywhere with him. They were his children—or, as it goes almost without saying scandal would soon hint, his harem. The favourites were always bitches—generally speaking more intelligent and making better pets than the male. Frederick was not the first nor the last among the lonely-hearted to take comfort in a boundless and unquestioning devotion—traditionally defined as 'dog-like' in every class of creatures—such as Frederick William had pined for all his life, and which one may lavishly requite without fear of disadvantage. Withal, even the most dearly beloved animal pet is more easily replaced than a human friend. Frederick, during those months in Bohemia, was suffering deeply from the death of two of the men he had counted closest to his heart. Étienne Jordan died late in May, Keyserlingk in August: when 13 September came round, Frederick wrote of it as the first month's anniversary of his Caesarion's death, as if that were the sole significance of the date.

The thirteenth September was the date of the Imperial Election.

Since July Frankfurt had been like a beleaguered city, with a French and a Pragmatic (Austrians, Hanoverians, Dutch) army respectively determined to 'ensure a free Election'. With Traun's weight thrown into the balance, the French were ousted from the region, and the freedom of the Election was all for Archduke Francis. On 13 September, then, Maria Theresa's husband received the splendid dignity of her father and forefathers, with a majority of seven out of nine Electoral votes: the representatives of Brandenburg and the Palatinate retired formally protesting. The Coronation was set for 4 October.

Vienna was all jubilation. If Francis was no Habsburg, his sons were; one broadsheet showed the infant Archdukes Joseph and Charles under a tree on which the Imperial eagle spread its wings, with the legend, 'Charles: *Look there, Joey, go catch Granddaddy's birdie!* Joseph: *I'm yet too little; run and call Papa, he'll catch it for me.*'

Maria Theresa, however, still repined: without its lost jewel of Silesia the Imperial Crown would not be worth wearing. Repeated messages from Vienna urged her brother-in-law to see to it that 4 October be celebrated worthily, with a victory over the Prussians to efface Hohenfriedberg for all time. Reluctant at first, Prince Charles in the latter part of September made up his mind to act in earnest.

The forces Frederick had with him in Bohemia had shrunk to half, considerable numbers having had to be rushed to Upper Silesia, where once again Hungarian troops were daily gaining ground. A second corps had gone to swell the Old Dessauer's army on guard in Halle by the Saxon frontier. The King with the remainder had decided to withdraw from the wasted Bohemian countryside ('I'm not the one who commands here: we are ruled by flour and forage.') and winter in Lower Silesia. Unaware that the enemy was moving too, he started for the hills.

As at Chotusitz in relation to Mollwitz, the situation before Hohenfriedberg was now reversed. This time it was Frederick who remained in ignorance throughout of the enemy's movements, and like Prince Charles before him he took too much for granted. Unnoticed, unbetrayed, the Austrians closed in till from the surrounding heights they had his army under complete observation as it made its way through the clefts and valleys leading to the plain between the Elbe and its tributary the River Aupa. On 29 September Frederick did get word that Prince Charles was also on the march, but still without the least intimation that the Austrians were anywhere near.

Heading for Trautenau, where a part of their force were already waiting with the bakeries, the Prussians halted for the night in a valley bounded by forests and downs. Under cover of the wooded hills, and aided by heavy autumn mists, the Austrians through the hours of darkness completed their encirclement. The main body occupied the crown of an extended rise running, like an obtuse V, north to south and roughly at right angles to the Prussian camp, whose lines pointed east towards Trautenau and, incidentally, an ambush of some further 12,000 Austrians laid in the defiles about Eypel. 'We hold them as though in the middle of a handkerchief,' one of Prince Charles's generals exulted. 'Tomorrow within an hour we'll have them pulled up by the four corners.' Prince

Charles advised him to keep a firm grip on his corners: 'You don't know the Prussians yet.'

On the morrow Frederick rose at four as usual and the generals assembled in his tent for the order of the day. Shortly after five a messenger broke in reporting that huge enemy cavalry formations were massing close by. The King ran outside, jumped on his horse and rode to the most westerly look-out post to see for himself. There was no doubt. The mists were clearing, and revealed far-stretching reefs of dust which bespoke the approach of an entire army, minute by minute adding to those already in position.

The Prussians were trapped in their valley. Every exit was dominated by narrowing, rocky cliffs. To stay where they were meant defending their camp to the death, with small hope of a better issue than just that. The only alternative was to attack, uphill.

The King collared the nearest drummer and bade him sound the call to arms. While all round tents were hurriedly struck and men obeyed the signal, he galloped on a last survey and detailed his final directions—which over and above the exigencies of haste involved nothing less than wheeling right about in a total change of front, to face the enemy who menaced right flank and rear. Inexplicably, the Austrian cavalry vanguard held back and allowed this manœuvre to be put in motion instead of blocking the attack by getting in first. Their artillery, however, commanding almost the whole field of Prussian operation, lost no time; the advancing ranks were thinned by as many as eight or ten men and horses at a time, without respite, and without effect upon the rest who went on 'with undiminished speed and quite unheeding', as the Austrian official report has it.

As at Chotusitz, Buddenbrock's cuirassiers opened the engagement, up a steep, rough gradient which the enemy had deemed unassailable, exposed to the raking fire which could not miss, yet pressing home the first attack with overwhelming impetus. Taking still more dreadful punishment, the infantry battalions of the same, right wing marched straight at the Austrian batteries, fell back decimated, renewed themselves, gained the top, overbore their adversaries, took the guns.

Centre and left followed suit; the Austrians yielded crest after crest, in cumulative disorder. Before the hour of noon they were in full retreat. Only a part of the Hungarian horsemen who had stood at Eypel appeared in time to have joined, and perhaps turned, the battle: but they fell on the Prussian baggage instead and occupied themselves with plunder and destruction until the decision was past and irrevocable.

The acts of collective and individual heroism, the tremors of the balance, the errors and lightning strokes of ingenuity are too many to be listed for a battle which, though the bloodiest yet of Frederick's experience, could not alter his strategic or political situation—not unless he had lost it, to be sure, as, according to himself, he deserved to have lost.

He had upheld the Prussian record of invincibility, albeit by a truly Pyrrhic victory. He had lost nearly 900 dead, over 2,700 wounded, over 300 missing; a fourth part of the infantry was gone. Gone also was the war chest, along with everything else contained in the camp; all the Hungarians had left behind were charred and mutilated corpses, mostly women and wounded. The Austrian losses were 800 dead, 2,780 wounded, 3,000 captured; the Saxons claimed 755 casualties altogether.* The pursuit was carried no further than the village of Soor, which gave its name to the battle; for honour's sake—said Frederick—the Prussians stayed five days in occupation of the field, and then slowly completed their withdrawal to Silesia.

Rightly the Hungarian hussars let it be known that they had left the Prussian King nothing but the shirt on his back. He had no change of linen; no books, no flute, no dogs, no snuff, no tableware, no Eichel—not even paper and ink. In pencil, on a scrap torn from his pocket notebook, Frederick scribbled the victory communiqué for Breslau: 'Austrians totally beaten; more another time.'

For a day or two he was dependent on the charity—so he expressed it—of his officers for a share of the odd hunk of bread stowed away in one or the other knapsack. At such times the comradeship of levelling grime and improvisation can carry a lofty sustenance of its own. And for a true heir to Frederick

* Frederick put the relative starting strengths at 30,000 allied troops to 19,000 Prussians; modern estimates vary between that and 40,000 to 22,000.

William's itch of omnifaisance, having to do everything for one's self had its stimulating compensations too. Some stationery being procured, the King among a host of other rôles had to act as his own secretary in his official as well as his private correspondence.

Fredersdorf, who was ill in Berlin, had to be told and reassured at the first opportunity (2 October):

> Just think what a scrap we had of it, 18 against 50! I was in the soup up to my ears all right. But you see? no bullet will touch me. . . . Annemarie is killed, Champion must be dead too [two of Frederick's horses]; Eichel and his decoder have not yet been found. Can you see that Köppen sends me ten thousand Thaler? If you had been here, I wouldn't have lost everything I had with me: but you know that silly old Rietzen, feckless as they come, and I had so many dangers round my neck, I couldn't possibly do anything about it [i.e. saving the camp!] myself. Now the campaign is sure to be over; so you can stop worrying. . . . Brave, honest Wedell is dead; Albert too [Frederick's wife's brother]—no great loss; Blanckenburg and Bredow too. May Heaven go on helping us. . . . God protect you. See to things in Berlin for me, take your medicine as you should, look after yourself, and get well!—Friedrich.

Citing his losses in the order of their importance to him, Frederick had omitted one which touched him painfully: the abduction of the whippet bitch Biche. After repeated requests the enemy returned the animal ahead of the other prisoners. The King's attendants surreptitiously let her into the room where he sat writing, and the reunion moved him to tears.

The next thing was to get replacements of his travelling library; Duhan was charged to send on a nucleus of Cicero, Horace, Lucian, Voltaire, Bossuet, and Montesquieu, to go on with.

Next came urgent orders to Fredersdorf for a snuff-box 'of jasper with brilliants and rubies, just like the one I had and which the hussars got' and two new flutes. Aside from the addiction itself, his snuff-boxes were becoming to Frederick what the Longfellows had been to Frederick William, and diamonds to Frederick I. Over the years his collection grew to 130—not counting what he gave away in presents from time to time—all ornate and costly; he liked to finger them as he carried them about. The psychological connotations of such fidgeting-talismans, and those attaching to the flute of all musical instruments, are too commonplace to need more than mention. Of less universal significance as a hinge and symbol of Frederick's crucial conflict with his father, the flute had also grown into an aid to thought, summoning inspiration whenever he got stuck in solving a problem.

Eichel, representing no private magic and thus not so immediately indispensable, was restored to service after eleven days of captivity. (With his usual efficiency he had managed to destroy most of the King's papers captured with him, on the way to Prince Charles's headquarters.) But before that the King had himself composed and fairly copied out the account of Soor for the newspapers at home, in which he underplayed his part as much as possible, 'in order that my respected ill-wishers, the Messrs. Gazetteers, may deign to consider it worthy of print.'

Another kind of dig was aimed at Wilhelmine, whom Frederick informed coldly of his victory over *her bosom friend, the Queen of Hungary:* while her brother was fighting for very life, the Margravine of Bayreuth had not found it in herself to keep away from Frankfurt and miss the Imperial Coronation; she had even gone to present her compliments in person to the new Empress.

Maria Theresa, pregnant once again, had made this first and only journey outside her own realm to witness her husband's investiture; but she was adamant in refusing to be crowned with him. Her pregnancy was the pretext; the truth was that she would not at any price detract from the two 'Couronnes masculines' she already bore in her own right, by accepting the diadem of a mere consort. She had changed not a little in the last five years, and though she would always love her husband tenderly, her autocratic pride, nurtured and hardened in the heat of perpetual emergency, came first. Sovereign dignity satisfied, she might let herself go in pure, homely sentiment, lustily crying, 'Vivat Kaiser Franz!' from the balcony on which she watched his ceremonial progress, and vigorously waving her handkerchief with the rest of the multitude.

Less than ever now would she hear of coming to terms with Frederick. If her armies were exhausted, so were his; if her people flagged in their enthusiasm for continuing the war, she would make Austria great as of old in spite of them. There could be no such thing as lasting peace within the Empire unless the King of Prussia were rendered too weak to cause future disturbance: those were her words to Robinson, who came to her with fresh designs for arbitration sketched out in Berlin.

It was not known either in Berlin or London that a further, 'fast and indissoluble' compact had been forged between Vienna and Dresden at the end of August, the basis of which was that neither Austria nor Saxony would under any circumstances whatsoever conclude a separate peace. Maria Theresa had promised to withdraw up to 12,000 troops from the Rhine and add them to the allied pool, Augustus III to throw in all his armed forces, so as to carry on the war even through the winter months and 'apply military pressure in such places where the enemy is most vulnerable'—which signified, in Brandenburg.

The Prussian army in Silesia, it was believed, was incapable of taking the field again before next spring. The Prussian army in Halle was dispersing, some regiments quartered as far north as Pomerania. The Saxon armies, on the other hand, were stationed so closely together that it would be possible to unite them within forty-eight hours, and the Austrian reinforcements from the Rhine were rapidly approaching the Saxon-Bohemian frontier. Provisionally the only hitch was that Prince Charles and the Saxon commander Count Rutowsky were so far unable to agree on a joint plan of action.

Behind the two powers' lapidary determination there was, all along, the Russian promise to Saxony of protection against Prussia. This, however, carried a proviso which now the Tzarina thought it well to reiterate—since too great a diminution of Prussia could not suit her any better than the reverse. The Russian promise would not apply if Saxony struck first at Brandenburg anywhere but in Silesia. She herself apprised Frederick of this. Frederick began to wonder, and tentatively to put two and two together.

Information had leaked out, concerning a continuous going and coming of Austrian troops in Bohemia. What if, on the basis of the Tzarina's declaration, the allies were hatching a scheme to embroil him with Russia? What if, by aiming a blow at Silesia via Saxon Lusatia, they hoped to lure him into Saxon territory?

Frederick's perspicacity was sharpened by a conviction, which had been slowly growing underneath his surface confidence that fighting would nowhere be resumed this year, that the key to peace lay in Saxony, the more accessible partner in the enemy alliance, and the one who looked to gain at the expense of Brandenburg a much-needed territorial link with Poland.

His surmise happened to be correct, but none around him would give it credence. Podewils and the Old Dessauer, both as a rule supremely militant in anti-Saxon suspicion, roundly told him that this was far-fetched to fantasy: even in Saxony one would not contemplate so insane a risk.

Presently corroboration came through some Swedish diplomats who were personal admirers of the King of Prussia, and who had got their information from none other than Count Brühl, King Augustus's Chief Minister and the crypto-regent of Saxony. Frederick would have preferred to be proved wrong. 'Shall I never be able to rest?' he exclaimed—one standard nightmare having superseded another: a labour of Sisyphus following on last year's impotence against Traun. 'To live like this is not living.' It was particularly the timing of the purposed blow which so dismayed him. But not for long. Perhaps the still persisting disbelief of his advisers helped steel him to override them.

To him the conclusive piece of circumstantial evidence was the character of Brühl himself, which therefore demands a glancing appraisal. Heinrich von Brühl, whose rise to power had begun in the last years of Augustus the Strong, was in his way a prodigy even among self-seeking politicians. Except in relation to his own material advancement and gratification, he seems to have lacked all practical sense and with it the faculty of co-ordinated, abstract thought. Ruled by vanity and greed and ruling others by the same, he lived, he governed, as it were, from hand to mouth: which made him unpredictable to those whose thinking proceeded by a less esoteric logic. Frederick thus was the last person to predict Brühl's actions, but he could understand them. In general, Frederick's understanding of human motives in all their diversity was so shrewd, so nearly unerring, that one is tempted to judge his misanthropy was founded in self-knowledge. In the case of Brühl, Frederick knew his gibes had in the past caught the other on the raw; with his kindred experience, he did not find it so difficult to believe that Brühl might even invite self-destruction, to destroy his detractor. Podewils and the Old Dessauer were happier, simpler, less self-conscious men. Strenuously opposing Frederick's plans to circumvent the allied plot, they now called *his* intention suicidal—without drawing the obvious parallel that, ironically, would have cleared the King of this charge.

In any event, they could not stop him. Frederick had received the Swedish warning on 11 November—the very day on which the trophies of Hohenfriedberg and Soor were deposited in the Garrison Church of Berlin. Five days later he was on his way to join the army in Silesia, 40,000 of which had been brought together near Liegnitz under the younger Prince Leopold. Under protest, the Old Dessauer was re-assembling his twenty-five battalions at Halle.

For once Frederick was determined to hold his defence till the attack on Prussia was demonstrably under way. He had not long to wait.

On 20 and 21 November two Austrian armies crossed into Saxon Lusatia, where their presence could have only one purpose. The army of Prince Charles was making for a rendezvous with Rutowsky's Saxons close to the Silesian border; the second Austrian army, led by General Grünne, headed straight north towards Brandenburg: for the Russian declaration contained no reference to any *Austrian* attack on Frederick's hereditary lands.

Directly the news was received, the younger Prince Leopold and Frederick with their 40,000 started from the Liegnitz area, by forced marches to prevent the junction of Rutowsky and Prince Charles. In the afternoon of 23 November, the Austrians were intercepted at Katholisch-Hennersdorf. The Saxon contingents attached to them were put out of action then and there; and Prince Charles, his retreat all but cut off, turned about and left Saxony faster than he had come—followed equally at speed by General Grünne, whose army had reached a point within thirty-five miles of Berlin. Their brief visit cost the Austrians 5,000 men, mainly prisoners,* and all their magazines.

The Prussians spread out over the south-eastern corner of Saxony as far as Görlitz. Through the offices of the British Minister at Dresden, Sir Thomas Villiers, King Augustus was invited to join the Convention of Hanover and make peace. Russia was arming, France turning a deaf ear to Frederick's urgent appeals for a subsidy. Augustus declined and allowed Brühl to spirit him away to Prague, where he would not see the ravages of war—and for that matter of his Austrian allies—in his own lands: lands so rich and civilized, incomparable with the barren wilds of Bohemia or Moravia, that Frederick for one was struck more forcibly than he had ever been by the agony one thus imposed upon a country.

The war had gone on too long for him, not only from the point of view of his resources. Frederick had proved himself as he had so passionately needed to do; in that sense, the war had already outlived its purpose. Thus his heart was open to pity and revulsion: he wished for peace as much from humane sentiments as in his own interests. But all his attempts to bring it about before any more harm was done continued fruitless.

> Everything is fine [he wrote to Fredersdorf in his atrocious German]. You'll have heard enough about all the good things that have happened, so I won't go into detail. . . . Our hussars are great lords one and all, loaded with fine horses and carriages and what-you-will; everything is to be had for a song. The enemy has lost over 1,000 baggage- and forage wagons. . . . My health is not too good; I don't sleep a single night for palpitations and stomach cramps and can hardly eat a thing. . . . I've been offering them peace, and if it won't do any good, my soul will be innocent of all these evils here as I am doing everything

* It was Frederick's set policy to convert prisoners as far—and as fast—as possible to service under the Prussian colours.

in my power to stop them. But an enemy army preying on the land is a great misfortune and ruination, from which God save anyone who can manage to avert it. . . . My heart bleeds for them: but still, better here than at home. . . . The whole frolic has cost us less than thirty dead and seventy wounded. . . . Here's to our going to the opera in Berlin on the 15th or 16th next!*

That was not to be. On 10 December, from Bautzen on the road to Dresden, the estimate was revised: 'I shan't be able to get to Berlin before the 20th, for because the old codger crawls so that one has to drive him the whole time . . .'

The crawling old codger was, of course, the Old Dessauer, and Frederick's mild if contumelious remark about driving him was an understatement paraphrasing the last word in tension.

Time was of the essence of the whole campaign, and that not only because winter conditions were already far advanced. If it was Frederick's vigilant despatch which had won him the first round, the second round was coming on and looked like being compromised from the start by the deliberate pace of the Old Prince. To begin with, he had delayed in Halle till 29 November, and although receiving the surrender of Leipzig the next day, thereafter proceeded with an excess of caution which Frederick interpreted as a demonstration against himself, and which certainly allowed the enemy to rally.

The Saxon main army was moving upstream towards Dresden along the left bank of the Elbe; the Austrian second army, likewise hale and whole, stood at Pirna; and Prince Charles, having reconstituted the first army in Prague, was on the way back to Saxony. Every day, every hour of procrastination increased the danger of the Old Dessauer's force being overcome by a united host of Austrians and Saxons—and the closer this occurred to Brandenburg, the wider the gateway to enemy invasion. In desperation Frederick sent 10,000 men to meet the old man at Meissen, where they were agreeably surprised to find the bridge across the river undestroyed and so gained the left bank without difficulty: only that the Halle army which was to have received them was not there, placing them in grave peril.

* A postscript reads: 'Have just had 3 Bichelets.' Biche, the returned prisoner of Soor, had littered.

The King was near distracted; at length, on the day before his relevant note to Fredersdorf, he launched his sharpest message yet at the Old Prince:

> . . . If anything could here plunge me into disaster, it will be Your Highness's dilatoriness. . . . It so happens that I always express myself so clearly that in all my days not one officer of my army has complained of being unable to understand me—my Field-Marshal is the only one who either can't or won't understand my plain and explicit orders. I cannot understand this and am most extremely displeased, for you are doing me out of all honour and reputation! . . . I have no sense of humour in these matters, and shall be obliged if Your Highness will not take me for some little Prince of Zerbst or Köthen, but just obey orders.

The King himself was racing ahead to get to Meissen before the enemy. Some saving delay now occurred in the allied camp, where the usual jealousies were flaring up, particularly after the Austrians' arrival in the neighbourhood of Dresden. The subterranean differences between Prince Charles and Count Rutowsky, coupled with the vandalism of the visitors, led to the allocation of strategically unsuitable quarters, widely scattered and some distance from the capital at that. Also, Rutowsky decided to advance no further. Dresden, part of whose fortifications had long since been turned into gardens, was too vulnerable. He would stay within call, and prepare a bloody reception for the Old Dessauer at a spot roughly level with Dresden. He chose a perfect position in hilly terrain between the Elbe and a village named Kesselsdorf.

But Frederick's insulting letter had done its work upon the Old Prince, throwing him into so rending a rage that to spite the King he would have rushed the portals of Hell. On Sunday, 12 December, he occupied Meissen, then marched on, in four columns ready for battle, trying to find the enemy.

In the course of the morning of 15 December the Saxon position was at last located. Rutowsky's forces were drawn out over three or four miles along a ridge overlooking slopes and chasms padded with frozen snow and glazed with ice; a little way off to the north-east the Austrians of the second army were ensconced in some rocky clefts descending towards the river.

All but Rutowsky's left wing, which rested on the village of Kesselsdorf itself, was impregnably arrayed atop natural battlements of rock, bristling with cannon. The village, too, was heavily protected with gun batteries, but appeared the only remotely likely point of attack. And attack the Old Dessauer would. He had been outrageously rebuked for going by the book with orthodox prudence and circumspection; now the father of the Prussian army, fifty years a soldier, maligned and chivvied by a conceited hothead less than half his age, would show what he and his could do when roused, and die in the attempt if necessary. He who had dismissed Brühl's suicidal impulse as impossible and castigated Frederick's as madness, had now been brought to the same pitch, himself.

Not that he threw away the book. It was the strength of the Old Dessauer's talent that he could combine method with the proposition of going head first through a wall; and he made his dispositions with great care. This took him till two o'clock. Then, having strung out his two lines of infantry to the length of Rutowsky's ridge, with cavalry support behind, and taking five battalions of his own élite to open the attack under his personal leadership, the old man took his place in front and prayed aloud, as was his pious habit.

This was his prayer at Kesselsdorf: 'Lord God, help me! and if you don't want to, then at least don't you help them villains of enemies either, but look on and see how it goes! Amen. In Jesus' name, MARCH!'

The grenadiers, the old man's pride and life-work, marched, with bared chests and shouldered arms, directly into the Austrian guns at Kesselsdorf—on and on, without themselves firing a shot, closing the breaches torn into them, true to their fame, terrifying as automata. Twice, all the same, they were beaten back by the murderous bombardment; the old Prince in the thick of it, weeping with the rage and misery of their dreadful toil as it foundered over and over in mangled debris—bent on seeking his own death, men asserted afterwards.

At the second repulse, however, the allied grenadiers—nine battalions of them—who stood at Kesselsdorf saw themselves winning, abandoned the cover of the village and with cries of 'Victory!' rushed down into the yielding Prussian ranks and after the fleeing, as they thought. But there was no flight, only a turmoil of hand-to-hand fighting: the Saxon artillery had to cease fire, as the combatants were inextricably mixed. This gave the Old Dessauer his cue to hurl in his waiting dragoons and cuirassiers in a great third wave, which within a few moments completed the break-up, begun under the intoxication of enthusiasm, of the enemy formations. Hardly any got away, hardly any unwounded. Another few moments, and the Saxon cavalry close by suffered the same fate; and, Rutowsky having omitted to provide a second line of defence, the village and its batteries were fast in Prussian hands.

So much for the action of the Prussian right wing. In the centre the youngest of the old man's three sons, Prince Maurice,* had the task of storming the glassy hillside to the east of the village. To this end his troops had first to descend an elongated slope, then ford a quaggy moat formed by the Kessel brook which there traversed the hollow 'frozen at the sides, but all the middle waist-deep, icy mud', and finally to clamber up the slippery rampart opposite. He himself, like his father in the lead, showed how it was to be done, inciting ardour to phrenetic pitch. Platoon by platoon, helping each other from foothold to foothold, the men clawed and scrambled up the rock, too steep for any fusillade to reach them, and so gained the top almost unscathed. Already the belief was spreading through the enemy host that black magic was at work against them, daemonic thunder growling from the bowels of the earth. Evidently bullet-proof as his sire, Prince Maurice in as short a space of time for his part made the impossible, fact; the heights were taken, resistance crushed and rolled away. The cavalry of the left wing was summoned to give chase.

At three o'clock the battle had been everywhere at its height. At five o'clock it was over. But for the terrain, which was unsuitable for cavalry pursuit, and but for the early nightfall of the season, the Saxon army would have been annihilated. Straggling back in disorder towards Dresden, it left 3,000 dead and wounded and 6,000 prisoners on the field, and never stopped in its retreat until, along with its technically unbeaten Austrian allies, it might rest in Bohemia.

* Aged thirty-three, like Frederick.

A previous, rueful quip of Frederick's, that, having defeated the Austrians without coming to grips with them, he had best chase the Saxons out of Saxony, had come true; and it was for his father's legacy and stand-in, the Old Dessauer, proudly to send word that he had sounded 'the Sodom's trumpet' to the enemy's perdition. Jericho rather than Sodom was the Biblical precedent the old man had in mind; but in truth that difference was immaterial.

Before the week was out the whole country lay under Prussian occupation, and Austria as well as Saxony sued for peace.

CHAPTER 26

EXIT FREDERICK WILLIAM

Frederick had won.

It was a fairy-tale triumph, the happy ending par excellence: the final transformation of ugly duckling into swan. What happens to the swan, as swan, is always necessarily another story.

A series of touching tableaux brought the transformation scene to a rousing finish. If Frederick made the most of every one, it was with great intelligence and breadth of mind.

The battle of Kesselsdorf was fought on Wednesday, 15 December. Early on Thursday the King set out at the head of his troops to honour the victors on their field. The Old Dessauer, tense and proud in his cloak shot full of bullet holes—his only hurt, as usual—met him at the spot where the first note of the 'Sodom's' trumpet had been sounded. On sight of the old man the King dismounted and, hat in hand, arms spread wide, ran to embrace him, thanked him 'in the most flattering terms to be mustered', and asked him to forget what had gone before. For two solid hours the old man—his ferocious countenance transfigured, those who knew him noted—was able to linger on the climax of his life, as he took the King over every inch of the ground in recapitulation of the battle, watched at a respectful distance by groups of sightseers, scavengers and Samaritans from Dresden.

Frederick, with all regard for the Old Prince's valour, was nevertheless conscious of acting with deliberate magnanimity;

the sentiments of a lifetime, and the intolerable anxiety of the last three weeks, were not easily erased.*

Magnanimity was the order of the day, stressed at every step when in the wake of the still retreating Saxon army the Prussians entered Dresden. Frederick did not omit to draw attention to the contrast with Charles XII's occupation of the city forty years ago. The contrast with the recent passage of friendly Austrian troops he had no need to underline. He declined to make his quarters at the royal palace, where the Queen-Electress and her younger children had been left behind, and went out of his way to show these helpless hostages kindness and respect. (Less courteously, he took a look at Brühl's profuse wardrobe and observed that it was certainly odd to find over three hundred wigs belonging to a man without a head.) 'Sui victoria indicat regem,' was the motto under which he would soon after publish the documents covering his negotiations with the Saxon Government.

The regal honour of self-conquest was not one which the Old Dessauer coveted either for himself or his men; he did not believe in coddling the vanquished, and saw no reason why his heroes of Kesselsdorf should not have a bit of fun now here and there. In this way, the celebrated conduct of the Prussian soldiery broke down somewhat, despite proclamations and exemplary punishments. But curiously enough, in the world at large the reputation now proved stronger than the incidents belying it; the Prussian soldier received more credit for his restraint and consideration of Catholic sensibilities in Saxony than he had five years ago in Silesia. The cynosure of the public gaze, the King himself, did everything to justify it.

For Sunday's Te Deum at the Church of the Cross in Dresden a throne had been made ready for him in the nave; Frederick spurned it with quiet rebuke and found himself a place among the congregation. Of course it made an excellent impression: yet few conquerors enjoying unconditional surrender have taken pains to impress themselves in that

* The Old Dessauer died of a stroke some fifteen months later; Frederick announced this to Fredersdorf en passant, 'The Old Dessauer's kicked the bucket,' plainly licensing his chamberlain's sympathetic reply to the effect of, 'Whereat there will be rejoicing in Hell.'

particular way upon a population at their mercy. If this conqueror indulged his vanity, at least its appetites were epicurean rather than cannibal. If his behaviour was calculated, it was not at variance with his genuine intentions.

To the astonishment and admiration of his contemporaries, Frederick contented himself with one million Thaler reparations from Saxony, levying no other tribute. To Austria he granted the same terms—recognition of Frederick's tenure of Silesia against Frederick's recognition of Francis as German Emperor—which had been repeatedly offered and rejected before Kesselsdorf. It was everywhere realized that just then he could have named any price, and got it. For the Russian Tzarina, on whose ire such hopes had been built and whose military preparations had now been completed, considered it inadvisable to attack Prussia without allied support; Maria Theresa was still at war with France, suffering dire reverses in Italy, and, informed that further English subsidies were out of the question, could not afford to let Saxony conclude a separate peace. But what Frederick wanted was a settlement that would last.

Imposing ruin and oppression on the defeated does not make for a safe future. So other conquerors have learnt to their cost, and proved that good sense, even without ideal goodwill, is none so common in a situation where an individual has absolute power to rationalize his human impulses into political decisions. Had Frederick kept his realistic calculations to himself, the world-wide applause might have been everlasting; but no, he had to publish them before very long. He was working systematically to lay the foundations of future friendship with all former enemies: surely Reason would present a sounder basis than a pretence of utter disinterestedness. So it did; but it spoilt the effect. Frederick cared nothing for that sort of effect; here as in all things else, he wanted recognition on his own terms.

He had got that, at thirty-four. The double peace treaty was signed on Christmas Day amid a clamour of international felicitations: in Saxony, which had witnessed Frederick's most public abasement as Crown Prince. 'I'll not attack a cat in future,' he vowed. He added, without guile, 'Unless I am forced.'

On Monday, 27 December, he left Dresden, travelling light in an open carriage with his two brothers. On Tuesday they paused to dine at Wusterhausen, of doleful memory confounded, and in the early afternoon reached the environs of Berlin.

His reception there was unprecedented. The acclaim at his accession when all was said had been part convention, part demonstration against Frederick William, part singing for largesse. Once Frederick's failure to implement the expected administrative reforms had sunk in, enthusiasm had simmered down. With his rash plunge into war, popular feeling in the paramount and therefore most politically conscious town of the Kingdom had turned right against him. The bloodless annexation of Silesia had helped, but without allaying apprehensions that were vindicated all too soon. The victory of Mollwitz was no merit of his; Chotusitz might have been a fluke. Ill-feeling had revived upon the outbreak of the Second War, hard on the heels of the First, and as it appeared hinging on the affairs of the Empire rather than on any direct concerns of Prussia.

The Sisyphus campaign of 1745 had wrought a change. For one thing, Frederick had become acknowledged as a new star in the martial firmament by all the nations. Then, the Frederick-legend, spreading outwards from Silesia, could not but flood his own country too, there to be appropriated as in a reservoir for the irrigation of the national self-esteem. By the time that the country was toppling on the brink of bankruptcy, the sudden threat of enemy invasion had held Frederick's subjects united behind him, their defender. And now that their King had turned the tables on his foes, now that it was evident he commanded luck as well as strength, gratitude and the obscure narcissist currents of tribal totemism joined forces, ready to deify him outright.

All this time Frederick had been away, and he was unprepared for the wild rapture with which he was greeted. The whole population had turned out to show him its feelings by every means in its power, marking a saturnalia of hero-worship. Coming on top of the immense relief from terrible strain and apprehensions and, no doubt, remorse—on top of the dream-like abruptness of salvation—it moved Frederick almost beyond control. Years hence, when he was used to mass adoration, he would sardonically dismiss it, 'Mount a monkey on a camel: that'll fetch just the same response.' But this was his first experience of it in the people among whom he had grown up. He had managed without praise for too great a part of his life, not to feel it when it came to him in such measure.

Tears in his eyes, powerless to smile, he could only salute and murmur words of thanks, over and over, as he was driven through the town, till at the palace esplanade he got out, fronted the multitude, took off his hat to them again and so stood silent and bare-headed a few moments before he went in.

Later in the evening he slipped out and through the streets bright and noisy with revelry edged his way to a withdrawn alley, where one person unable to come to his welcome, Duhan, lay dying. 'I am as though widowed and orphaned already; remember you are almost the only one left of the friends I have counted my family, and do get well.' This service Duhan could not do him: but at least they had both been granted the crowning boon of their association—that he had lived to see the day. He died in the early hours of 3 January.

There remained the old King in his grave at Potsdam, where, he had threatened, he would sit up and laugh at his son if Frederick made a hash of things.

Frederick had a dream, which with slight variation recurred once or twice over the years.

He dreamt he saw his father coming towards him with soldiers to put him under arrest; for what crime? 'for not loving his father enough.' Then the scene changed. He was on campaign. Again, suddenly his father stood before him. 'Have I done well?' the dreamer asked, and Frederick William answered, 'Yes.' 'Then I am content. Your approval is worth more to me than that of the whole world.'

One could not dream fairer than that.

* * *

Frederick had won. He had got everything his own way. He had squared himself with his father, and had settled accounts with him. The son had cast the father's every reproach back in his teeth, and at the same time treated the father's memory with a forbearance in the heroic style. He had had a proxy to hand—the Old Dessauer—in whom the son was able now to kick, now to pat the father; and an enemy, the House of Habsburg, on whom the son could piously avenge the father yet also show himself the better man.

Frederick had won; already men styled him 'the Great'. His greatness, Maupertuis wrote, now was such that only by the works of peace could he still add to it. That suited Frederick, who not long before had confided to the lamented Jordan: 'You are right in thinking I work hard. *This I do to keep alive: for nothing resembles death so closely as idleness**.' Having made his mark in a manner all the world accepted, Frederick might safely return to the pursuit of what he too accounted higher achievement, without having this decried as the most that the little man's sedentary talents were equal to. Nobody would dispute that the victor of two wars in which he had won every battle, laboured in the vineyard of Peace from choice, not by default. The comparison with Solomon would ring more soundly now that in the same breath Frederick was likened to Alexander. And the compulsive industry that was in his blood, fostered to near-mania by the happenings of his youth, henceforth might have full play on the best of positive grounds: it would not square simply with fear of impotence, sterility—death. 'A king is the first servant of the State.' Frederick would prove it.

He had won, all along the line. The world's image of the crushed and beaten Crown Prince of Prussia had been blotted out. Admitted into the ranks of poets and thinkers by the foremost living authority in the field, Frederick was in the pleasant position of being able to feel superior to his intellectual friends because they knew nothing of war, and to his generals because they knew nothing about art. Where other men of action could but hope for the best at the hands of the historians, he could put his own pen forward. Artists and scientists looked towards that Cinderella capital, Berlin—where a specially erected temple of Janus had been ceremonially closed during the peace celebrations—as a new sanctum of Apollo. Princes trembled, armies faltered at the name of Frederick of Prussia; diplomats respected his wits; the common people, not only in his own dominions, idolized him; clever men extolled his conversation and would travel far to partake of it; and the

* My italics.

custodians of Thought and Virtue, the philosophes, lauded their crowned member, whose cause they were making their own, come aggression, come arbitrariness. The concept of *enlightened* despotism, with a trick of masterly dialectical legerdemain reconciling two irreconcilables, was born.

Another concept, that was moribund, had been dealt the coup de grâce, although the institution in which it was embodied would not completely expire till sixty years hence. That concept, that institution was the Holy Roman Empire of the German Nation, a remnant of theocracy and thus a historical fossil, a deadweight upon Progress and consequently an abomination in the sight of all Enlightenment. As Frederick had predicted to Voltaire on the eve of the Silesian coup, by it 'the System' had been shattered though the pieces were still standing. Apologists of Frederick, anxious to condone the means because of the desirable end, could advance the argument usual in such cases, that you can't make an omelette without breaking eggs.

Furthermore, the author of the *Antimachiavel* had brought a new guise to kingship, with the idea of Service, the introduction of authority based on Reason and maintained by deserts, into an office hitherto founded only in its sacrosanct nature. It was the beginning of the end of the ideal of Louis XIV which had set the tone of royalty for so long—an empty, costly, and self-defeating form among the Sun King's teeming little imitators. Nothing succeeds like success: already there were princes awakening to the new fashion and limbering up again for the sincerest form of flattery.

Whether for good or ill remained to be seen.

Interpretations of Progress depend on the vantage point in time and space from which the past is judged. From Frederick's pinnacle of triumph, all that had led and goaded him to it now looked right and good. There was no more conflict. The period of reaction was closed. Thus far it had been Frederick against his father; from now on it would be Frederick acting for and by and as himself.

But, 'There's a Frederick William in you after all,' his father had once grudgingly conceded. How much of a Frederick William, neither of them knew.

APPENDIXES

Offspring of Frederick William I and Sophie Dorothee

Genealogical Table

Some Principal Dates

Offspring of

Frederick William I 1688–1740

and Sophie Dorothee 1687–1757

married 28 November 1706

A son (*Friedrich Ludwig*), born 23 November 1707, died within six months.

Friederike Sophie WILHELMINE, born 3 July 1709, died 1758.

A son (*Friedrich Wilhelm*), born 16 August 1710, died 1711.

Karl FRIEDRICH (*FREDERICK II*), born 24 January 1712, died 1786.

A daughter, born and died 1713.

Friederike LOUISE, born 28 September 1714, died 1784.

Philippina CHARLOTTE, born 13 March 1716, died 1801.

A son, born 1717, died 1718.

SOPHIE Dorothee Maria, born 25 January 1719, died 1765.

Louise ULRIKE, born 24 July 1720, died 1782.

August Wilhelm (*AUGUSTUS WILLIAM*), born 9 August 1722, died 1758.

Anna AMALIE (*AMELIA*), born 9 November 1723, died 1787.

Friedrich Heinrich Ludwig (*HENRY*), born 18 January 1726, died 1802.

August FERDINAND, born 23 May 1730, died 1813.

GENEALOGICAL TABLE

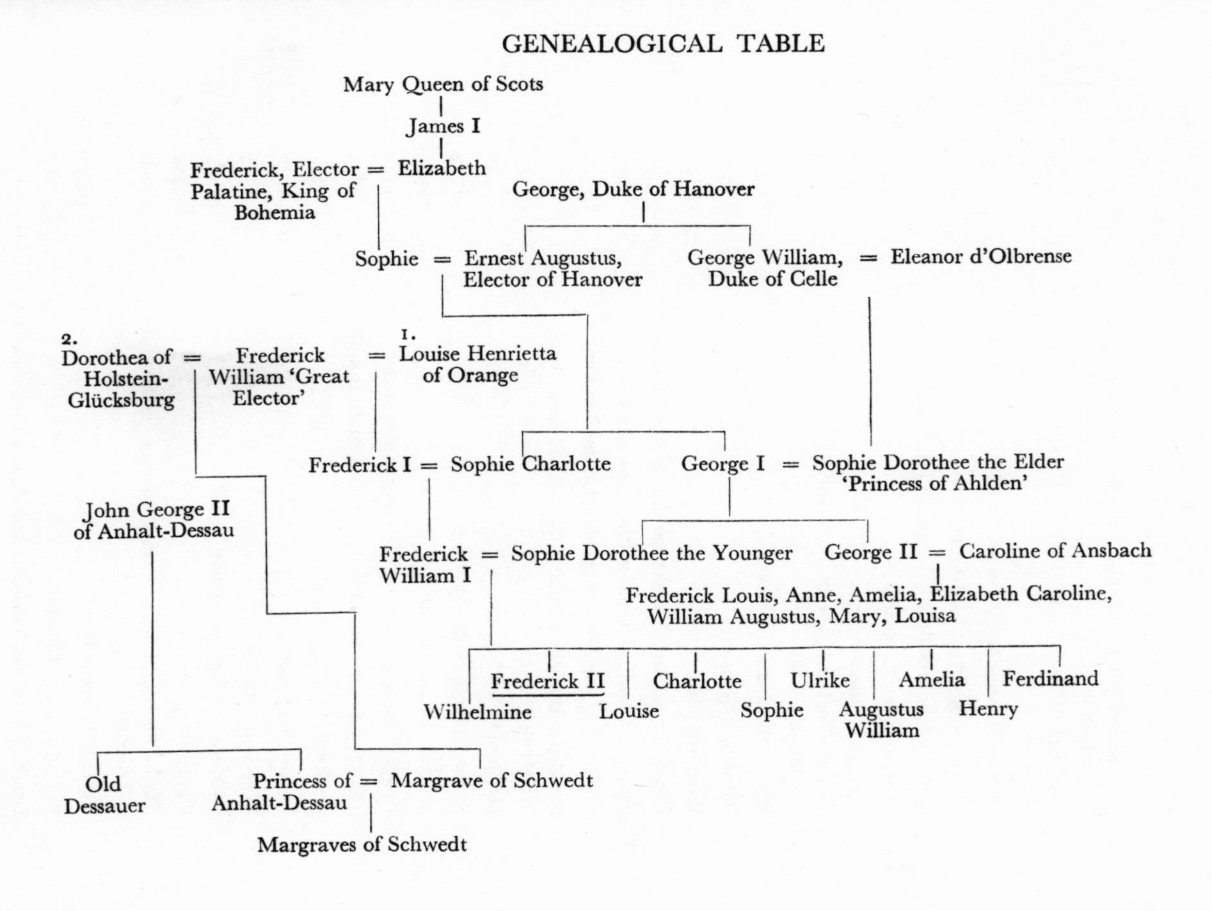

Some Principal Dates

Margravate of Brandenburg established	1140
First Hohenzollern Margrave and Elector of Brandenburg	1415
Frederick William, 11th ('Great') Elector, born	1620
reigned	1640–1688
Peace of Westphalia, terminating Thirty Years War	1648
Future King Frederick I born	1657
Prince Leopold of Anhalt-Dessau ('Old Dessauer') born	1676
Edict of Nantes repealed	1685
Frederick William born	1688
Elector Frederick III of Brandenburg becomes first King in Prussia	1701
War of the Spanish Succession	1701–1713/14
Battle of Malplaquet	1709
Frederick born	24.1.1712
Death of Frederick I; accession of Frederick William I	25.2.1713
Emperor Charles VI moots Pragmatic Sanction	1713
Elector of Hanover becomes King George I of England	10.8.1714
Frederick William's Pomeranian expedition, April–December	1715
Death of Louis XIV	1.9.1715
Maria Theresa of Austria born	13.5.1717
Pragmatic Sanction promulgated	1724
Death of George I; George II King of England	21.6.1727
Treaty of Seville, terminating Anglo-Spanish troubles	1729
Frederick's abortive flight	4.8.1730
Execution of Katte	6.11.1730
Frederick married	12.6.1733
War of the Polish Succession	1733–1735/8
Rhine campaign	1734
Maria Theresa marries Francis Stephen of Lorraine-Tuscany	12.2.1736
Turkish-Austrian War	1738–1739
War of Jenkins' Ear starts	1739
Death of Frederick William; accession of Frederick II	31.5.1740

SOME PRINCIPAL DATES

Death of Emperor Charles VI; accession of Maria Theresa	20.10.1740		
Frederick invades Silesia	16.12.1740	First Silesian War	War of the Austrian Succession—continued till 1748
Battle of Mollwitz	10.4.1741		
Alliance of Prussia and France	4.6.1741		
Agreement of Klein-Schnellendorf (Prussia–Austria)	9.10.1741		
Franco-Bavarian invasion of Austria	24.10.1741		
Prague falls to Bavarians	25.11.1741		
Austrians overrun Bavaria	December 1741–Jan. 1742		
Elector Charles Albert of Bavaria elected Emperor Charles VII	24.1.1742		
Frederick invades Moravia	5.2.1742		
Battle of Chotusitz	17.5.1742		
Peace of Breslau (Prussia–Austria)	28.7.1742		
Battle of Dettingen	27.6.1743		
Treaty of Worms (Austria, England, Holland, Sardinia)	13.9.1743		
Union of Frankfurt (Frederick–Emperor)	22.5.1744		
Treaty of Paris (France–Prussia)	5.6.1744		
Austrians invade Alsace and Lorraine	1.7.1744		
Frederick invades Bohemia	15.8.1744	Second Silesian War	
Frederick retreats to Silesia	November 1744		
Union of Warsaw (England, Austria, Holland, Saxony)	8.1.1745		
Death of Emperor Charles VII	20.1.1745		
Peace of Füssen (Bavaria–Austria)	22.4.1745		
Battle of Fontenoy	11.5.1745		
Battle of Hohenfriedberg	4.6.1745		
Charles Edward Stuart lands in Hebrides	2.8.1745		
Convention of Hanover (Prussia–England)	26.8.1745		
Archduke Francis elected German Emperor	13.9.1745		
Battle of Soor	30.9.1745		
Battle of Kesselsdorf	15.12.1745		
Peace of Dresden (Prussia–Austria, Saxony)	25.12.1745		

Bibliography

Acton, Lord: *Lectures on Modern History*. London, 1960.

Adelung, J.C.: *Leben und Charakter des königl. Polnischen und Churfürstl. Sächsischen Premier Ministre Grafens von Brühl, in vertraulichen Briefen entworfen*—1760.

Alderfeld, G.: *Military History of Charles XII*. London, 1740.

Arneth, A. von: *Geschichte Maria Theresias*. Vienna, 1863–79.

Arnheim, F.: *Der Hof des Kronprinzen* (*Geschichte des preussischen Hofes*, Vol. II). Berlin, 1912.

Besterman, Theodore: *Voltaire Essays*. Oxford, 1962.

Biographisches Lexikon des Kaisertums Österreich. Vienna, 1856–91.

Borcke, Gebrüder von: *Briefe Friederichs des Grossen und seiner Brüder aus der Zeit von* 1727–62. Potsdam, 1881.

Bourdeau, E. H.: *Le Grand Frédéric*. Paris, 1900–1902.

Brode, R.: *Friedrich der Grosse und der Konflikt mit seinem Vater*. Leipzig, 1904.

Broglie, Duc de: *Frederick the Great and Maria Theresa*. London, 1883.

Carlyle, Thomas: *History of Frederick II of Prussia, called Frederick the Great*. London, 1858–65.

Carsten, F. L.: *The Origins of Prussia*. London, 1954.

Catherine II of Russia: *Memoirs*, transl. K. Anthony. London, 1927.

Catt, Henri de: *Brouillon de mes mémoires*.—1758–60.

Churchill, Winston S.: *Marlborough, his Life and Times*. London, 1933–38.

Clausewitz, Carl von: *Oeuvres*, Vol. 10. Berlin, 1881.

— — *Strategische Beleuchtung mehrerer Feldzüge etc*. Berlin, 1863.

Craig, Gordon A.: *The Politics of the Prussian Army*, 1640–1945. Oxford, 1955.

Curas, Hilmar: *Anekdoten und Karakterzüge aus dem Leben Friedrichs des Zweiten*. Berlin, 1887.

Dahlmann-Waitz: *Quellenkunde*. Leipzig, 1906.

Dette, Erwin: *Friedrich der Grosse und sein Heer*. Göttingen, 1914.

Earle, Edward Mead and others: *Makers of Modern Strategy: Military Thought from Machiavelli to Hitler*. Princeton, 1943.

Elze, Walter: *Friedrich der Grosse, Geistige Welt, Schicksal, Taten*. Berlin, 1936.

Encyclopaedia Britannica: 1911 (XI) and 1962 editions.

Ergang, Robert: *The Potsdam Führer: Frederick William I, Father of Prussian Militarism*. New York, 1941.

Fassmann, D.: *Merkwürdigster Regierungsantritt Sr. Preussischen Majestät Frideric II*. Frankfurt & Leipzig, 1741–44.

Fester, R.: *Die Bayreuther Schwester Friedrichs des Grossen*. Berlin, 1902.

Fontane, Theodor: *Die Katte-Tragödie* (*Wanderungen durch die Mark Brandenburg*) Berlin, 1925.

Francis, Louis: *La Vie Privée de Voltaire*. Paris, 1948.

Frederick II of Prussia: *Die Werke Friedrichs des Grossen in deutscher Übersetzung*, ed. G. V. Volz. Berlin, 1913–14.

— — *Examen du Prince de Machiavel, avec des notes historiques e politiques*. 1741.

— — *Histoire de mon temps* (1740–1745), *Oeuvres*.

— — *Die Komödien des grossen Königs*, ed. Carl von Niessen. Berlin, 1937.

— — *Die Briefe Friedrichs des Grossen an seinen ehemaligen Kammerdiener Fredersdorf*, ed. J. Richter. Berlin, 1926.

— — *Das militärische Testament Friedrichs des Grossen*, ed. von Taysen. Berlin, 1879.

— — and F. W. von Grumbkow: *Correspondance. Publikationen aus den Preussischen Staatsarchiven*. Leipzig, 1898.

— — and U. F. von Suhm: *Correspondance familière*. Berlin, 1787.

Frederick William I of Prussia: *Briefe an Fürst Leopold von Anhalt-Dessau*. Acta Borussia, 1905.

Gaxotte, Pierre: *Frederick the Great*. London, 1941.

Gibson, J.: *Locke's Theory of Knowledge and its Historical Relation*. Cambridge, 1917.

Gooch, G. P.: *Frederick the Great: The Ruler, the Writer, the Man*. New York, 1947.

— — *Maria Theresa and other studies*. London, 1951.

— — *Catherine the Great and other studies*. London, 1954.

Green, J. R.: *A Short History of the English People*. London, 1907.

Hart, B. H. Liddell: *Great Captains Unveiled*. London, 1927.

Hegemann, Werner: *Fridericus, oder das Königsopfer*. Hellerau, 1926.

Hoffbauer, —.: *Die Kattetragödie in Cüstrin und ihre Stätte*. Posen, 1905.

Holke, F.: *Strafsrechtspflege unter Friedrich Wilhelm I: Beiträge zur brandenburgischen Rechtsgeschichte, III*. Berlin, 1894.

Horn, D. B. *The British Diplomatic Service*, 1689–1789. Oxford, 1960.

James, D. G.: *The Life of Reason: Hobbes, Locke and Bolinbroke*. London, 1949.

Jewish Encylopaedia. New York and London, 1901–5.

Jungfer, Hans: *Die Juden unter Friedrich dem Grossen*. Leipzig, 1880.

Klepper, Jochen: *In Tormentis Pinxit*. Stuttgart-Berlin, 1938.

König, A. B.: *Biographisches Lexikon aller Helden und Militairpersonen, welche sich in preussischen Diensten berühmt gemacht haben*. Breslau, 1788.

Koser, Reinhold: *Geschichte Friedrichs des Grossen*. Stuttgart–Berlin, 1921.

— — *Die äussere Erscheinung Friedrichs des Grossen*. Hohenzollern-jahrbuch. 1897.

Koser and Droysen, ed: *Briefwechsel Friedrichs des Grossen mit Voltaire*. Leipzig, 1908–11.

Krauske, O.: *Vom Hofe Friedrich Wilhelms des Ersten.* Hohenzollern-jahrbuch. 1902.

Kugler, Franz: *Geschichte Friedrichs des Grossen.* Leipzig, 1840.

Landwehr, H.: *Die Kirchenpolitik des Grossen Kurfürsten.* Berlin, 1894.

Lavisse, Ernest: *La Jeunesse du Grand Frédéric.* Paris, 1891.

Lehndorf, Ahasuerus Heinrich Reichsgraf von: *Dreissig Jahre am Hofe Friedrichs des Grossen.* Gotha, 1907.

Leopold, Fürst von Anhalt-Dessau: *Selbstbiographie.* Dessau, 1860.

Lévy-Bruhl, L.: *L'Allemagne depuis Leibniz.* Paris, 1890.

Ludovici, C. G.: *Ausführlicher Entwurf einer vollständigen Historie der Wolff'schen Philosophie.* 1736–38.

Macaulay, Thomas Babington Macaulay, Baron: *Critical and Historical Essays*, 1843.

Mann, Thomas: *Friedrich und die grosse Koalition* (*Rede und Antwort*). Berlin, 1922.

Martin, Kingsley: *French Liberal Thought in the Eighteenth Century.* London, 1962.

Maurice, Comte de Saxe: *Mes Rêveries.* Paris, 1877.

Meier, Burkhard: *Potsdam.* Berlin, 1937.

Mirabeau, Honoré Gabriel Riqueti, Comte de: *De la monarchie prussienne sous Frédéric le Grand, etc.* London, 1788.

Mittler, Ernst Siegfried und Sohn: *Miscellaneen zur Geschichte Königs Friedrich des Grossen.* Berlin, 1878.

Montesquieu, C. L. de Secondat Baron de la Brède et de: *L'Esprit des Lois;* ed. J. Brethe de la Gressaye. 1950–58.

Neuville, R. P. de: *Mémoires du maréchal duc de Belleisle.* Paris, 1761.

Nicolai, F.: *Anekdoten von König Friedrich II.* Berlin, 1789.

— — *Freimüthige Anmerkungen über des Herrn Ritters von Zimmermann Fragmente etc., von einem brandenburgischen Patrioten*, 1791.

Nicolson, Harold: *The Age of Reason.* London, 1960.

Pariset, G.: *L'État et les Églises en Prusse sous Frédéric Guillaume Ier.* Paris, 1897.

Pertz, G. H.: *Über die Merkwürdigkeiten der Markgräfin.*—1851.

Phillips, T. R.: *Roots of Strategy.* London, 1943.

Pöllnitz, Ch. L. von: *Mémoires pour servir à l'histoire des quatre derniers souverains de la maison de Brandebourg.* Berlin, 1791.

Posner, Max: *Zur literarischen Tätigkeit Friedrichs des Grossen; Erörterungen und Aktenstücke.*

Preuss, J. D. E.: *Friedrich der Grosse, eine Lebensgeschichte.* Berlin, 1834.

Preussischer Generalstab: *Die Kriege Friedrichs des Grossen.* Berlin, 1890–1904.

Prussian: *Schreiben eines Preussens an den Herrn Zimmermann.*

Ranke, Leopold von: *Zwölf Bücher preussischer Geschichte.*

— — *Friedrich II, König von Preussen* (*Werke*, vols. II and III).

Reddaway, W. F.: *Frederick the Great and the Rise of Prussia.* London, 1904.

Reiners, Ludwig: *Friedrich*. Munich, 1952.

Reinhold, Peter: *Maria Theresa*. Vienna, 1957.

Rivington, J.: *Criticism of the Henriad*. London, 1758.

Russell, Bertrand: *Critical Exposition of the Philosophy of Leibniz*. London, 1937.

Schevill, Ferdinand: *The Great Elector*. Chicago, 1947.

Saint-Simon, Louis de Rouvroi, Duc de: *Mémoires*, ed. G. Truc. Paris, 1947–61.

Schmidt, O.E.: *Minister Graf Brühl und Karl Heinrich von Heinechen*. Leipzig–Berlin, 1921.

Schöning und Selle: *Krankheitsgeschichte des Höchstseligen Königs von Preussen, Friedrichs des Zweiten*. Berlin, 1786.

Schultz, W. von: *Die preussischen Werbungen unter Friedrich Wilhelm I und Friedrich dem Grossen*. Schwerin, 1887.

Seckendorf, Ludwig Heinrich von: *Journal Secret du baron de Seckendorf*. Tübingen, 1811.

Seidel, P.: *Die Bildnisse Friedrichs des Grossen*. Hohenzollernjahrbuch. Berlin, 1897.

— — *Friedrich der Grosse und die bildende Kunst*. Berlin-Leipzig.

Thiérot, A.: *Voltaire en Prusse*. Paris, 1878.

Trenck, Friedrich Freiherr von der: *Merkwürdige Lebensgeschichte etc*. Berlin and Vienna, 1787.

Valentin, Veit: *Some interpretations of Frederick the Great*. (*History*, 1934).

Vollständige Protocolle des Köpenicker Kriegsgerichts über Kronprinz Friedrich, Leutnants von Katte, von Kait usw. Aus dem Familienarchiv der von der Schulenburg. Berlin, 1861.

Voltaire, François Marie Arouet de: *Mémoires pour servir à la vie de M. de Voltaire écrits par lui-même*. 1784.

— — *Précis du Siècle de Louis XV*. Paris, 1819.

— — *The Age of Louis XIV*. London, 1962.

— — *Correspondence*, ed. Theodore Besterman. Geneva, 1953–62.

Voltz, G. B.: *Aus der Welt Friedrichs des Grossen*. Dresden, 1922.

Vorberg, G.: *Der Klatsch über das Geschlechtsleben Friedrichs des Zweiten*. Bonn, 1921.

Waddington, A.: *Le Grand Electeur et Louis XIV*. Paris, 1905.

Weber, Carl von: *Moritz, Graf von Sachsen etc; nach archivalischen Quellen*. Leipzig, 1863.

Wedgwood, C. V.: *The Thirty Years War*. London, 1957.

White, Jon Manchip: *Marshal of France, the Life and Times of Maurice de Saxe*. London, 1962.

Wiegand, W.: *Friedrich der Grosse* (Monographien zur Weltgeschichte). Leipzig, 1922.

Wilhelmine (Frédérique Sophie) de Prusse, Margrave de Bareith etc.: *Mémoires, écrit de sa main*. Brunswick, Paris, London, 1812.

Wurzbach's Biographisches Lexikon. Leipzig, 1792–94.

Zimmermann, J. G. Ritter von: *Fragmente über Friedrich den Grossen, etc*.

— — *Über Friedrich den Grossen und meine Unterredungen mit ihm kurz vor seinem Tode*. Leipzig, 1788.

INDEX

FRAN